# INVESTING IN COMMUNITY

Evan (left) and Eric Nord flank the plaque dedicating the new Nordson Corporation building in Amherst, Ohio, to their father, Walter, ca. 1968. (Reproduced courtesy of Nordson Corporation)

NORD HISTORY PROJECT COMMITTEE

Patricia Murphy, *Project Manager*

Eric T. Nord

Evan W. Nord

William D. Ginn

Patricia Holsworth

Daniel D. Merrill

Marlene D. Merrill

# INVESTING IN COMMUNITY

## THE HISTORY AND LEGACY OF THE NORD FAMILY OF OHIO

Martha M. Pickrell

Oberlin Historical
and Improvement
Organization

Oberlin, Ohio

Oberlin Historical and Improvement Organization /
Oberlin Heritage Center
73½ South Professor Street
P. O. Box 455
Oberlin, Ohio 44074-0455


Library of Congress Cataloging-in-Publication Data

Pickrell, Martha M.
  Investing in community : the history and legacy of the Nord
family of Ohio / Martha M. Pickrell
     p.    cm.
  Includes bibliographical references and index
  ISBN 0-9759929-0-2 (alk. paper)
    1. Nord family.   2. Swedish-Americans—Ohio—Oberlin—
Biography.   3. Business people—Ohio—Oberlin—Biography.
4. Philanthropists—Ohio—Oberlin—Biography.   5. Charities—
Ohio—Lorain County   6. Corporations—Ohio—Amherst.
7. Oberlin (Ohio)—Biography.   8. Ohio—Biography.   I. Oberlin
Historical and Improvement Organization.   II. Title.
CT274.N655P53 2004
338.092'2771—dc22

                                                   2004019756


ISBN 0-9759929-0-2
Printed in the United States of America on acid-free paper.

Composition by Sarah MacLennan Kerr, Ph.D.
Editorial and Production Services
Oberlin, Ohio 44074-1440

# CONTENTS

FOREWORD

I am deeply honored that Evan Nord asked me, in early 2001, whether the Oberlin Historical and Improvement Organization (O.H.I.O.) and I would be willing to help him and his brother, Eric, undertake a project they had hoped to accomplish for quite some time. Evan, with whom I had enjoyed working for many years on preserving and sharing Oberlin's history and historic buildings, asked me to direct a project to research, write, and publish a history of his family, their business interests, and their contributions to the community. Evan and Eric wanted an amply illustrated publication that would help younger members of the Nord family, the corporation's and the foundations' new staff members, and others understand and appreciate the Nord legacy, the family's values, and the tradition of community service they had always practiced. This history is far more than a typical American success story and much more than the story of an illustrious American family's beginnings in Ohio. It is an important story that can inspire all of us to think about how we can effectively contribute to our communities in our own ways.

In talking with Evan and Eric about their ideas and goals for the project I quickly learned that each wanted, above all, to honor the memory of their parents, Walter and Virginia Nord. The modest, soft-spoken brothers attained their exceptional achievements in business and philanthropy without thought of claiming personal credit. Neither desired a publication that could be seen as self-congratulatory or self-serving. Indeed, initially they believed the book should be not about them but about their parents and the early history of the Nordson business. Happily, they eventually recognized that they, too, were an important part of the story. We decided to focus on the first two generations of the family: Walter and Virginia Nord and their children and spouses—Mary and Joe Ignat, Eric and Jane Nord, and Evan and Cindy Nord.

Having had the great pleasure of working closely with various members of the Nord Family, especially Evan, with staff of The Nord Family Foundation and The Nordson Corporation Foundation, and with staff from a number of the other nonprofit organizations the Nord family has supported over the years, I viewed the book as a logical extension of our collaboration and a natural undertaking for O.H.I.O. as our community's historical society. The more deeply we became involved in the project the more ambitious an undertaking it seemed; it encompassed not only local and family history but also the inextricably linked and important topics of corporate and industrial history, the history of the Nords' philanthropy, and the twentieth-century history of Lorain County.

It was indeed a joy to ask others for their help because everyone I approached was thrilled to hear that the project was being undertaken, agreed it was long overdue, and was eager to participate. Producing this publication has truly been an amazing team effort and collaboration. I salute and applaud Martha Pickrell, the primary researcher and writer for the project, who uncovered marvelous source materials and worked with extraordinary skill and determination to bring the volume to fruition. Martha is the author of two business histories and has extensive experience working with archives and historical societies. I am particularly indebted to the members of the project steering committee, who joined me in this worthy endeavor and without whom it could not have been accomplished: Evan Nord, Eric Nord, Bill Ginn, Pat Holsworth, Dan Merrill, and Marly Merrill. Each brought special skills and insights, helped locate documents and illustrations, provided good counsel, and contributed very generously of his or her time. Each also carefully reviewed and augmented various drafts of the manuscript, as did Cindy Nord, Gini Barbato, Ed Campbell, Jack Clark, Constance Haqq, David Ignat, Henry Libicki, John Mullaney, and others. My deep gratitude also goes to Sarah MacLennan Kerr, who masterfully pulled it all together, helping in ways that extended far beyond her official role as editor/compositor. I thank everyone who joined in this massive undertaking; I am grateful to all who shared resources and images; and I apologize that space precludes me from mentioning each and every one. I would be remiss, however, if I did not also thank the board, staff, and volunteers of O.H.I.O. for their support and help with all the details. Above all, heartfelt thanks to Evan and Eric, who, with typical Nord generosity, provided the funding essential to achieve a premium product without straining O.H.I.O.'s limited resources.

There is far more to this expansive story than could be covered fully in the pages that follow; many topics only touched upon here deserve much more extensive study. As custodians of history, we hope to foster further such explorations and collaborations in the years ahead.

—Patricia Murphy
Executive Director
Oberlin Historical and Improvement Organization /
Oberlin Heritage Center

June 2004

$F$or almost half a century the unique contributions of the Nord family—Walter and Virginia Nord, their daughter, Mary Nord Ignat, and their sons, Eric and Evan, and their families—to the communities of Lorain County, Ohio, and beyond have won appreciation from employees, friends, neighbors, nonprofit agencies and their clients, leaders in the world of business, industry, and philanthropy, and citizens throughout the area. This book is an effort to put into lasting form some of the highlights of the Nords' lives and of the business and philanthropic enterprises that have grown to prominence and success under their leadership.

What follows is the product of a research project begun by the Oberlin Historical and Improvement Organization (O.H.I.O.) in 2001 at the request of Evan and Eric Nord. It brings together information from many sources pertaining to the history of the Nord family, as well as Nordson Corporation and The Nord Family Foundation and their predecessors. It focuses on the family from the arrival in the United States of Otto Nord, Walter's father, through the generation of Walter's children, Mary, Eric, and Evan.

The book draws on several earlier historical projects, each of which has made its own important contribution. As early as the 1940s Marilyn Pietch Jenne, longtime secretary to Walter Nord and then to his sons, Evan and Eric, began to save items that seemed to have historical importance. In later decades additional efforts were made by the Nords and by James Doughman, a former director of public affairs of Nordson Corporation. In the mid-1970s, at the family's request, Fred R. Powers, a retired Amherst, Ohio, educator and Walter's close friend, wrote articles and speeches, now in manuscript form at the Amherst Historical Society's headquarters, that contain many facts and priceless anecdotes about family, company, and community history.

By the 1980s Nordson Corporation officials, looking back at more than fifty years of history under Nord leadership, began to compile chronologies and search for a historian. A draft history of the corporation up to the 1950s was prepared in 1992 by Mary Ann Hellrigel of Case Western Reserve University. In 1995 the business historian Barbara S. Griffith was hired to conduct an extensive oral history project that comprised interviews, an historical essay, and chronologies. And in 1997 a scrap-

# PREFACE

book on the company's history was created internally to honor Eric Nord on his retirement as chairman of the corporation.

In 1992 the trustees of The Nord Family Foundation, wishing to document and learn more of the foundation's history, which dates back to 1952, commissioned their own oral history project, consisting of a videotape and numerous interviews conducted in 1992 and 1993 by Jeanne Harrah, an oral history expert associated with the Western Reserve Historical Society in Cleveland. The foundation also made provision for the future by depositing its records with the Western Reserve Historical Society. In 1999 family members at a foundation retreat videotaped more oral history with Eric and Evan.

Much had been accomplished, yet by the millennial year Evan, in particular, wanted something else done to draw together the many threads of the story he knew so well. He provided the spark, asking Patricia Murphy, executive director of the Oberlin Heritage Center / O.H.I.O., to undertake and oversee publication of a history aimed at a general audience. In addition to Eric and Evan, Murphy selected the following people to serve with her on the project's volunteer steering committee: Marlene Deahl Merrill and Patricia Holsworth, historians for O.H.I.O.; William D. Ginn, longtime legal adviser and close associate of the Nord family; and Daniel D. Merrill, a retired Oberlin College professor. I was hired as the primary researcher and writer for the project.

The manuscript of this book was carefully reviewed by the steering committee, members of the Nord and Ignat families, chief executives of Nordson Corporation, The Nord Family Foundation, The Nordson Corporation Foundation, the Community Foundation of Greater Lorain County, and others. Yet its viewpoint is my own, and I take responsibility for any errors. This is a basic history. I hope that it will draw you, the reader, into the story with a reasonably fast-paced narrative broken into readable segments, along with a plentiful selection of illustrations.

Sarah MacLennan Kerr, Ph.D., of Oberlin did the editorial, graphic, and design work for the volume and wrote the section on "A Loss in the Family."

I wish to personally thank the steering committee members for their efforts and support. Working with Eric and Evan Nord was a pleasure. Thanks especially to Pat Murphy for her patience, help, and good judgment throughout and to Pat Holsworth, an experienced genealogist, who quickly and efficiently found a great deal of information and also provided invaluable insight into genealogical issues. Bill Ginn was most responsive to many time-consuming and perplexing questions. And without the help and inspiration of Marly and Dan Merrill, my work would simply not have been possible. Sally Kerr provided the highest level of expertise and substantial education in the intricacies of electronic publishing. In addition, I thank each of the committee members for making significant improvements and amplifications to the text.

Others in, or closely connected to, the Nord family who were helpful in the research include Cindy Nord, Jane Nord, David Ignat, Joseph N. Ignat, Marilyn Jenne, Clifford Berry, Henry Libicki, Jeptha and Demaris Carrell, John R. and Kathleen Clark, Beth Bauknight, Rosemary Lancaster, and Julie Miller. In addition, valued assistance came from John Mullaney and Ann Allison of The Nord Family Foundation, from Anne Marie Cronin, formerly with the foundation, and from many people at Nordson Corporation, including Edward P. Campbell (chairman / chief executive officer); Constance Haqq, Cecilia Render, and Eddie Williams (The Nordson Corporation Foundation); Robert A. Schneider and Richard J. Bort (Nordson Visual Communications Center); and Brenda Bookshar, Lucy Garza, John Kirschner, Tom Petredis, Christine Reed, Barbara Shehan, Sherry Kerner Szczepanski, Robert E. Veillette (assistant general counsel and secretary), Bruce Waffen (director, corporate public relations), and Nancy Scott (a former employee).

I owe a huge debt of gratitude to Barbara S. Griffith and Jeanne Harrah for their earlier work in eliciting and recording the memories of leading figures of the family, the corporation, and the foundations. In the case of Barbara Griffith, this also included writing a very useful but unpublished historical essay. For the early years of the corporation, Mary Ann Hellrigel's work was very helpful as well.

I am grateful to staff and volunteers at many libraries and archives, including Mary Roberts, Ruth Haff, Orville Manes, Karen Mounsey, Denise Karshner, and John Dietrich at the Amherst Historical Society, Margaret Burzynski-Bays at the Western Reserve Historical Society, Janet Turner, Don Dovala, and Maxine Miller at the Amherst Public Library, Ric Consiglio at the Ashtabula County District Library, Elsie Berg and May Collins at the Ashtabula County Genealogical Society, Al Doane at the Black River Historical Society, Helen Conger and Tom Steman at the Case Western Reserve University Archives, Anne Colucci at the Jefferson Public Library, Linda Greenaway and Karis Lyon at the Lorain County Historical Society, Susan Paul at the Lorain County Community College Library, Ramona Flores at the Lorain Public Library, Roland Baumann, Tammy Martin, and Ken Grossi at the Oberlin College Archives, Michael Hibben at the Oberlin Public Library, Lynn Ayers at the Wilberforce University Library, and the reference staffs of the Cleveland Public Library, Orrville Public Library, and Youngstown Public Library, all in Ohio; and in South Bend, Indiana, Mary Waterson, Jane Spencer, John Kovach, and other reference staff at the St. Joseph County Public Library; and

Michele Russo, Cassandra Toth, Raymond Jorgeson, Nancy Colborn, and other staff of the Schurz Library at Indiana University South Bend; also the Harvard University Archives, Cambridge, Massachusetts.

Special thanks to Margaretha Talerman, curator of the American Swedish Historical Museum, Philadelphia. Also helpful were the Swenson Swedish Immigration Research Center, Augustana College, Rock Island, Illinois; the Consulate General of Sweden in New York; Byron J. Nordstrom of Gustavus Adolphus College, Minneapolis; and Hendrik Nordström, also of Minneapolis.

Staff members and volunteers at institutions connected with the Nord family were most gracious in supplying information, including: Mac Bennett, Central Carolina Community Foundation, Columbia, South Carolina; Ronald Cocco, Clark and Post Architects, Lorain; Richard Lothrop, Christ Episcopal Church, Oberlin; Teresa McCoy, Common Ground retreat center, Oberlin; Betsy Manderen, Firelands Association for the Visual Arts, Oberlin; Terry Kovach, Kendal at Oberlin; Ellen Payner, Lorain County Board of Mental Retardation and Developmental Disabilities, Elyria; Tracy Green, Lorain County Community College Foundation, Elyria; Tina Salyer, Lorain County Joint Vocational School; Dan Martin and Rebecca Voit, Lorain County Metro Parks; Brian Frederick, Margo Hirth, and Cheryl McKenna, Community Foundation of Greater Lorain County, Lorain; Carol Peck, Lucy Idol Center for the Handicapped, Vermilion; Tim Donohue, The Nord Center, Lorain; Ann Fuller, Oberlin Community Services; Nancy Sabath, Oberlin Early Childhood Center; and Dale Rosenkranz, Amherst Outdoor Life Association. Thanks too to former Mayor John Higgins of Amherst and his assistant, Sally Cornwell.

Heartfelt thanks to O.H.I.O. supervolunteer Dick Holsworth for assistance in many ways during all phases of producing this book, especially for traveling with his wife, Pat, to South Carolina to scan dozens of family photographs at Evan and Cindy Nord's home and for sharing some of his own superb photographs. Thanks also to O.H.I.O. Museum Fellow Morgan Franck, who gave me good instruction in some of the fine points of oral history, to Museum Fellow Hans Petersen, Collections Assistant Prue Richards, and Intern Tom Reeves, who helped with research and photographs, to Assistant to the Director Mary Anne Cunningham, for reading the manuscript, and to O.H.I.O. members Sigrid Boe and Keith Koenning, for their input regarding the Splash Zone.

The Franklin D. Schurz Library at Indiana University South Bend provided a welcome haven, where I wrote the narrative that follows. It is truly an honor to have had a part in researching and sharing the inspiring story of the Nord family.

—MARTHA M. PICKRELL

I<sub></sub>t was just after lunchtime in Oberlin, Ohio, in the comfortable lobby of the Oberlin Inn on Main Street. Two elderly gentlemen, Eric and Evan Nord, sat together on a couch, huddled over a set of landscape plans for the local arts center. Excitement was in their faces and in their gestures.

Oberlin, about an hour southwest of Cleveland in Lorain County, is centered around Oberlin College. Founded in 1833, the college was the first coeducational institution in the United States and a leader in the education of African Americans. Eric Nord and his wife, Jane, had been part of the Oberlin community since the World War II era. Evan and his wife, Cindy, had lived near Columbia, South Carolina, since 1978, but Evan had worn a path through the roads and skies with his frequent trips back to Oberlin and to Amherst, the town 10 miles north of Oberlin where both men were born and spent their youth and young manhood.

These two good-humored, soft-spoken, unassuming engineers, nominally retired, were still fully involved in many community projects, and they and their late father, Walter G. Nord, had been at the center of a very successful combination of industry and philanthropy that transformed this part of Ohio and touched faraway places.

Nordson Corporation, which had its beginnings in Amherst as the U.S. Automatic Company, a screw machine products shop, not long after the turn of the twentieth century, has become one of the world's foremost manufacturers of industrial equipment for applying coatings, adhesives, and sealants. Top executives at the corporate headquarters in Westlake, Ohio, preside over a company with more than 3,000 employees and more than $600 million in annual sales. Nordson is truly international in scope, for more than 60 percent of its market is outside North America. It has reached and maintained its position by internal development and judicious acquisitions.

Nordson's largest manufacturing facility is located in a sprawling campus on Jackson Street in Amherst. Just a mile or so to the west, in a renovated nineteenth-century sandstone house with a large recent addition, is the new headquarters of The Nord Family Foundation. With current assets of nearly $77 million, since the late 1980s the foundation has dispensed more than $53 million in grants that have strengthened health and social services, education, civic leadership, and cultural op-

# INTRODUCTION

portunities, primarily in northeast Ohio but also in South Carolina, Colorado, and Massachusetts, where Nord family members live. The 160 grants totaling more than $3 million in 2003 ranged from $123,000 to the Center for Leadership in Education, to $50,000 for the Ohio Dance Theatre, to $30,000 for the Boys & Girls Club of Lorain County, to $30,000 to the Conflict Center in Denver.

The corporation's own foundation, The Nordson Corporation Foundation, gave nearly $1.5 million in grants in 2003 to agencies and programs in northeast Ohio and in areas where the corporation's plants are located: greater Atlanta, the Monterey Peninsula of California, and San Diego.

Both foundations stem from the original small charitable trust begun by Walter G. Nord in 1952. Both are expressions of his magnanimous philosophy and that of his wife, Virginia, passed down to their children and grandchildren, of sharing whatever wealth might come their way. And both the company and the foundations are expressions of a lifework seen as filling a need, as devising or inventing solutions that work. Throughout the Nord story is a sturdy tradition of altruism, curiosity, and realism, of meeting difficulties and surmounting them, of investing in community.

# THE NORD FAMILY TO 1913

In the summer of 1938 Eric Nord, then a twenty-year-old college student, left his traveling companions and bicycled on alone, exploring the unpaved back roads of a hilly, rural area in the far western region of Sweden, a place peppered with farms, villages, and small towns. He was searching for relatives of his grandfather, Otto Nord, and his grandmother, Mary Erickson Nord, who had come to America in the late nineteenth century. By the end of his search he had indeed found one or two people who were probably relatives.

## OTTO AND MARY NORD

Eric remembered Otto and Mary Nord well. When he was a small child he, his older sister, Mary, and his younger brother, Evan, would take summertime trips in the family car with their parents, Walter and Virginia Nord, to visit Otto and Mary at their farm in Denmark Township in Ashtabula County, Ohio, near the Pennsylvania border. The two-story wooden farmhouse, the barn, the orchards, the cornfields, the horses, cows, and chickens were a source of warm memories. Otto was a tall, quiet man, still muscular and strong in his seventies, with a large, bushy beard; Mary, a small woman, not much taller than a child, who loved to please her grandchildren and often had a joke to tell in her thick Swedish accent.

## A VILLAGE TRADITION

Sweden is a long, narrow, rugged land where making a living has not been easy, and it has bred strong, hardworking, clearheaded men and women for some 2,000 years. Vilhelm Moberg, a much-beloved Swedish novelist and historian, wrote the following in his book, *A History of the Swedish People* (1972), about the ancient heritage of the Swedes and their life together: "Out of sheer self-preservation people brought their dwellings together, seeking in such a cluster protection against their enemies, against robbers and predatory beasts, against criminals and against the starving wolves that strayed about the land in winter."

Villagers came to each other's aid in times of illness, work, joy, and mourning. As Moberg put it, "If a cow fell sick, it was handy to have a neighbour who knew how to cure it. Birth and marriage, death and funerals, all were the common concern of the village council. Agriculture too was carried on jointly by the men of the village."

By the mid–nineteenth century, however, the world had become much more complex. Swedish peasant families were suffering great stress. They felt a growing resentment against the demands and restrictions of the government and the Lutheran Church that was an integral part of that government, against entrenched traditions of social and economic inequality, against scarce, poor, and expensive land that often was not available to younger sons.

## OTTO'S SWEDISH ANCESTORS

The Scandinavian countries are famous for the complexity of their naming system and the difficulty of tracing ancestors back through history. In a traditional pattern, sons and daughters took the first name of their father as the first part of their last name, adding to it "son" or "dotter." Mary Erickson Nord, whose parents were Erik Pettersson and Britta Olafson, followed this pattern only partially: Although she was probably called "Mary Eriksdotter" in Sweden, she was generally known as "Mary Erickson" in the United States, so that is the name used in this history. In contrast, men who went into professions such as teaching or into the military chose a new surname, and that name followed their children and other descendants. Thus it was with the Nord family.

According to Swedish research commissioned in 1953 by Walter and Virginia Nord, Otto was the son of Jonas Olofsson Hedqvist and Johanna Eriksdotter. Johanna, born on October 28, 1805 in Högsäter Parish of the Church of Sweden, was the daughter of the soldier Erik Tängberg and Malin Eriksdotter, both of Kråksrud. Johanna moved from Högsäter to Torp Parish in 1826 and there married Jonas Olofsson Hedqvist on January 2, 1831. Jonas was born at Kollerö, Väne-Ryr Parish, in 1804, the son of Olof Jonasson Blomberg and Helena Hansdotter of Tägnebyn. Until 1832 Jonas was registered in parish and civil records with the family name of Hedqvist, but after the family moved to Skällebo, in the same parish, he was known only as Jonas Olofsson. Otto Jonasson, Jonas and Johanna's fourth child, was born on June 3, 1848 at Blaggarnstorpet under Wrine, in Ödeborg Parish (see Appendix 1). Jonas died there on June 14, 1855.

Widowed, Johanna moved to Färgelanda Parish, where she and Jon Olsson Nor were married on July 16, 1856. Jon, who became a soldier like his father, was given the soldier name "Nor." Johanna Eriksdotter died on April 4, 1875; Jon Olsson Nor, on May 30, 1895.

Otto was only eight years old when his mother remarried. Nor raised all four of Johanna's children as his own, and all of them took his last name. Because of the way the name was pronounced, however, the spelling was erroneously changed to "Nord." Thus Otto became a Nor(d) by adoption, a tradition repeated in later generations by his grandson Evan Nord, who adopted his wife's children when they married, and by his great-grandson Eric Baker Nord, who also adopted his wife's daughter when they married.

# SWEDISH PIONEERS IN AMERICA

## TAKING THE RISK

Early pioneers, earlier than Otto, heard of America and resolved to risk everything for a chance to live a freer, more prosperous life. After a long period of struggle—difficult voyages of many weeks across the ocean on small sailing ships, followed by long inland journeys to find a

Mary Erickson Nord (left), ca. 1872. The other young woman is probably her older sister Anna. (Photograph by Olle Prestos Fotographi-Atelier, Wenersborg, Sweden; reproduced courtesy of Evan and Cindy Nord)

place to settle—they discovered a near-paradise where virgin land was plentiful, religion was not imposed by the state, and people enjoyed a sense of control over their own destiny.

These pioneers encouraged others to join them in long, glowing letters to their relatives back home in Sweden. By the 1860s severe food shortages and the advent of faster, safer, steam-powered ships and railroads had helped swell the number who emigrated to America from a stream to a mighty river. The flood of Scandinavian emigration also included Norwegians, Danes, and Finns. In all, nearly 2 million Scandinavian men, women, and children made the journey to America between 1861 and 1910.

The Swedes came as individuals, families, and groups of neighbors and soon founded their own communities. Whereas, in Sweden, communities were stratified according to a person's occupation and wealth, in America the Swedish settlers worked extremely hard to achieve a community based on equality.[1]

Britta Olafson and Erik Pettersson, Walter Nord's maternal grandparents, with Frank, one of his older brothers, ca. 1882. (Reproduced courtesy of Eric and Jane Nord)

## OTTO COMES TO ASHTABULA

Not much of Otto Nord's early life is known, but he appears to have left Sweden with little money. According to one family tradition, he boarded a steamship after signing an agreement with the steamship company that he would pay for his passage by later sending it a portion of his wages from whatever work he found. Handwritten documents confirm that Otto arrived at New York Harbor on May 24, 1872; but, for reasons that are not clear, his naturalization papers list two immigration dates, May 24, 1872 and August 31, 1879.

According to another family tradition, Otto first traveled from New York to Minnesota, where many thousands of Scandinavians were settling, to check out prospects there. It may have been in Minnesota that he found others who knew of a growing Scandinavian community in Ashtabula County, Ohio.

In 1874 Scandinavian immigrants began to settle at Ashtabula Harbor, on the southern shore of Lake Erie east of Cleveland. It was an important outlet for the booming iron industry, and workers were needed to load and unload iron-bearing ships. Otto found work as an iron-ore shoveler, surely one of the most taxing occupations that could be imagined.

In about 1876, in the United States, Otto married Mary Erickson. Born on April 12, 1856, Mary was the daughter of Erik Pettersson and his wife, Britta Olafson of Ladängen, Väne-Åsaka Parish. Mary had six siblings, two of whom died as children. She emigrated to the United States on April 7, 1874. Her parents and her surviving four siblings emigrated later, the last one on March 4, 1881.

Otto and Mary had six children: Herman Joel Nord, born on March 31, 1877; Frank Victor Nord, born on October 17, 1878; Emily Augusta Nord, born on February 4, 1881; Walter Godfrey Nord, born on January 30, 1884; Ann Sophia "Anna" Nord, born on November 21, 1886; and

Olive Dorothy Nord, born on September 30, 1889. The 1880 census revealed a large Scandinavian colony in Ashtabula. One household was headed by Mary's brother-in-law, Andrew Peterson, and comprised nineteen people: Mary's mother; her sister, Anna Peterson; Mary, Otto, and their two sons, Herman and Frank; Andrew Peterson's brother; and eleven male boarders, all laborers. Otto clearly meant to remain in the United States, for he became a citizen on March 17, 1881.[2]

## THE MOVE TO DENMARK TOWNSHIP

The group of Scandinavian immigrant families at Ashtabula grew into a sizable settlement. But shoveling iron ore all day in a noisy harbor city was not what Otto wanted for the rest of his life. Along with many other Ashtabula Swedes, he and his family had their eyes on buying enough land to support themselves by farming. Attractive, wooded land beckoned some 12 miles to the south, in Denmark Township.

According to a county history, Scandinavian settlement in Denmark Township began in the late 1870s when a man named Fitch, a lawyer in Jefferson, the county seat, "convinced many of the workers [at Ashtabula Harbor] of the reasonably priced, woodsy land available in Denmark township." At first, and for many years, the doggedly persistent men "commuted" on foot each day to the harbor to earn their laborer's wages while developing their farms. "The men of these families," the account

Otto and Mary Erickson Nord and their children at the farm in Denmark Township, Ashtabula County, Ohio, ca. 1893. Left to right: Walter, Frank, Herman, Otto, Mary, Emily, Ann Sophia "Anna," Olive. (Reproduced courtesy of Eric and Jane Nord)

continues, "walked the 20 to 25 miles to the harbor and back. They worked for 50 cents per day. Sometimes in bad weather, they would stay overnight in the Harbor or 'Swede town.' "

On August 7, 1882 Otto purchased 30 acres in Denmark Township from another Scandinavian, August Ekberg. Otto's third son, Walter, the first of the Nord children born in the township, noted that, during several winters, when the docks were closed Otto had cleared land for their farm. Walter also learned from his parents that they spent $275 to build their little wooden house. Otto had help in the actual construction of the house. According to Eric and Evan, the Denmark township settlement was a community of families who truly cared for and aided each other, including pitching in to build each other's homes. Thus the old village tradition from the homeland described in Moberg's history was carried into the New World.

About a half-mile from the Nords' farm was a little crossroads called Denmark, with a store, a church, and a one-room schoolhouse. The roads were primitive, and rural electrification was decades away. Horses provided the power for tilling Otto's fields. By 1900, the year of the next available federal census, Otto was more than fifty years old and may have stopped commuting to Ashtabula Harbor; he was listed simply as a farmer. Through thrift and hard work, Otto and Mary not only succeeded as farmers but also helped launch two sons, Herman and Walter, on notable careers.[3]

## WALTER'S YOUTH AND YOUNG MANHOOD

### LESSONS OF THE FARM

Walter Godfrey Nord, Otto and Mary's fourth child, born on January 30, 1884, grew up in a small house crowded with people. Outside were the farm grounds with their animals, outbuildings, and innumerable chores to be done. Beyond this, the world was more open: a quiet landscape where a young person could be alone with the sun and the clouds, the moon and the stars, and dream of the future.

Every day, as a small child, Walter saw his father wrestle with the demands of farming as they existed before the advent of power machinery. No doubt with the help of Walter's older brothers, Herman and Frank (about seven and five years older than Walter), Otto planted, tended, and harvested his acres of oats, corn, and wheat. In addition, the horses and equipment had to be cared for, the cows milked, a vegetable garden and chickens tended, and eggs gathered. Some of those chores fell to Walter's mother, along with all her household duties, and to his sister Emily (three years older than Walter). All needed to do their part, even, eventually, Anna and Olive (two and five years younger than Walter).

*Axel Hallstrom [an innovator in the field of agriculture] and I had much in common. We both had Swedish parents and were born and reared on a farm where economy was a prime necessity. We both lived on our parents' farms until we reached the age of 18. . . . I worked in the earlier years in heavy crops such as oats, corn, wheat.*

—Walter Nord, "Axel Hallstrom in Memoriam," *American Swedish Historical Foundation Yearbook,* 1966

Making a living from farming could be precarious at times, and it is probable that throughout Walter's early years his father was still making the exhausting daily trek with other men of the neighborhood to work at the Ashtabula Harbor docks, in all seasons except winter. Industriousness, persistence, and frugality were primary values in the Nord home, and Walter began to do his share at an early age.

Life in the Nord home taught many other important lessons as well. Walter learned to love the outdoors, where he spent most of his time. His parents taught their children to respect each other and to see the value of sharing whatever one had with people who were less fortunate. The family attended church regularly. From Mary Nord her children learned that the load of life could be lightened by carrying it with a sense of humor. And, as in many immigrant homes, great importance was placed on acquiring an education.

Theirs was a Swedish-speaking household, but just a few minutes' walk away, down a country road, was a one-room school where all of the Nord children were sent when they were old enough and where they learned English. In Walter's case, even before attending school, he must have heard and learned many English words from his older siblings.[4]

*Above:* Anna and Olive, younger sisters of Walter Nord, ca. 1905. (Photograph by Loomis Studio, Jefferson, Ohio; reproduced courtesy of Evan and Cindy Nord)

*Below:* Walter Nord, at about the time of his graduation from the Jefferson Educational Institute in 1904. (Photograph by F. B. Way, Ashtabula, Ohio; reproduced courtesy of Evan and Cindy Nord)

## LESSONS IN THE CLASSROOM

Walter grew to be a sturdy, muscular youth, though not tall like his father. By 1900 he had reached the age of sixteen and, being the only boy still at home, spent much of his time helping his father on the farm; indeed, in the 1900 census he was listed as a farm laborer. His older brothers were already part of the wider world. Herman, the oldest, studious and thoughtful and articulate, was well on his way to becoming a lawyer. He received his degree in law from Western Reserve University, in Cleveland, in 1904. Frank, the second oldest, did not attend college but taught school as a young man.

Although Walter looked up to his older brothers, he had his own way of approaching life. He loved the farm and all the challenges it presented to his keen, analytical, inventive mind. It was often necessary to improvise when dealing with farm machinery. He became intrigued by how things worked and how they could be improved. He set his sights on an education that would answer some of his questions and looked toward using his refined and developed skills one day in a business of his own.

His parents sent him to the only local high school, the Jefferson Educational Institute, in Jefferson, some 6 miles to the west—far enough away that arrangements were made for him to board there. School records indicate that Herman had studied there as well, graduating in 1896. The institute was described in a 1908 catalog as "a high school of the First Class in the classification provided by the School Laws of Ohio . . . on the accredited list of Ohio State University and other colleges. Its graduates are admitted to these institutions without examination."

Courses accommodated both the typical student and those who planned to go on to college. Three tracks were offered: the English Course, the Scientific Course, and the Latin-German Course. Walter pursued the Scientific Course and received his diploma in 1904, at the age of twenty. Among the subjects in the four-year course were algebra and geometry, physiology, botany, physics, chemistry, Latin and German, English, history, and civics.

The catalog further noted that "the school is supplied with sufficient apparatus and material for the experimental study of the sciences, and much individual work is required of the pupils. A Tiffany Industrial Cabinet, costing seventy-five dollars, is included in the equipment." Typical of schools of the period, student "societies" presented exercises every Friday afternoon, including "essays, orations, recitations and music." It was certainly an education with a degree of diversity: Few other Scandinavian names appear in lists of students in Walter's class or in previous classes, and his class consisted of nine girls and seven boys.[5]

## A CASE MAN FOR LIFE

Next, Walter took a bolder step. Following in his brother Herman's footsteps, he enrolled at Adelbert College, a men's college at Western Reserve University (now part of Case Western Reserve University). In 1909, after more than three years of study there and two years of additional study at the nearby Case School of Applied Science, he received two degrees, a bachelor of science in mechanical engineering from Case and a bachelor of arts from Western Reserve.

Throughout his college years Walter worked at various jobs in order to meet his expenses. Custodial work and cooking in university buildings were among his duties. According to Eric, Walter "inherited" from Herman a job as janitor at Guilford House, a dormitory at Mather College, the female counterpart of Adelbert College.

Working and studying at Adelbert were not always easy for Walter, and his average grade was "fair." His best marks were in physics, followed by English, German, mathematics, and the Bible. He had three failures, which he made up satisfactorily. His junior year class load was especially heavy and difficult, and the records show that by the fourth year he was

*Like Walter Nord, many first- and second-generation Swedish Americans achieved distinction in technology and business in the United States between 1850 and 1950. Others include:*

*Vincent Bendix, 1882–1945, inventor of the Bendix drive and four-wheel brakes for automobiles and of braking systems for aircraft.*

*John Ericsson, 1803–1889, inventor of the screw propeller, designer of the Civil War ship* Monitor.

*Amandus Johnson, 1877–1974, historian of the Swedish in America, founder of the American Swedish Historical Museum in Philadelphia, 1926.*

*John Erik Jonsson, 1901–1994, founder of Texas Instruments, mayor of Dallas.*

*Andrew Lanquist, 1856–1931, noted Chicago builder whose many major structures include the U.S. Steel plant in Gary, Indiana, and the Wrigley buildings in Chicago.*

*John W. Nordstrom, 1871–1963, founder of the Nordstrom chain of department stores.*

*Emil Tyden, 1865–1951, inventor of the self-locking railroad car seal and firefighting sprinkler systems, developer of the Idaho baking potato.*

*—American Swedish Historical Foundation; Göran Blomé,* Twelve Ways to the Top: Swedish-American Success Stories, *1985*

taking all but one course at Case, which specialized in the challenging technical subjects he enjoyed.

He made a number of close friends at college. Among them were Swen Emil Swanbeck and his wife. A native of Sweden, Swanbeck was a professor of modern languages, much admired by students over a long career. George Saywell was among the first people Walter met at college, an older "brother" at the Phi Gamma Delta fraternity and a graduating law student who, as a patent attorney, later advised Walter on many of his inventions. Fellow Case engineering students Robert Fitzsimons of Cleveland and James Atlee Wilson of Youngstown, Ohio, became lifelong friends. Walter Hollstein of Amherst, Ohio, became a business associate.

All of the mechanical engineers in Walter's class at Case wrote senior theses on various facets of industrial machinery; for example, "Testing and Investigating a Wellman Steam Turbine" and "A Design of a Mechanical Brake for Hoisting Machines." Walter's thesis was on "The Cost of a Horse Power per Annum." He compared the cost of operating a number of industrial plants, using coal, under various conditions, trying to arrive at some averages that would be of use to engineers. Walter maintained his connections with the university and with the city of Cleveland throughout his life.

He matured into a unique young man of action and ideas, thrifty in his habits, an early riser, and very industrious indeed, not only in completing whatever project he was engaged in but with vision flowing con-

Walter Nord (first row, right) and a few of his fellow graduates of the Case School of Applied Science, 1909. His friends James Atlee Wilson and Robert Fitzsimons are on the left and right in the second row, respectively. (Reproduced courtesy of Evan and Cindy Nord)

stantly toward new possibilities. His analytical, inventive mind was full of curiosity, always watching and listening. In his heart, sustenance came from the outdoor life he had enjoyed so much in his youth, from his faith, from his brothers and sisters and friends. With his soft-spoken manner, a gentle, appealing personality, and a well-developed sense of humor, he had learned early to cultivate his gifts of making friends and entertaining them with witty stories.[6]

## ONWARD AND UPWARD

Walter, now twenty-five years old, quickly found responsible positions as an engineer. In 1909, after moving to Youngstown, home city of his friend

Elizabeth Stabe Grieve, her husband, Thomas Grieve, and their eleven-month-old daughter, Virginia, Walter Nord's future wife, 1889. (Photograph by Carrick and Weiler, Cleveland, Ohio; reproduced courtesy of Evan and Cindy Nord)

*Above, left:* Katherine Weaver Stabe, maternal grandmother of Virginia Grieve Nord, ca. 1862. (Photograph by Hopkins' Studio, Cleveland, Ohio; reproduced courtesy of Evan and Cindy Nord)

*Above, right:* Virginia Grieve as a young child, ca. 1892. (Photograph by Pifer & Becker, Cleveland, Ohio; reproduced courtesy of Evan and Cindy Nord)

*Left:* Virginia Grieve as a young woman, with her brother, Thomas, ca. 1907. (Photograph by Milton Studio, Bellevue, Ohio; reproduced courtesy of Evan and Cindy Nord)

Walter Nord and Virginia Grieve, at about the time of their marriage. (Reproduced courtesy of The Nord Family Foundation)

Atlee Wilson, he worked as a steam engineer at the Youngstown Sheet and Tube Company. He remained there for three years, rising to the job of master mechanic. In 1912 he went to Harvey, Illinois, where he served as superintendent of the Western Conduit Company. The following year he returned to Youngstown. Later that year, or early in 1914, he signed on as a master mechanic for the Cleveland Stone Company, to be based in Amherst, known for its huge sandstone quarries employing hundreds of workers.

Perhaps it was during his college years that Walter met the attractive young woman who became his wife. Virginia Grieve, born in Cleveland on May 25, 1888, came from a poor family. Her father, Thomas, was a Scotsman from Canada; her mother, Elizabeth Stabe, was born in New York State of German immigrant parents. Thomas, who worked as a steward and bartender, died in 1901, leaving Elizabeth, Virginia, and Virginia's younger brother, also named Thomas, in dire straits. Elizabeth worked as a seamstress to make ends meet.

In the 1890s Virginia attended a Lutheran German-language elementary school in Cleveland. Later she became a member of the Episcopal Church. After she graduated from high school, Virginia found work as a secretary. She soon showed herself to be skilled and hardworking in both business and the domestic arts, as well as a lover of flowers and dancing. Family lore has it that Virginia and Walter met through ballroom dancing lessons she taught.

Virginia Grieve Nord holding her bridal bouquet, 1913. (Photograph by Webb Studio, Cleveland, Ohio; reproduced courtesy of Evan and Cindy Nord)

Walter and Virginia were married on April 2, 1913 at Grace Episcopal Church in Cleveland. As part of the Episcopal wedding liturgy of the time, Walter pledged "to love and to cherish"; Virginia, "to love, cherish, and to obey." According to Eric and Evan, their parents' marriage was a harmonious one: They remembered hearing no harsh words between the two. This harmony extended also to the relationship between the couple and Virginia's mother, Elizabeth. Within one or two years Elizabeth came to live with the Nords in Amherst, and Virginia enjoyed a close partnership with her mother until Elizabeth's death in 1938.[7]

# THE NORDS IN AMHERST, 1914–1928

Each of Walter's early jobs had been more challenging than the last. Now, as master mechanic for the Cleveland Stone Company, he was in charge of the derricks, hoisting machinery, and other equipment used in several of the company's sandstone quarries.

## WALTER AND VIRGINIA SETTLE IN AMHERST

### "SANDSTONE CENTER OF THE WORLD"

The size of the booming sandstone industry—and of some of the quarries themselves—was impressive. Lorain County, Ohio, had been an important center of the industry since the mid–nineteenth century. Below the soil of most of the county lies a layer of this durable gray or buff-colored stone, formed ages ago when the shores of Lake Erie extended farther south than they do today. First used primarily to manufacture grindstones for mills, by the post–Civil War period sandstone had become a popular building stone with many uses, and a number of quarries were established near the towns of Amherst and South Amherst. A particularly strong demand came from the city of Chicago after its disastrous fire in 1871.

By the turn of the twentieth century a degree of mechanization had made large-scale operations possible. In 1901 No. 6, the biggest of the Cleveland Stone Company's quarries in the area, 2 miles southwest of Amherst, was called "the largest sandstone quarry in the world." It was hundreds of feet deep, employed more than 400 men, and shipped 30 cars of stone daily over the quarry's special tracks to the Lake Shore & Michigan Southern Railroad.

The sandstone industry, and the railroad that came in the early 1850s, had transformed the small village known first as Plato (1827–1836), then Amherstville (1836–1872), then North Amherst (1872–1909), and finally just Amherst. Josiah Harris and Caleb Ormsby of Massachusetts, Jonas Stratton of Amherst, New Hampshire, and others had brought their New England village culture to the settlement in the 1820s and 1830s. In time it became a typical small, midwestern town with its Baptist, Congregational, and Methodist churches. Beyond the town lay a well-developed agricultural area.

Even in 1908 the scale of operations in Amherst's sandstone quarries was awe inspiring, and peril was ever present. (Reproduced courtesy of the Amherst Historical Society)

As the sandstone industry blossomed in the later decades of the nineteenth century and the first decades of the twentieth, Amherst, though still a small town—1,595 people in 1880; 2,425 in 1920—began to achieve something of the look, atmosphere, and feel of a small city. It welcomed immigrants from Germany, Switzerland, England, Scotland, and other countries. Soon the town had Lutheran, Roman Catholic, and German Evangelical churches, German tradesmen and merchants, and a German bank. A town charter came in 1873, and in 1884 a large, handsome, three-story sandstone Town Hall was built at the central intersection. In 1894 a substantial sandstone building known as the Central or Union School—which all of Walter and Virginia's children later attended—was erected. Both buildings inspired community pride.

With great foresight, the Lake Shore & Michigan Southern Railroad tracks, so vital to the quarrying industry, were raised on a series of viaducts, so that no one traveling through town by horse and wagon or on foot needed to wait for a train to pass. In 1893 a passenger station was built; across from it, on Franklin Street, a freight depot was constructed in

No. 6 was the largest Cleveland Stone Company quarry in the Amherst area. The derricks shown in this 1929 photograph are no longer at the site, and the quarry hole is filling up with water. (Reproduced courtesy of the Amherst Historical Society)

*Left:* An early view of the Amherst, Ohio, Town Hall, built in 1884 on the site of Josiah Harris's first cabin. (Reproduced courtesy of the Amherst Historical Society)

*Below:* A postcard view of Park Avenue, Amherst, looking east from Main Street during homecoming festivities in 1914. (Reproduced courtesy of the Amherst Historical Society)

1905. Many of the quarry workers boarded the trains at the passenger station and went south, reaching the quarries via spur lines. Cars filled with heavy sandstone blocks traveled in the other direction.

Work in the quarries was extremely difficult. The men labored in the open, exposed to sun and rain from morning to evening, performing the labor-intensive operations of stripping, cutting (channeling), wedging, drilling, and splitting the huge blocks in preparation for their being hauled to the surface and transported to mills to be cut and shaped. The men risked their lives every day on rickety wooden ladders, worked with steam equipment that could explode, and used saws that could suddenly come apart. Accidents were frequent, and many lives were shortened by inhaling sandstone dust that caused silicosis, a lung disease.

Moreover, the pay was notoriously poor. In 1910 the workers at the Amherst quarries went on strike, but they returned to work on the company's terms after losing a total of $15,000 in pay. Three years later about 800 workers at Quarry No. 6 struck for 1½ cents more pay per hour.

The Amherst area was also home to cut-stone factories. There, highly skilled artisans who had learned their trade in England and Scotland produced fine, finished stonework that was used widely in large buildings and bridges.

The importance of the sandstone industry to Amherst and the countless hours of labor by its workers were commemorated by the erection of a sandstone bandstand next to the Town Hall. Incised into a panel in the base of the bandstand are the words, "This building dedicated to Amherst through the generous spirit and labor of the citizens[,] stone cutters[,] cut stone co's.[,] and quarries [in] 1915."[1]

## AN EVENTFUL TIME FOR WALTER

This was the industry in which Walter now immersed himself. Possibly the fact that some of the work was outdoors appealed to him, but no doubt he did not anticipate all of the demands and complexities that awaited him, both as an engineer and as a human being. Considerable travel was involved: As master mechanic, working with some of the largest steam-driven machinery in the world, he was needed not only at the quarries in the Amherst area but also at Cleveland Stone's quarries in several other communities in Ohio and Michigan. The company appears to have been cutting costs all along the line in its race to compete with other companies, including Ohio Quarries, which operated the mammoth Buckeye Quarry in South Amherst.

Life was full for Walter and Virginia. They became parents for the first time on February 22, 1914, when their daughter, Mary Elizabeth, was born in Cleveland. Walter spent a few weeks beginning his new job in Amherst and boarding with the Rice family, who lived in a farmhouse on Quarry Road close to Cleveland Stone's Quarry No. 6. Before long Virginia and the new baby joined him, and they moved into a rented house on Elyria Avenue near Church Street, known as the "Holle home." Elizabeth Grieve, Virginia's mother, soon came to live with them.

Margaret Rice Egeland, who grew up in the Rice farmhouse near the quarry, provided a glimpse of how Walter responded to the pressures of his new life: "I remember his first night with us. He was interested at the time in working on clocks as a hobby and he told us all about the different ones he had. Later he gave up clocks and took up furniture-making as a hobby. . . . He had a wonderful sense of humor. He ate dinner at our place long after he was living in town and my mother used to say that she could tell when he turned into the driveway (walking, of course) if he had a joke to tell, because, already, there would be a faint smile on his face. Often something had happened at the quarry or he had something on one of the other men eating there." Virginia balanced Walter's tendency toward levity with a dignified, serious demeanor.

During his eight years with the Cleveland Stone Company Walter developed a loyal core group of skilled mechanics. Both a talented engineer and a good manager, he became known as someone who "was always very kind to take in people who needed work — even if they weren't very dependable. He was willing to give anyone a chance at the quarry."

Walter occasionally encountered opposition, however, from the rank-and-file stone workers. Eric noted that "the quarry jobs were very, very hard jobs from a physical standpoint, and Dad had the idea that he could mechanize some of those jobs. . . . He spent a fair amount of time making equipment to do some of the more undesirable jobs. But the guys in the quarry didn't think that was a good idea, they thought that eventually they

*Top:* Mary Elizabeth Nord, 1915. (Reproduced courtesy of Evan and Cindy Nord)

*Bottom:* Mary Elizabeth Nord pushing Eric in his baby carriage, ca. 1918, probably at their grandparents' Denmark Township farm in Ashtabula County, Ohio. (Reproduced courtesy of Evan and Cindy Nord)

would lose their jobs. . . . So they saw to it that all sorts of things happened to the machinery he had made. You know, like dropping it down a quarry hole."[2]

## BECOMING PART OF THE AMHERST COMMUNITY

As Walter struggled with the problems of the quarries in Amherst and beyond, the years passed and the Nords became more and more involved in the community. On November 8, 1917, not long after the United States entered World War I, their son Eric Thomas was born; nearly two years later, on August 22, 1919, their son Evan Walter entered the world. Both were born in Amherst. On January 22, 1920 Walter and Virginia purchased a lot at 144 Spring Street, with the intention of building a house. In the meantime they lived in a rented house on Harris Street.

Now they were a household of six: two parents, three children, and Grandmother Grieve, who was a great help with the babies.

According to Eric and Evan, the house on Spring Street was a prefabricated one ordered from the Sears Roebuck catalog, something rather fashionable at the time. Walter and Virginia built it with the help of a $4,000 loan from the Amherst Savings and Banking Company. Eric recalled that the rooms in the house were quite small. Next door was an attractive sandstone building, a former school that had been converted to serve as a church. St. George Mission was founded by the rector of Christ Church, Oberlin, in 1912 to serve the Episcopalians of Amherst. Its congregation numbered somewhere around fifteen to twenty people and was served by a priest part-time. The Nord family attended services there on Sunday afternoons.

By 1920 the town of Amherst, with just under 2,500 people, had a vibrant, well-organized community life. In addition to the Town Hall and the Central School, Amherst had its own hospital, Carnegie Library, town park, six churches, two movie theaters, an opera house (on the third floor of the Town Hall), a hotel, a bowling alley, streetcar service, more than thirty civic, fraternal, social, and religious organizations, a town band, and many athletic teams, both student and adult. The year was packed with traditional events: spring cleanup day, high school graduation, Memorial Day and the Fourth of July, annual community and quarrymen's picnics, band concerts, baseball games, county fairs, school openings, Armistice Day (now Veterans Day) observances, Thanksgiving services, and Christmas celebrations.

Forming the economic backbone of the community, in addition to the quarries, were more than forty businesses and industries—stores, restaurants, banks, livery stables, blacksmiths, automobile agencies and gasoline stations, and a few manufacturing concerns. The largest of these was the U.S. Automatic Company, founded in 1908, which made small steel parts for industry on what were called "screw machines." U.S. Automatic was established by A. J. Uthe and William H. Schibley—thus its name, "U.S." They had deliberately located it on Jackson Street near the railroad's freight depot to make shipping as easy as possible. Producing parts for the growing automobile industry, the company expanded considerably in its early years.

By 1919 U.S. Automatic was employing 135 men and had completed a large, all-electric-powered addition to the original plant. Its 65-foot-high smoke stack was the tallest structure in Amherst. The company's owners not only distributed annual bonuses to the workers but also shared the profits with them and offered life insurance to employees who worked for the company for more than five years. Another prominent business was started in 1917 by August Nabakowski, whose roofing and sheet-metal shop later experienced much growth.

The editors of the *Amherst News-Times* sometimes did not think the town was working hard enough to modernize and make a good showing, compared with neighboring towns such as Elyria. But Amherst, as is evident from articles in the same newspaper, had something just as important: a family feeling and an ethic of service to the community. For example, when a disastrous train wreck took place in 1916, the mayor rang the bell at the Town Hall, and residents flocked to help the injured. In August 1921, merchants provided trucks to take 1,500 Amherst residents to the beach for their annual picnic. And, in 1920, a committee of the Business Men's Association purchased the Redington building as a memorial to those who had died in World War I. It served as American Legion headquarters and a social hall for the community. On that committee was Walter G. Nord.

St. George's Episcopal Chapel on Spring Street in Amherst, earlier a one-room schoolhouse, was next door to Walter and Virginia Nord's home. The Nord family attended this church, which closed its doors in about 1930. Eventually it was dismantled and reconstructed as part of the Amherst Historical Society's Sandstone Museum Center (see p. 148). (Reproduced courtesy of the Amherst Historical Society)

An early photograph of The American Specialty Company on Mill Avenue, Amherst. (Reproduced courtesy of Evan and Cindy Nord)

The American Specialty Company building was still recognizable in March 2004, evoking thoughts of the early Nord companies. (Photograph by Sarah MacLennan Kerr)

Walter formed lasting friendships with the town's leaders, including John J. Smythe, a lawyer who was elected Amherst's youngest mayor at the age of twenty-three in 1919; and Fred R. Powers, an Oberlin College graduate and much-beloved educator who served as superintendent of schools from 1918 to 1956. Both men contributed to the Amherst ethic: For example, Mayor Smythe performed marriages at no charge, and Superintendent Powers started a night school for foreign-language speakers. Before long, Walter became a community leader too: He was elected to the school board and took an interest in local government.[3]

# WALTER SPREADS HIS WINGS

Walter's frequent automobile trips for the Cleveland Stone Company gave him ample time to think about his life. He was working full-time basically to maintain and repair machinery. His desires and even attempts to make innovative contributions were not being encouraged. He really wanted to be his own boss. And he was away from his young, growing family far too often. So it is certainly not surprising that between 1919 and 1922 he gradually made a break with his life as a staff engineer and became an entrepreneur. He began by starting two businesses: The American Specialty Company of Amherst, while he was still working for Cleveland Stone; and the General Stone Company, three years later. His two older brothers and his sister-in-law Elizabeth, Herman's wife, helped him take both courageous steps.

## THE START OF AMERICAN SPECIALTY

The American Specialty Company's articles of incorporation, dated April 14, 1919, specified that it was to manufacture and sell iron and steel products. Those products were largely of Walter's own design. Among the earliest was a steam trap for industrial pipelines. The steam trap kept the pipelines free of water that condensed from cooling steam. Another quite early product that Eric remembered, from his early visits to his father's shop, did not involve iron and steel at all but wooden cabinets for radios, assembled to the specifications of radio manufacturers. Already, at the age of six or so, Eric was fascinated with machinery. As he later told the business historian Barbara Griffith, "I would go up to the shop with my father and play around with the stuff even when I was a very young kid."

Another part of American Specialty's business, according to a 1924 advertisement in the *Amherst News-Times*, consisted of repairing many different kinds of engines, including "gas, gasoline, oil and steam engines and boilers, cream separators and dairy equipment, harvesting machinery and all types of mechanical farm equipment." School Superindendent Powers, who years later wrote informal histories of the Nords' accomplishments, noted that American Specialty began in an old cut-stone-manufacturing building but soon moved to a two-story former lumber company, later a cloak factory, on Mill Avenue near the passenger station. Fragmentary records indicate that American Specialty made $2,292.01 in sales in its first year.

The company was incorporated in Cleveland, with the help of Herman, by then a successful Cleveland attorney who also served as Swedish vice consul, and Elizabeth, who purchased a $2,000 mortgage on the Mill Avenue property. Incorporators included Walter's other brother, Frank, and some of Frank's associates in both a garage and a sight-seeing busi-

*[In 1909 John Strohmeier] came to [U.S. Automatic,] where 15 automatics, a gas engine and a good wheelbarrow, all housed in a wooden frame building, served as shop, power, and delivery service respectively. Thirteen of the machines were single spindled, two of them were multiple spindled. . . . John Strohmeier remembers easily our three great building eras of 1910, 1914 and 1917. . . . Blue prints were nonexistent during John's earlier days. All parts were made from samples and comparison of the original part with the new part as the measuring gage. Micrometers were unknown. The rise of the automobile industry brought the first blue prints and the first precision gages.*

—Jerome McFadden, "These Thirteen Lead in Years of Service," *Chips,* September 1941

ness in Cleveland. Chief among them was Charles E. Shields, who remained actively involved with American Specialty throughout its history.

According to Eric's and Evan's recollections, at least four members of Walter's crew at the Cleveland Stone Company followed him from the quarries to his new company: Rudy Berger, Fred Mathes, Louis Schieferstein, and Herb Van Keuren. These men and others ended up staying with Walter for many years, but at first they took a gamble, for the company operated on a shoestring and some of its machinery was not up-to-date. Eric pointed out that Walter had additional help from Virginia, who served as her husband's secretary and bookkeeper for the first ten years or so.[4]

## GENERAL STONE COMPANY

Walter founded the General Stone Company at about the time he left Cleveland Stone. Shields was among the incorporators of this business as well. Incorporated in Cleveland on January 5, 1922, General Stone was to own, control, and sell stone quarries and to buy, sell, and deal in stone and stone products. Among the stockholders were Walter, Herman, and Frank Nord. J. H. Gillman served as secretary and production manager.

Still pursuing the idea of greater use of mechanization in quarries, Walter developed designs for machinery to fashion large grindstones for the wood-pulp industry, known as pulp stones. He and his crew at American Specialty built the equipment and hauled it to a small quarry he had purchased in Opekiska, West Virginia, on the Monongahela River between Morgantown and Fairmont. Powers noted that, over the next fifteen years, Walter served as either "president, master mechanic or salesman"—or all three—operating out of his office at American Specialty and making periodic trips to the quarry. He had good technical support from some expert stonecutters and from Gillman, who had worked at the large quarries. As with American Specialty, Walter had office help from his wife.

According to Eric, Opekiska sandstone was harder than the Amherst variety. As Walter and his workers developed their equipment for shaping and finishing the pulp stones and refined their manufacturing processes, a superior-quality stone was produced. At one point a competitor offered Walter a great deal of money to buy him out, but Walter declined the offer.

The drive to Opekiska took seven hours. When the two Nord boys were old enough, Walter took them with him, and the trips became true family excursions. Evan and Eric remembered that they had to be up and ready to leave at about 3:00 in the morning. As a boy of ten Eric was fascinated by watching as the quarried blocks were gradually transformed into large grinding wheels 6–7 feet in diameter.[5]

*My grandmother [Nord] had a real sense of humor. In those days there were guys who went around selling seed potatoes. And of course they were all bragging about the marvelous characteristics of their particular seed potatoes. And so she bought some seed potatoes from this one fellow and they planted them. When they were eaten, they were just as hard as rocks. "So Grandma," we said, "How did you serve those potatoes?" "Well," she said, "I took the potatoes onto the chopping block, and I chopped them up into pieces and then I boiled them for three or four hours, and then I threw them away and ate the chopping block."*

—Eric Nord, interview with Martha Pickrell, August 23, 2002

## FAMILY MEMORIES

The children, including older sister Mary, also enjoyed their family excursions to Otto and Mary's farm in Ashtabula County. About twice a year the family would visit the small wooden farmhouse, where their grandfather and grandmother would greet them and offer warm hospitality. Eric especially remembered his grandmother offering them a "shicken" to eat, cooked on a wood stove, and telling humorous stories that have stayed with them for more than seventy-five years. The youngsters enjoyed exploring the barn, riding the horses, fishing in the pond, and climbing trees in the orchard. Transportation was still primitive there: Automobiles had not yet replaced horses, and a corduroy road, reinforced with logs to keep wagons out of the mud, ran in front of the house. Electricity had yet to come to the farm. One special memory is of their Aunt Emily, Walter's widowed older sister, who lived for a time in a tent on the property. Walter's two younger sisters, Anna and Olive, had married after serving as nurses during World War I.

Otto died at home in Denmark Township on October 10, 1926, at the age of seventy-eight. He left a debt-free estate of more than $5,000, as well as 46 acres of property. Eric well remembered his grandfather's funeral at the Denmark Center Church, the many flowers, and a tearful tribute by the minister. (As he recalled, the other Scandinavians present were—typically—less demonstrative.) Walter's brothers and sisters and their families were there as well. Otto was buried in Ashtabula's Edgewood Cemetery. Mary soon moved to West Springfield, just across the Pennsylvania border, to live with her daughter Anna Colvin. Five years later, on February 19, 1931, she died there.

In a 1992 interview Eric and Evan provided more details of their family life in Amherst. The boys slept in twin beds in one of the small bedrooms in the house on Spring Street. Their parents "kept them in line" with gentle but firm discipline; if anyone was especially strict, it was their Grandmother Elizabeth. She and Virginia sometimes spoke in German if they did not want the children to understand. In fact, Elizabeth's

*Top:* Otto and Mary Erickson Nord's farmhouse in Denmark Township, as it looked in 1951. (Reproduced courtesy of Eric and Jane Nord)

*Bottom:* A young child with chickens at the Nord farm in Denmark Township, ca. 1920. (Reproduced courtesy of Eric and Jane Nord)

*Top:* A family gathering at the Nords' Denmark Township farm, ca. 1920. Front row: Mary Erickson Nord (left) and Elizabeth Grieve. Back row: Emily Nord Tracy, Walter's older sister (left), and an unidentified woman, possibly Olive, Walter's youngest sister. (Reproduced courtesy of Eric and Jane Nord)

*Middle:* According to Evan, showing off the Nord bald heads was a frequent feature of reunions at Otto and Mary's farm in the 1920s. (Reproduced courtesy of Eric and Jane Nord)

*Bottom:* Herman Nord, Walter's oldest brother, with their father, Otto, on their farmhouse porch, ca. 1922. (Reproduced courtesy of Eric and Jane Nord)

A watermelon feast at the Denmark Township farm, ca. 1920. Mary Erickson Nord is on the far right; her daughter Emily Nord Tracy is standing by the corner of the house. (Reproduced courtesy of Eric and Jane Nord)

Mary and Otto Nord, at left, outside their farmhouse in Denmark Township with their son Walter and two of their grandchildren, ca. 1922. Walter is holding the arm of his nephew Otto; Eric appears to be scratching his chin. (Reproduced courtesy of Eric and Jane Nord)

*Well, there were one or two rich people at Amherst, rich by our standards. And, my father had a car and we lived in a house that was a four-bedroom house. The bedrooms were probably not much bigger than this room. There was room for a double bed in each one of them. My brother and I slept in twin beds. We had a little tiny living room. We thought that was great. That's what you'd live in if you were below the poverty line now. The town was very diverse, but there was a sense of community there.*

—Eric Nord, interview with Jeanne Harrah, September 10, 1992

*They both believed I think in dividing up the work that was to be done around the house. In other words, Dad would do whatever housework he thought was his fair share. He would always wash the dishes in the evening and the kids were always there to wipe the dishes. . . . Mother did the laundry and occasionally we helped scrub the clothes. . . . You'd put the clothes on a boiler and put it out on a double hot plate and boil the clothes, and wash them and scrub them on the old scrub board. So, there was never lack of anything to do.*

—Evan Nord, interview with Jeanne Harrah, July 23, 1992

and Virginia's command of German was useful in their communication with German-speaking townspeople.

Virginia was industrious, sewing dresses, upholstering chairs, handy with tools she kept in her own tool box, tending the flower garden she loved. Evan would occasionally help his mother with the laundry, boiling the clothes in a wash boiler and scrubbing them on the washboard. Walter, too, did his share of the housework, including cooking breakfast and doing the dishes after dinner. At night Walter and Virginia sometimes went dancing.

Theirs was a home permeated by religious faith but not by sectarianism. They often said grace at dinnertime and regularly attended St. George's Episcopal Chapel next door. Yet Eric believed that the denomination of their church was relatively unimportant. It was the basic values taught there, and at home, that counted. The three children were extremely close to each other, forming bonds that no one could ever break.

As brothers usually do, the two boys early developed distinct personalities. Eric, with the traditional oldest son's advantage, developed traits of quiet confidence, studiousness, discipline, careful observation, and good judgment. At the age of six he already knew he wanted to be an engineer like his father. Evan was somewhat less studious, a lover of pony riding and other active sports and also more sensitive, more influenced by feelings, more of a worrier. According to later interviews, the two boys had their share of typical sibling fights, but they did not last long. Mary exerted a loving influence over her brothers. Eric remembered her as something of a caregiver, even as a child, and as a good listener.[6]

## COMMITMENT TO THE COMMUNITY

On April 5, 1920 the *Amherst News-Times* reported, "W. G. Nord was elected by the members of the school board to take the place made vacant by the resignation of E. A. Little. Mr. Nord is an able man and is sure to make a satisfactory member on the Amherst Board of Education." Thus began Walter's long involvement with the Amherst schools. Incidentally, that newspaper article may be the first time the nickname "W.G.," by which Walter was universally known until the end of his life, appeared in print.

Walter was elected president of the board in January 1923. Superintendent Powers—like Walter, a young man in his thirties—and his board had been actively pursuing plans to build an addition to the overcrowded Central School, which held all the grades and the high school. The high school principal was a woman, Marion L. Steele, like Powers an Oberlin College graduate. Walter helped lead this project to acceptance by the taxpayers and helped oversee the construction of a large, three-story addition in 1922–1923. More than 150 students were added from smaller schools through consolidation. Departments such as domestic science, physical education, shop, business education, music, art, and laboratory sciences were added or much improved. Walter spoke at the school's public dedication on December 7, 1923.[7]

The Central School addition, designed by Silsbee and Smith, Architects, marked the beginning of a long association and close working relationship between the Nord family and the firm that today is known as Clark and Post Architects, Inc., located in Lorain, Ohio. According to the retired firm principal John R. "Jack" Clark, the firm went on to design many buildings for Nordson Corporation, including its headquarters in Westlake and many of its engineering and manufacturing facilities, as well as quarters for many organizations supported by the Nord foundations.[8]

The difficulties of running local schools were powerfully illustrated in the spring of 1924, when a shortfall in funds from the state forced the Amherst Board of Education to end the school year several weeks early. After a close vote by the board, Walter announced the reason for the closing, and Powers explained that Amherst received less money per pupil than did twenty-four of the twenty-eight school districts in the county.

## TRYING POLITICAL LEADERSHIP

By then Walter was facing other challenges as well. In November 1923 he had been elected mayor of Amherst for a two-year term. A Republican, he had narrowly defeated the incumbent Democratic mayor, his friend Smythe.

This was an era of corrupt big-city politics and national scandals surrounding President Warren G. Harding, the Teapot Dome, Prohibition, and other well-known matters. Amherst, however, should have offered few rewards for corruption. The governing structure headed by the mayor and his council worked fairly well, and the council took care of business through a number of committees.

But a few practices apparently had become somewhat lax in Amherst prior to Walter's service as mayor. Contemporary sources point to difficulties in enforcing the Prohibition laws in northeast Ohio. Amherst Village Council records and the *Amherst News-Times* do not always make it clear whether Walter or a council member initiated ordinances. On January 15, 1924, however, at Walter's second council meeting, a new

Evan riding "Molly" at Otto and Mary's farm in Denmark Township, ca. 1922. (Reproduced courtesy of Evan and Cindy Nord)

The Central School in Amherst, ca. 1940–1950, where Mary, Eric, and Evan Nord received their primary and secondary education. (Reproduced courtesy of the Amherst Historical Society)

fund was established to pay detectives, Secret Service men, attorneys, court costs, and other expenses involved in "the enforcement of laws prohibiting the liquor traffic in Amherst." According to the newspaper account, this new "Secret Service fund" was to be financed by 25 percent of any fines paid into the town treasury for liquor-law violations.

The evidence seems strong that the following month Walter had a role in tightening up law enforcement in the town. At the February 5 meeting he read an ordinance "making it an offense to destroy or injure the property of said village or any departments thereof, or of any person, firm or corporation within the said village." The ordinance was passed.

In Amherst the mayor himself served as judge over many minor criminal offenses in what was called the Mayor's Court. Unlike his predecessor, Walter virtually never charged a traffic offender more than $1 of the customary $10 fine, but when it came to drunk-and-disorderly cases he increased the penalty. One man was fined $200 for public intoxication.

Eric and Evan recalled that Walter and Virginia did not serve alcoholic beverages, even after Prohibition ended in the 1930s. Yet they did not preach to others on the subject of alcohol, although for a time Virginia was a member of the Women's Christian Temperance Union. For example, the Nords tolerated the home brewing of beer by Germans and Hungarians in the town.

Walter and his council addressed many other issues. In 1924, apparently for the first time, speed-limit and stop signs were erected, and parking regulations were enacted. An officer was appointed to arrest speeders, and later a "police judge" was named to take care of traffic cases when Walter was in West Virginia, visiting his quarry.

As mayor, Walter occasionally stated his positions in letters to the *Amherst News-Times*. On February 21, 1924 he condemned the practice of attaching a sled to the back of a automobile and pulling it through the streets of the town. "In nearby towns," he wrote, "several very regrettable accidents have occurred and we feel it is our duty to take action to prevent similar accidents here. We therefore ask that the hauling of sleds or sleighs of any description by motor cars be discontinued. Flagrant abuse of this request must be considered as disorderly conduct and we hope that this notice will serve to end participation in this sport."

Walter's style of leadership can be seen in a newspaper reporter's comment about a severe sewer backup problem after a storm: "Mayor Nord said he had more than twenty-five complaints last Saturday and Sunday from residents of the N. Main street district. He advised the Council to investigate and remedy the trouble at once. Mr. Nord said he believed part of the trouble was caused by many residents allowing their roof water [to] run into the sewer, thus creating an overflow at the end of the sewer pipe line." An outside expert was called in, possibly at Walter's suggestion, to resolve the problem.

On June 28, 1924 a devastating tornado struck the cities of Lorain and Sandusky, causing many deaths and great damage and homelessness. Mayor Nord helped rally Amherst's residents to come to Lorain's aid. William Schibley, president of U.S. Automatic, Amherst's largest manufacturer, chaired the initial meeting of a citizens' committee. On July 12 Walter and Conrad Zilch, president of the Amherst Business Men's Association— of which Walter was also an active member—delivered a check for $2,500 to the Red Cross in Lorain.

Walter served as mayor for another year. But the world of politics was not truly his world, and he never returned to it after that. The schools, however, were another matter. As president of the Amherst Board of Education, Walter had a most capable superintendent in Fred Powers, who attended to every detail of managing the schools. He also had the satisfaction of seeing many of the positive values that he and Powers shared put into practice. For example, in 1924 the entire school, from the first grade through high school, appeared on the Town Hall stage in an Armistice Day performance to benefit the hospital. That fall the schools began a once-a-week religion class for fifth through eighth graders, held in the children's own churches.

Walter took a personal interest in the high school, especially its scientific and technical curriculum and facilities. No doubt he had a hand in arranging a talk at a high school assembly by Charles Howe, president of the Case School of Applied Science. "His talk," wrote the *Elyria Chronicle-Telegram,* "was one of the vocational addresses scheduled for the chapel services this year and was on 'Engineering as a Life Work.' " Walter served on the Amherst school board for two decades.[9]

## OUTDOOR LIFE

The Amherst Outdoor Life Association was yet another major community creation in which Walter took a leading role. Southwest of town, off

*He [Walter] got Eric and Evan off to a good start scientifically by buying them chemical sets, etc., when they were just little children. . . . One day, the boys were fussing around the kitchen on Spring Street while Grandmother [Grieve] was taking a nap. When she woke up, she found the kitchen door locked. After much insistence, they opened up. She found that they had been cooking some sort of compound on the stove with a resulting explosion and a big splotch on the ceiling. The boys had hoped to get it cleaned off—but the ceiling had to be painted.*

—Margaret Rice Egeland, quoted in Fred R. Powers, manuscript notes, undated

—Evan Nord, interview
with Jeanne Harrah,
July 23, 1992

*Dad went into this gas station and told the attendant . . . to fill it up. And the attendant says, "Hey Nord, tell me something, how did you get to be successful, you know, the president of the school board and the mayor of Amherst, how'd you do that?" And Dad says, "Well, I'll tell you, you work ten or twelve hours a day . . . and you save every penny you got." The guy says, "That's enough. I don't want to know any more about it." . . . He wasn't interested in making those sacrifices. But that was Dad's philosophy that you work hard, you save your money . . . but you help wherever you can help.*

—Evan Nord, interview
with Jeanne Harrah,
July 23, 1992

Quarry Road, was an unused former quarry area. Eric believed that his father planned to purchase the land in order to salvage some equipment that was still on the property, rehabilitate the equipment at American Specialty, and sell it. American Specialty did purchase the property on February 20, 1920 from E. O. S. and Clara Brown.

But the story did not end there. According to Eric, a group of Walter's friends discussed with him the idea of leaving the land "natural" and forming a conservation organization. With his love of the outdoors, Walter readily agreed. In the spring of 1924 the *Amherst News-Times* reported that American Specialty was leasing the 66-acre tract, including two small quarry holes, to a new organization, the Amherst Outdoor Life Association, which was to maintain the private park for its members' use.

Many types of outdoor activities were envisioned for the park. Representatives of the Ohio Sportsmen's League and the gun editor of the Cleveland *Plain Dealer* addressed 75 people at an organizational meeting, and a membership drive recruited 107 members. Among the association's first activities were setting up a rifle range for trap shooting, starting to stock a quarry hole with fish, and ordering three deer from the U.S. government, which had thousands available from national forests.

Four years later, in April 1928, the *Amherst News-Times* reported that the project was coming along nicely. The quarry holes had been stocked with hundreds of fish procured from state hatcheries. Over a two-year period volunteers had planted 25,000 fir trees, obtained from the state department of forestry. Today many of these trees stand tall on the grounds at the Outdoor Life Park, which the association still maintains for the use of its members.

Evan and Eric had keen memories of family excursions to the park. The children planted many of the thousands of small fir seedlings, and in winter the whole family enjoyed ice skating there. In later years the brothers marveled at the fact that their parents allowed them to dive and swim in the deep quarry-hole lakes unsupervised. Often with them was Evan's best friend, Bud Jenne, whom Evan called "more of a daredevil." Evan remembered that Mary went to the park, too, with her friends, and that the girls would stay close to the banks at the other end of the quarry hole. Even in retirement Evan enjoyed visiting the park, pointing out to Jack Clark and other friends the massive trees that he, his brother, and his father had planted years ago as saplings.

These years, so full of work, family, and service, set the pattern for Walter's life over the next forty years: committed and involved in as many matters as he could handle, in his business, in his own restless creativity, in his family, and in the community.[10]

Like every community in the United States, Amherst was greatly affected by the dramatic and prolonged business slowdown that became evident nationally when the stock market collapsed in September 1929. In Amherst, however, trouble had begun several months earlier.

## PROBLEMS AND OPPORTUNITIES

On December 20, 1928 the *Amherst News-Times* announced that the Amherst Savings and Banking Company had closed and was in the hands of bank examiners, after rumors of bank losses caused depositors to start withdrawing money. "There is scarcely a phase of town activity remaining unaffected by the closing," wrote the newspaper two weeks later. "Even the churches report diminished collections." The Village Council had no cash and had to borrow funds for current expenses.

### RECEIVERSHIP

As if to further discredit the bank, on January 24, 1929 the *Amherst News-Times* revealed that a Lorain County grand jury had indicted William H. Schibley, president of the bank and also of the U.S. Automatic Company, on "12 counts charging embezzlement, misapplication and abstraction of funds." For one thing, Schibley had transferred more than $20,000 from various bank accounts into the account of U.S. Automatic, which had fallen on hard times and had severe problems paying its creditors.

The banking authorities assessed the bank's seventy-four stockholders a total of about $100,000, and the bank reopened in April with a new president. Schibley, who protested that he had eventually replaced the funds, went to the state penitentiary. At the end of January the U.S. Automatic Company found itself in receivership. The petition demanding a receiver came from the Fitzsimons Steel Company of Youngstown; U.S. Automatic had not paid for more than $14,000 in materials. The steel company, owned by the family of Robert Fitzsimons, Walter Nord's classmate at Case, had its own choices for a dual receivership, but John J. Smythe, attorney for U.S. Automatic, protested that this was far too cumbersome. The judge of the Lorain County Common Pleas Court then appointed Walter as receiver.

3

# THE DEPRESSION ERA, 1929–1939

35

According to Fred Powers, important factors in Walter's appointment were "his rapidly growing reputation as a successful businessman, plus his record of stability, progressiveness and absolute fairness, which had been forcefully called to public attention during the time he served as mayor of Amherst." And according to another reliable source it was Smythe, Walter's opponent in his mayoral race, who recommended him. Eric noted, "John was a director in this bankrupt company so he had an in-

An early photograph of the U.S. Automatic Company plant in Amherst. (Photograph by Bill Harlan; reproduced courtesy of Evan and Cindy Nord)

side position and he had an inside reason for wanting to get someone in there to run that company who would do a good job."

The court gave Walter just thirty days to establish whether the company was making money. If not, it would probably be sold immediately. But after only two weeks Walter sent an optimistic report to the editor of the *Amherst News-Times.* "Practically every machine in the plant is in operation," he wrote, adding that production was increasing, quality was improving, and prices had been raised. He believed that, given enough time, much of the indebtedness could be erased. On March 7, 1929 the paper reported that the court had granted permission to the company to "operate indefinitely under the receivership of W.G. Nord." With the largest sales in several years, the shop was working night and day, and work was plentiful for two months.

Exactly how Walter accomplished this turnaround is not known, but it must have been encouraging to everyone who was involved with U.S. Automatic. The screw machine industry, operating on a job-shop basis, was always unreliable and cyclical, and poor managers had apparently nearly driven the company under. Its survival over the next five years is the first striking example we have of Walter's abilities in the field of industrial management. He no doubt utilized his many connections to help keep the company afloat in difficult times, including the advice of his brother Herman, the confidence of his friend Robert Fitzsimons, and the resources of American Specialty. In 1935, although it remained in debt, the company still employed 100 workers, just 35 fewer than in its expansive period in 1919.[1]

## DEPRESSION AND RESPONSES

But it was a time of difficulty in Amherst as the Great Depression hit with full force. The savings bank continued to have problems, closed a second time, and was sold to a Lorain bank. Powers and the Amherst Board of Education—of which Walter had been elected president again in January 1930 after a hiatus—struggled to meet expenses. A special levy was necessary that year just to keep the schools in operation. Eventually, teachers took a succession of pay cuts, as did other government employees. The Amherst Village Council, looking for ways to save money, began to consider building a municipal light plant even though it obtained a rebate on its light bill in 1932. In March 1933 the township trustees requested additional poor-relief funds from the county commissioners. Relief drives organized by the Red Cross and other organizations aided the poor of Amherst. In December 1930 the Colonial Theatre offered children a free movie in return for a can of food.

A feeling of solidarity imbued the town. According to Eric, "This community of Amherst was composed of widely different backgrounds of people. The one background that was probably pretty universal here, was that none of them were rich." With a decent income, living in a modest house, Walter and Virginia were frugal themselves but did their part to help needy families. As Eric recalled, "Mother was always for the guys who were not well off. She'd had enough experience with that her-

U.S. Automatic's workforce outside the plant on Jackson Street, Amherst, probably before 1930. The man in shirt sleeves partially shown at the far right may be Walter Nord. (Reproduced courtesy of Nordson Corporation)

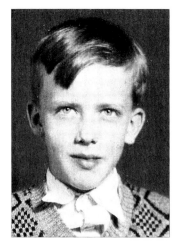

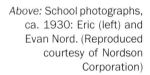

*Above:* School photographs, ca. 1930: Eric (left) and Evan Nord. (Reproduced courtesy of Nordson Corporation)

*Below:* Evan, Mary, Virginia, and Eric Nord, possibly at the Outdoor Life Park in Amherst, ca. 1929. (Reproduced courtesy of Evan and Cindy Nord)

self. . . . You never heard her complain about anything much. She was for the underdog. And, of course my father had been brought up with practically nothing, so they were kindred spirits." And they knew their neighbors well.

One of the most frequent sights in those years was that of homeless men riding the rails, stopping off in Amherst for the night. In April 1931 the *Amherst News-Times* reported that in the past three months 300 had stayed at the jail, located at the Town Hall. Eric, who was thirteen that year, and Evan, who was eleven, had fond memories of homeless men coming to their door, knowing they were sure to get a good, nutritious meal cooked by Virginia or Elizabeth, perhaps chuck roast or Swiss steak—the same plain, nourishing food they themselves remembered eating. The railroad was nearby, and Eric and Evan believed that some sort of message system existed among the men directing them to the Nords' hospitable home.

Already busy managing three companies, active with the school board and the Amherst Outdoor Life Association, Walter somehow found time to respond in additional ways to problems in the community. He cemented his close connections in Amherst by joining the Noon Day Club, organized by Smythe and August Nabakowski in December 1931, which met weekly with the goal of civic and social improvement as well as good fellowship. An active member of the Business Men's Association, he served in 1932 as its representative on the Executive Committee of a new watchdog organization, the Lorain County Taxpayers' League, which put pressure on local governments to reduce their expenditures. For the Business Men's Association he also devoted time to the Village Council's light-expense problem, to collecting donations for the needy, and to promoting the Hoover administration's campaign to "end the hoarding of money" by fearful Americans, returning it to circulation through the issue of "anti-hoarding" bonds.[2]

## Keeping Afloat

As the depression reached its depths, the national administration of Franklin Delano Roosevelt swept in with bold new policies. For his part, Walter, a strong Republican, found some cause for optimism. A few opportunities came along to help keep U.S. Automatic and American Specialty going, provide a livelihood for their workers, and boost the economy of Amherst.

Eric remembered well the work U.S. Automatic obtained from a sheet-metal-stamping company in Sandusky, making parts for cigarette rollers that tobacco companies offered as premiums to thrifty cigarette smokers who preferred to buy bulk tobacco and "roll their own." Eric noted, "I remember as a kid that they made these cigarette rollers by the millions. They ran three shifts a day" until the demand for them died down.

American Specialty, too, soon had a new kind of product, developed by Walter around 1931. In an anecdote now famous in company lore, he drove into a filling station one day for a "lube." The attendant complained that he could not get grease into the bearing of the spring and the shackle using the "Zerk fitting," a fitting to which a grease gun could be applied. Walter considered the problem and, that very night, came up with a "chuck device" to grip the fitting and force grease into it. The company soon began to manufacture the Griptight coupler—and sold many thousands. Then Walter came up with a replacement for the fitting itself. That, too, sold well.

Another product that benefited both U.S. Automatic and American Specialty came out of the blue. It was the Rotoscope, invented by L. R. Wottring, owner of the Wottring Instrument Company in Lorain. A device for eye doctors' offices, the Rotoscope was used to correct eye-muscle problems such as crossed eyes. Eric recalled that Wottring came to Walter, having spent all of his funds on developing his invention, and asked for help: "Somehow or other this guy talked him into it and we started making those machines. And they just sold like crazy. . . . American Specialty was the only company that had any money, and that wasn't very much. So, American Specialty . . . bought the parts from U.S. Automatic [and assembled them,] and that kept both U.S. Automatic and American Specialty going."

Best friends Bud Jenne (left) and Evan Nord with a pony in Amherst, ca. 1929–1930. (Reproduced courtesy of Evan and Cindy Nord)

Mary Elizabeth Nord as a
young woman, ca. 1931.
(Photograph by Rudy Moc
Studio, Lorain, Ohio;
reproduced courtesy of
Evan and Cindy Nord)

Manufacturing of the Rotoscope began about 1933 and continued for several years, until the market was saturated. Today a Rotoscope is in the collections of the Black River Historical Society in Lorain.

Eric and Evan, as they grew into their teens, began to pick up basic mechanical skills by working during their summer vacations with seasoned employees of American Specialty. Eric remembered especially working with the mechanic Rudy Berger and the machinist Fred Mathes. In addition to the fine points of metal-parts manufacture, these mentors taught the boys by their example valuable lessons about dedication to work, about not only how to work hard but also how to enjoy it.

At the same time, all three Nord children were broadening their horizons in other ways. A graduate of Amherst High School, Mary, the oldest, earned a bachelor of arts degree in 1936 at Bluffton College in Bluffton, Ohio, where she was active in the college theater group and YWCA and was an editor of the student newspaper. There she met Joseph Allen Ignat, her future husband. Joe, a handsome, dark-haired, gregarious young man with a well-developed sense of humor, shared Mary's enjoyment of theater and journalism. Coming from a poor Slovakian family in Cleveland, he and his seven brothers and sisters were raised by his mother, Anna, after her divorce from their father.

At Amherst High School, Eric edited *The Record,* the student newspaper; and Evan was beginning his lifelong love affair with tennis. Evan recalled, "We played 'pick-up' sports, baseball and football and basketball. . . . I played on the tennis team. . . . I played that sport throughout my high school years."

The Amherst mission church (St. George's Chapel) having closed in about 1930, on Sundays the family now drove to nearby Oberlin to attend Christ Episcopal Church. Eric was confirmed in Christ Church in 1931 and remembered the fact that, in his confirmation class, he came to know African Americans for the first time. Oberlin, with its long heritage of higher education, racial diversity, and zeal for moral and social reform, was a far different world from the industrial town of Amherst. Evan's confirmation at Christ Church took place in 1933.

The family was saddened by the death of Grandmother Mary Erickson Nord at the age of seventy-four on February 19, 1931 in Pennsylvania. She was buried near Otto in Edgewood Cemetery in Ashtabula.

As her children grew older Virginia had begun to spread her wings. In addition to the Parent-Teacher Association and the Women's Christian Temperance Union, she joined the Amherst Study Club, became active in the Amherst Garden Club, and served on the board of the public library. She also began what became her famous collection of fans from all over the world. Walter put in many hours helping her repair them. He continued to enjoy such hobbies; one of the qualities remembered by his children was that he seemed not to bring his troubles home with him.

One of the papers Virginia presented to the Amherst Study Club, according to the *Amherst News-Times*, was on "Athens and Sparta." She was seeking to fill in some of those broadening delights of learning that had been so lacking in her early life. For years she had grown rather quiet in the company of friends who were college educated.

Despite trying conditions, as long as Walter was involved, all was not bleak in Amherst. On July 3, 1933 the *Amherst News-Times* proclaimed that "Prospects for Local Industries Are Looking Up," noting new projects for the struggling quarries and, at U.S. Automatic, "a spurt that has been the best in many months." And on January 2, 1934 Walter and Virginia and other school board members and their wives, along with Mr. and Mrs. Fred Powers, enjoyed their annual party at the Oberlin Inn. Nothing but hilarity seems to have been permitted. After a series of comic speeches, Walter ended the program with what one hopes was a partially serious one on "Optimism for 1934."[3]

# PERSISTENCE

## BUSINESS UPS AND DOWNS

The middle and late 1930s were a time of economic instability. Despite new safety-net programs of the federal government, the Great Depression showed no signs of ending.

Walter was surely gratified that Eric was following in his footsteps, entering the Case School of Applied Science in Cleveland in the fall of 1935. But business news was not especially good. Walter's quarrying venture, the General Stone Company, which had seemed so promising, was now in trouble. The Carborundum Company of Niagara Falls, New York, which specialized in various forms of abrasives, had developed an artificial grindstone for use in pulp-paper manufacture that effectively put Walter's operation out of business. A rare handwritten record from December 1936 shows an operating loss for the General Stone Company of more than $3,000 and a deficit of nearly $55,000. Walter's response was, no doubt with great regret, to close the business.

The U.S. Automatic Company, though it kept going, was not doing particularly well either. But by 1935 Walter was ready to put together a more comprehensive effort to improve the company's chances not just to survive but to thrive. As described in company documents researched by Mary Ann Hellrigel, Walter worked step-by-step with his attorney brother and legal adviser, Herman. On October 17 of that year the company was reconstituted as a corporation under the laws of Ohio. The incorporators

*I was just fascinated with working around the machines and that sort of thing in the shop. . . . My father only had two or three employees. One of them was an old machinist, . . . probably 45 when I first knew him. He wasn't educated with any formal education, but he was a very ingenious sort of a guy. He showed me how to run a lathe and a milling machine, and a drill press and all that sort of thing. I remember that he had a box, a wooden packing box that he kept there by the lathe so that I could reach the controls. . . . As I look back on it, a lot of the machinery that we had was really pretty junky. . . . And you really had to be a mechanic to make things with it. He would cobble attachments up and improvise ways of using these machines and would make a lot of good stuff. . . . I never really appreciated as much then as I do now in later years how ingenious this guy was. I think he felt that he could do anything with a machine. That rubbed off on me, I think, and those were valuable lessons I learned there at a fairly young age.*

—Eric Nord, interview with Jeanne Harrah, September 10, 1992

of the new U.S. Automatic Corporation were Walter Nord, D. C. MacDonald (a partner in Herman's law firm), and Samuel Deitsch.

More than 2,000 shares of stock were issued in order to meet the obligations of the old company. At the first stockholders' meeting, held in Cleveland on November 1, 1935, seven directors were elected: Walter and Herman Nord; Robert Fitzsimons, Walter's Case friend and creditor; the lawyer John J. Smythe; D. C. Lowles, a Cleveland accountant; Walter Hollstein, an Amherst farmer and fellow Case graduate; and William A. Miller, another Amherst area investor. The Executive Committee was headed by Walter, as president and treasurer, and included Smythe, as vice president, and Miller. Marcella Kelch served as assistant secretary.

Minutes of the corporation, as documented by Hellrigel, show that steps were taken in 1936 to provide more operating funds, including selling $3,600 worth of stock to The American Specialty Company; authorizing the sale of additional stock and borrowing of money; and, at Walter's suggestion, paying him only a minimal salary. That same year, with little money to spare, the directors authorized Walter to purchase three rather expensive but much-needed machines. The next year they did so again, at even greater expense. This gamble of Walter's and the hard work of his 100 plant workers paid off, for the corporation posted a net profit of more than $17,000 for the year ending October 1936 and more than $30,000 in October 1937. The situation looked good enough in July 1937, in fact, that the company was considering expansion.

Positive factors, in addition to modernization of the company's equipment, must have included Walter's close connection with Fitzsimons and his efforts to find business, as well as a limited upturn of business in general in those years. But very important, too, in the 1930s and in the decades to come, was the corporate culture Walter nurtured in his factory. Clifford Berry, who started at U.S. Automatic as a turret lathe operator in 1935, had many happy memories of working in the plant that felt like a family, where Walter walked through the shop each day and took time to listen to his employees, showed a personal interest in them, and was willing to lend assistance if necessary. Among the workers, Evan and Eric remembered, were a few who suffered from blindness and other disabilities. In cooperation with an in-plant union, the Amherst Screw Products Workers, Inc., chartered in April 1937, the company for the first time offered each worker a paid vacation that summer. The union helped pay for employee activities such as parties and picnics, and it provided a small death benefit.[4]

## SUPPLYING INNOVATION

A general slowdown in business came in the years 1938–1939, and this was reflected in reduced work at U.S. Automatic. But rather than lay off workers, Hellrigel noted, in the spring of 1938 Walter convinced his directors to let him shut down the plant's machinery for three months and employ the workers in reconditioning it. He also found additional financial help again from The American Specialty Company. By the early months of 1939 the company's situation was slightly better, new machinery was on order, and a Christmas bonus was given to the employees.

At American Specialty, however, a serious problem had developed with the Zerk automotive fitting devices. In about 1935 the Stewart-Warner Corporation, on behalf of its subsidiary, the Alemite Corporation, had brought suit for infringement of patent; and American Specialty, not having the funds to defend itself, eventually stopped producing the devices. During the case, because Walter was ill, Eric was drafted to go to Chicago and meet the large corporation's lawyers, supposedly for a discussion of the issue, but it was more a case of being dictated to. Eric recalled the intimidating experience vividly.

Handwritten financial statistics show small profits for 1934–1936 and a small loss in 1937 for American Specialty, but in those same years Walter and his assistants were developing and refining new products that, later, boosted business considerably. These were products closely related to Walter's earliest loves, the outdoors and farming. First, according to Eric, came a device to aid in crop irrigation, then a vegetable-washing machine. On August 19, 1938 the *Amherst News-Times* published a long article describing a large, boxlike contraption fitted with an array of high-pressure water-spray nozzles and a conveyor that held rows of picked plants such as carrots, onions, celery, and radishes. Rotating the vegetables

Christ Episcopal Church, Oberlin, as it looked in the 1950s. Various members of the Nord family have attended Christ Church since about 1930. (Reproduced courtesy of Christ Church, Oberlin)

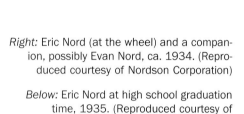

*Right:* Eric Nord (at the wheel) and a companion, possibly Evan Nord, ca. 1934. (Reproduced courtesy of Nordson Corporation)

*Below:* Eric Nord at high school graduation time, 1935. (Reproduced courtesy of Nordson Corporation)

on a track, it sprayed them eight times from several directions. The washer had been requested by a truck farmer near Hartville, south of Kent, Ohio, in an area of rich former swampland used for growing vegetables. The machines eliminated the time-consuming chore of washing harvested vegetables by hand.

The vegetable washer had been developed over the past three years and tested locally, and by 1938 sales were expanding. "The scope of the sale," wrote the *Amherst News-Times* on August 19, "is extending into Michigan and even into Texas." The newspaper reported that Walter and his friend Powers had just driven to Hartville to pay a visit to the vegetable farms. Powers "had his movie camera along and took nearly a complete series of pictures showing the process used in cleaning the vegetables." With his eye on wider sales, Walter sent his salesman, Harold Ricket, to take the films to potential customers.

Boating at Amherst's Outdoor Life Park, ca. 1938. Evan Nord is rowing; the man standing in the stern may be Joseph A. Ignat. (Reproduced courtesy of Evan and Cindy Nord)

A meeting al fresco, possibly at the Outdoor Life Park in Amherst, ca. 1937. Seated, left to right: Joseph A. Ignat, Eric Nord, Evan Nord. Standing: American Specialty employee George Cox, an unidentified man, Fred Powers, Walter Nord. (Reproduced courtesy of Eric and Jane Nord)

Joseph and Mary Ignat
on their wedding day,
October 15, 1938. Mary's
cousin Rose Stabe is at the
right. (Reproduced courtesy
of Evan and Cindy Nord)

*You just get to thinking
about how a certain piece of
machinery works. You notice
the difficulties encountered
and you decide to see if there
is some way to make it work
easier and faster.*

— Walter Nord,
quoted in Alvin Silverman,
"He Must Be an Inventor,"
*Case Alumnus,* April 1945

Several variations on the vegetable washer
were developed; some of the machines
reached considerable size, up to 20 feet long.
Evan worked on the vegetable washers during his summer vacations. He described the
typical design process, how his father would
tell Rudy Berger what he wanted, "and then
. . . Rudy Berger would make it. He was a
welder and a machinist. Then after they made
it," Evan quipped, "they'd draw the blue-
prints, as is."[5]

## A TIME OF TRANSITION

During these years Walter continued to play
a prominent part in the Amherst community.
Marilyn Pietch Jenne, a niece of Superintendent Powers who later played
an important role in the history of the Nord family and companies, remembered as a girl delivering agendas to Walter's home for her uncle on
the Sunday nights before school board meetings.

Among the issues the board discussed was the hiring of married
female teachers. At a meeting in August 1937 Walter voted to rehire a
teacher who had recently been married, despite a policy against it. Another measure Walter surely approved of was providing agricultural education for rural boys in the Amherst and neighboring Brownhelm schools.
The public turned down the prospect of another school addition in 1938.
In a March 18 *Amherst News-Times* article, an unidentified member of the
board—possibly Walter—praised the Amherst schools under Powers for
producing fine college material and vocational graduates, for a harmonious atmosphere within the school, for intelligent management, and for
good relations with the board.

Though no longer holding an elected office, Walter continued to be
drawn into municipal issues. The town went through a heated controversy over whether to build its own electrical plant, as some neighboring
towns had done, rather than be subject to the rates of the Ohio Public
Service Company. Walter played a useful role by helping form a committee that brought in a professional engineer to study the probable effects
of the two competing plans. At a special election on February 22, 1939,
Amherst voters gave a mandate to construct the plant, despite the engineer's recommendations to the contrary.

As an employer of disabled persons at U.S. Automatic, Walter became
especially interested in the plight of blind workers. In the 1930s he became active in an organization based in Elyria known as the Center for
the Sightless, whose mission was to promote the welfare of the visually

handicapped. He became president of this organization in 1938 and remained so for the rest of his life.

Walter's beliefs in service corresponded with those of Rotary International, formed in Chicago in 1905 to foster service, high ethical standards, and international connections among businessmen. Now, with worsening conditions in Europe, the formation of an international network seemed especially important. On January 2, 1938 the *Amherst News-Times* announced the chartering of the Amherst Rotary Club. Walter served as the group's first president.

More than 200 Rotarians and their wives attended the Charter Night dinner in the school gymnasium. At the head table, along with the mayor, Rotary officials and others, were Walter and Virginia Nord and Herman and Elizabeth Nord. Herman, a Rotary member in Cleveland, served as

Herman J. Nord (1877–1939), Walter's oldest brother, was an attorney and Swedish vice consul in Cleveland. This portrait was taken in his later years. (Photograph by Blackstone Studios, New York City; reproduced courtesy of the American Swedish Historical Museum)

toastmaster that night. Dr. Allen D. Albert, a past president of Rotary International, presented the charter to Walter and described the group's purposes, including those of the Rotary peace movement: "Rotarians want peace," he said, "not the coward's peace, but the strong man's peace of knowing he is right. This may not come in my life, but might in the lifetime of younger men, but not unless I do my part now." A year after its founding, the entire chapter joined thousands of Rotarians at an international convention in Cleveland. Rotary continues to be important for Amherst.

In 1939 Walter was fifty-five years old. It was a time of transition for the Nord family, as it was a time of change in the entire world. The year before, on June 14, 1938, Elizabeth, Virginia's mother, had died at the age of seventy-two. Three days later she was buried in Woodlawn Cemetery in

Cleveland after a funeral service at Christ Church in Oberlin. On October 15, 1938 Mary and Joe had been married, also in Oberlin's Christ Church. After her graduation from college, Mary had worked as a secretary in Cleveland, and her husband worked for the state highway department. The two made their home in Painesville, Ohio, in the early years of their marriage. With his outgoing personality, his skills in writing and salesmanship, and his Democratic Catholic background, Joe brought an important element of diversity into the Nord family.

In the fall of 1937 Evan had joined Eric in the study of mechanical engineering at the Case School of Applied Science in Cleveland. Both brothers belonged to the Phi Kappa Psi fraternity and enjoyed participating in campus activities, Eric in student clubs and government, Evan in the yearbook and tennis. On June 5, 1939 Eric received his bachelor of science degree.

Just three days later, however, on June 8, came a great blow: the death of Herman Nord. Herman was laid to rest at Lake View Cemetery in Cleveland. Surviving him were Elizabeth and three children, Otto, Sarah, and Margaret. Young Otto soon took his father's place on the Board of Directors of the U.S. Automatic Corporation.

All his life Walter had sought the counsel and friendship of his older brother. In later years they had become business associates as well. Furthermore, through Herman's influence as Swedish vice consul, Walter had begun to take a special interest in other people of Swedish and Scandinavian origin or parentage. Before long, honoring his brother's memory, Walter became active in the cause of Swedish-American relations and history.

Walter himself had often kept going through sheer force of will during recent years. According to Eric, his father suffered from a number of ailments, one of which, hyperthyroidism (overactive thyroid gland), was debilitating and poorly understood at the time.

In September 1939 the 125th Anniversary Homecoming Celebration of the town of Amherst was a happy occasion for Walter and his family. Walter served on the Program Committee, headed by Beral Powers, Fred's wife. Hundreds of people participated in the historical pageant commemorating all the years since Josiah Harris had come looking for a site for a town. The entire September 22 issue of the *Amherst News-Times* was dedicated to the celebration and the town. Walter must have taken satisfaction in the stories and photographs on the U.S. Automatic plant and the large advertisements, one for U.S. Automatic, declaring "1814–1939 Congratulations," and the other for American Specialty, "Washing the Vegetables You Eat."[6]

Difficult times can bring out the best in us. This has never been truer than when Americans joined people throughout the world in the righteous cause of defeating Nazi tyranny. Looking back from sixty years later, the response of the United States to this threat seems to have been truly remarkable in its quickness, strength, unity, organization, tenacity, and degree of self-sacrifice.

## WARTIME UNITY

In the Amherst area alone, more than 1,000 men and women served in the armed forces. As of November 1946, twenty-nine men had died in the war, and three were missing. Amherst's service people, including many already in the ranks before Pearl Harbor under the Selective Service Act of 1940, mustered in at Camp Perry or the Great Lakes Naval Training Station, went through basic training, and were sent overseas, where they served in most of the world's battle areas.

As in communities throughout the nation, corresponding home efforts involved nearly every Amherst resident in civilian defense, conservation of materials, scrap drives, victory gardens (home gardens to boost nutrition in a time of food shortages and rationing), war-bond and blood drives, and war production. The U.S. Automatic Corporation transformed itself into a large wartime manufacturing plant. With its night-and-day operations employing at their peak several hundred workers in three shifts, it truly occupied a central place in the Amherst wartime community and economy. In addition, hundreds of Amherst area workers traveled daily to Elyria and Lorain for war work.

For the Nord family, too, these years were a time of challenge, gathering together, and regeneration. In the early 1940s, despite various fatiguing, sometimes debilitating health problems, Walter maintained a demanding schedule at the helm of two struggling companies as well as frequently attending to the community's needs. Like everyone else, he was increasingly conscious of a climate of approaching war.

As the U.S. government geared up to produce armaments for England, France, and its own defense, the draft began. The *Amherst News-Times* wrote of meetings on implementing industrial training in the high school in response to the National Defense Training Program. The Rotary Club featured a talk by Peter C. Rhodes, an international correspondent for United Press, on Adolf Hitler's conquest of Norway.[1]

## HOMECOMING

U.S. Automatic began its production of parts for military armaments in a climate of improving business. In 1940 the company purchased nearly 5 acres of property south of the plant for expansion and installed a fire-fighting system that included a tall water-storage tower. That year Eric, a mechanical engineer just a year out of college, came back to Amherst to join Walter at U.S. Automatic. He had been working for a company in Cleveland, but his father's favorite physician, Dr. H. L. Knapp of Elyria, spoke to him confidentially about Walter's ill health. He urged Eric to come home and help out, saying something like, as Eric put it later, "Your father is very stressed out and I don't know how long he can hang on." Eric soon heeded the doctor's advice.

Then, not long after graduating from the Case School of Applied Science in June 1941, Evan, who had studied mechanical engineering like his brother, also came home to be part of his father's business efforts. And around that time, Mary and Joe Ignat left Painesville and moved to Oberlin. Joe performed a number of special roles for U.S. Automatic; Mary made an important contribution as well. Another new member of Walter's team, one who was almost a member of the family, was young Marilyn Pietch, who began work as Walter's secretary in January 1941 at the recommendation of her uncle, Fred Powers, for whom she had worked at the high school. Her fiancé, shortly to be her husband, was Evan's closest friend, Bud Jenne, who had grown up next door to the Nords on Spring Street.

Eric quickly became indispensable to his father at U.S. Automatic. He began in the toolroom but soon, because of his father's illness, assumed management responsibilities. One of his tasks was to create and fill new positions and to supervise employees as business increased. Eric had been elected assistant secretary and treasurer of the firm in January 1941. That September, after William Miller died, Eric became a director of the firm.

The U.S. War Department's Cleveland Ordnance District supplied most of the company's wartime contracts. U.S. Automatic's first major war product, however, came as a subcontract from a larger company, Robbins & Myers. This was the job of making parts for the Norden bombsight used in bomber planes, an extremely high-precision instrument that directed the gunner exactly when to drop a bomb in order to hit his target. Eric later described the Norden bombsight as "one of the United States' few secret weapons in the early period of World War II."

To provide space for this production, ground was broken in the spring of 1941 for a 181-foot-long, 40-foot-wide addition to the south side of the plant. The company purchased more land in July for future expansion.

By the end of September 1941 U.S. Automatic had complied with government requirements for facilities serving as defense plants by enclosing its grounds with secure fencing, employing armed guards, and requiring identification badges. An old cold storage plant, which had housed U.S. Automatic in its first years and more recently had been devoted to ice making, was close to the company's buildings. In order to complete the fencing properly, in July 1941 U.S. Automatic purchased the Amherst Cold Storage Company. By November a "Defense Plant" sign had been posted outside U.S. Automatic.

Evan, arriving in the summer of 1941, tackled a variety of engineering tasks and problems. At U.S. Automatic, before long, he became assistant production manager and took charge of the bombsight parts—"to make sure that they got made and to make sure they got made on time and to make sure they were right," he later said. This involved such minute measurements that the parts at times needed to be completed in a bath of oil to keep them at a consistent temperature. Even in recent interviews Eric marveled at Evan's zeal and skill in this work.

Somewhere around this time, too, Evan handled the conversion of the plant from belt-driven to motor-driven machines. He introduced other time- and money-saving innovations as well. For example, according to Cliff Berry, Evan noticed that U.S. Automatic had an inefficient method of disposing of the metal chips that were left over from the machining process: trucking them out in wheelbarrows. He purchased an automatic conveying system in a company sale in Michigan and soon had it installed. Berry noted, "The conveyor just took them [the chips] down to the dumpster. It made our work a lot easier and saved a lot of money for the company."

At American Specialty, Evan continued to work on improvements to the vegetable washing and irrigation equipment. And he had an idea for the newly acquired Amherst Cold Storage building. Assisted by a team of workers, he transformed the old ice plant into Amherst's first frozen meat locker facility. Two hundred sixty-five individual lockers were installed to store the frozen products of the on-site meat-processing plant, as well as other foods the customers wanted to bring. A grand opening tour in November 1941 drew a reported 600 people, and soon afterward manager Hollis Reighley of Oberlin had rented all of the lockers. Evan was elected assistant treasurer of the U.S. Automatic Corporation in January and a director that December, filling the term of D. C. Lowles, who had died.

*In the early days of the present emergency, when the defenseless countries of Europe were being overrun by the armies of dictators, we were just starting to manufacture parts essential to defense. . . . By far the greater percentage involved a high degree of skill in engineering and production. . . . As the tempo of the global emergency increased, our production increased with it, requiring additional sacrifices from you to meet the greater demand for more and better parts. When the Pearl Harbor tragedy overtook us, we of the Automatic were well on our way to an all-out production for the defense of our own country and for the aid of our allies. But with this new impetus we were spurred to greater efforts and a deeper determination to do everything in our power to avenge this unbelievable, humiliating blow to our national pride and prestige. I need not recount what has taken place in this plant since then—how we have worked long hours continuously day after day, night after night, seven days a week, week in and week out without interruption. Many of our employees have not lost a single day since the beginning of the war. It has been a grueling fight and one that has severely tried our physical and mental endurance. No one knows what such a strain means until he has tried it.*

—Walter Nord, in his "E" Award acceptance speech, January 13, 1943

Evan and a fellow U.S. Automatic employee, James Miskovsky, also performed the feat of painting the word "Amherst" in 15-foot-high letters on the roof of the new bombsight building, along with an arrow directing any airplanes passing overhead to the Lorain airport. Walter had volunteered this service to the community to fulfill a new government regulation. Clearly, U.S. Automatic was the center of vital activity in Amherst. By December 1941, according to a press account, the company had 376 factory employees.[2]

## THE START OF CHIPS

*We ain't going to go to Michigan
And work for Henry Ford;
We're going to stay in Amherst
And work for Mister Nord.*

— Employee skit song,
remembered by
David Ignat

Morale was good as production increased. In response to a suggestion by a worker, George Washburn, *Chips,* a monthly publication by and for U.S. Automatic employees, made its debut in September 1941. It was named for the leftover pieces at a screw machine operator's work station. Joe Ignat, who had been hired to assist purchasing agent Ray Wasem, was a talented writer and served as editor of *Chips.* An editorial by Walter, entitled "Defense at Home," appeared on the first page of the first issue. "Our business," he wrote, "is no longer that of merely producing parts. We are now an important cog in the first line of defense."

Because it was also sent to employees who were serving in the armed forces, *Chips* featured news of the company and its workers. As Joe wrote in the first issue, "This is your paper. It's up to you to make it just what you want it to be. No person should feel at any time that he or she is not welcome to contribute stories, pictures or ideas." One item that readers could count on in every issue was a sports column by George Innes, secretary-treasurer of the Amherst Screw Products Workers. Joe also had assistance from other members of the new U.S. Automatic Press Club, one of several groups that augmented the usual recreational activities of the union.[3]

## ENTERING THE WAR

The next year, as the United States entered the war following Pearl Harbor, men and women began to be sent abroad, and the nation suffered terrible losses. It was a time of greater and greater effort on the part of war manufacturing plants. Walter, now fifty-eight years old, worked extremely hard, concentrating his efforts and relying on his two energetic sons and all the others around him.

Early in 1942, Hellrigel noted, the board of U.S. Automatic approved another large new addition, a new building on the south, which was completed in a few months. It was designed expressly for the manufacture of M-48 fuse bodies (for timing devices installed on the leading edges of bombs). As workers left for the armed services, replacements

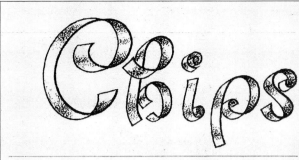

# Chips

VOL. 1                    SEPTEMBER 25, 1941

## DEFENSE AT HOME

### W. G. Nord

Unquestionably the most important thing facing us all today is the matter of national defense and the preservation of the principles of democracy.

Many men have left lathes, automatics, grinders and other jobs to aid in an all out for defense campaign. Most of these men have exchanged comfortable homes for military barracks at meager pay. The sacrifice on their part is great. Can we do half as well as they? Will we defense workers, manufacturers of parts bɛck these men to the best of our ability?

For the first time in more than a hundred years we are preparing ourselves against possible armed invasion. To carry the armament program to a successful conclusion the entire democratic world calls on all American industry to put forth its greatest effort.

Our business is no longer that of merely producing parts. We are now an important cog in the first line of defense. Our machines turn out vital defense items, any one of which can stop the assembly of a war tank if its delivery is not made.

Every man must consider himself a worker on the front line of defense. He takes his place along side of his brother who drives the tank he helps make.

Times like these call for discipline. Regimented discipline for those away from home in some cases is severe and for that reason we at home should begin a self-disciplinary program. Let us all place ourselves under obligation to produce more rings and pins than has ever been produced before.

Let us stop waste. We owe it to our country, our plant and ourselves. Each moment of delay, every inefficient move, every lapse of memory, may become a cause for regret.

Yours is an important mission. You are a soldier of America without uniform. Keep your head and heart clear and your eye on the stars and stripes. "AMERICA AND YOU"—a combination that must not be licked!

*Left:* Walter Nord's lead editorial in the premier issue of *Chips,* published in September 1941. (Reproduced courtesy of Nordson Corporation)

*Below:* Evan Nord at his graduation from the Case School of Applied Science, 1941. (Reproduced courtesy of Evan and Cindy Nord)

came not only from Amherst but also from the surrounding communities. The first female factory workers were hired. The plant operated day and night, seven days a week. When summer came, many workers took the company's offer to add the customary vacation pay to their wages if they would stay and keep the machines running. By year's end, according to Joe's statement in the local press, U.S. Automatic had 590 employees, including 198 women.

Berry remembered the extensive modernization of U.S. Automatic's equipment during the war. Among the items produced were parts for airplanes, locomotives, trucks, tanks, ships, Jeeps, and scout cars; munitions; parts for radios, telephones, electric motors, and starters; parts for guns; and parts for anti–aircraft equipment. On top of their superhuman working efforts, U.S. Automatic employees responded to Walter's call and committed an extraordinary average of 12 percent of their pay to U.S. war bonds. This included taking their yearly bonus in the form of bonds.

The American Specialty Company had also geared up for war production. Photographs of American Specialty workers doing cadmium plating for U.S. Automatic in a new site on Park Avenue appeared in the February 1942 issue of *Chips*. The newly expanded workforce divided itself into three shifts, handling the plating, inspection, and packing. Eric noted that cadmium plating was used on some parts, including fuses, and that later U.S. Automatic had its own plating department.[4]

We're In to WIN

# The Battle of Amherst

You are a veteran of the Battle of Amherst. No mention is ever made in the headlines about this battle. No casualty lists are compiled; No next of kin need be notified of your loss. But a bloody, important and monumental battle has been raging here since long before the treachery of Pearl Harbor.

Somewhere in Nazi-dominated Europe, or perhaps in the nest of the little yellow men of Nippon, there is a counterpart of our own plant. In this enemy plant, the instruments of war are being manufactured that soon will be used to kill young Americans who have gone out to defend us who have been kept at work at home.

The men and women who work in that plant are the foe against whom we here in Amherst are waging our battle.

To win we must produce, and yet, to produce is not enough, so long as that factory is also producing. To win, we must out-produce that plant, and the bigger the margin by which we can out-produce them, the sooner will we have defeated them.

No slave-manned factory in Europe can ever whip an American factory run by free Americans, if we freemen will only comprehend the battle we must win. The only barricade that can be erected to prevent our winning is the lack of realization of the vital importance of our part in this struggle.

Come on, let's snap out of it! Corregidor is no more important in this war against tyranny than is Amherst. Bataan will go down in history as one of the most valiant stands ever made by man—the Battle of Amherst will never be recorded on history's pages. And yet, there will be more and more Bataans, with their inevitable downfalls, unless there are more and more victories in battles such as ours — the Battle of Amherst.

If you don't want to pitch in and do more than your share to win this battle—move over and let a free American, proud of his heritage and jealous of any threat to his future, take hold. No battle shall ever be lost in Europe because one was lost in Amherst!

## RECOGNITION

June Strehle at her engine lathe at U.S. Automatic. Looking on is army Maj. Herbert S. Karch, who visited the plant when the Army/Navy "E" Award was presented to the company on January 13, 1943. (Reproduced courtesy of Nordson Corporation)

It was not long before the U.S. Automatic Corporation, and by extension the town of Amherst, began to receive official recognition from the federal government for its extraordinary war efforts. First came a "Minute Man Flag" from the U.S. Treasury Department, in recognition of the employees' generosity in purchasing war bonds. In early September 1942 Walter congratulated the entire workforce, massed outside the plant, noting that U.S. Automatic was "the first war plant in the county, and one of the first employing more than 100 men, in the state, to be signed up 100 per cent [to purchase war bonds]." A. J. Plocher, chairman of the county war-bond drive, presented the flag to Frank Lach, union president, and Hannah Tompkins, representing the female workers.

Then, in December 1942, came a great announcement: U.S. Automatic became one of forty-three industrial plants in Ohio, and the first entirely in Lorain County, to receive the Army/Navy "E" [for excellence] Production Award. According to the January 14, 1943 *Amherst News-Times,* U.S. Automatic was "the first exclusive screw machine production company in the U.S. to be given this high award." Robert P. Patterson, under secretary of war, sent a letter of notification. "This award," he wrote, "symbolizes your country's appreciation of the achievement of every man and woman in the U.S. Automatic Corporation. It consists of a flag to be flown over your plant, and a lapel pin which each of you may wear as a sign of distinguished service to your country."

On the afternoon of January 13, 1943 the awards were officially presented before an immense crowd of employees and special visitors, all gathered in the large new addition, by Maj. Herbert S. Karch of the Cleveland Ordnance District. Karch praised U.S. Automatic's efforts highly, saying, "You are making hundreds of vital parts for our war machine. You are far ahead of the average production figures for the screw machine products industry. . . . Thanks to your rigid inspection system, your rejection figure has been very low, in spite of the fact that much of your output is made to extremely close tolerances." He went on to describe the progress of the war, how American armed forces were turning from a primarily defensive effort to an offensive one. Further changes in production, and even greater efforts on the part of workers and their families, were needed.

In his response, Walter said, "I know that I speak for every one of you when I say that this is one of the proudest days of our lives." He reviewed briefly each stage the factory had passed through in gearing up its production. Congratulating his employees, he added, "We know that, in spite of the long hard fight we have made, we are not exhausted, but rather that we are trained and seasoned to embark upon even greater campaigns in the field of production."

Among other speakers, Lach, representing the workers, responded, "We thank you for the great honor which was bestowed upon us here today," and pledged to continue until victory. Others singled out to have their lapel pins put on by armed forces officials were John Strohmeier, the longest-term employee at thirty-five years, and Ruth Jewett, one of the first of the female shop workers.

That afternoon the special guests enjoyed a tour of the plant. Visitors viewed the first stage of the manufacturing process, watching and listening to the "mechanical thunder" of more than 100 automatic screw machines in which "rough bars of solid steel are cut into primary parts for almost every war instrument in existence," to be finished in other parts of the plant. Both the *Amherst News-Times* and *Chips* showed their pride in the event by printing special "E" Award editions. Items also appeared in the Case alumni magazine and the trade journal *Screw Machine Engineering.*

Walter Nord cutting an "E" Award cake during the banquet held at the Oberlin Inn after the award was presented to U.S. Automatic in January 1943. On his right is army Maj. Herbert S. Karch; on his left, navy Lt. Comdr. William J. Maurer. Seated is the Hon. Dan A. Cook, judge of the Lorain County Common Pleas Court. (Reproduced courtesy of Eric and Jane Nord)

That evening Walter hosted a banquet at the Oberlin Inn for many of the special guests who had attended the afternoon's events. After dinner, with a military official on each side, he cut an "E" Award cake. Some weeks later every guest received a souvenir: a booklet written by Walter containing introductions of each guest and also some entertaining stories. It is obvious that great pains had been taken to invite every person who had been of help in any way to Walter, Virginia, and the business—more than twenty employee representatives, as well as relatives, friends, associates, customers, college classmates and professors, public officials, even competitors—about 135 guests in all.

The booklet gives a rare glimpse not only of Walter's wit but also of his deepest thoughts and feelings. Paying tribute to his late brother Herman, he wrote, "I have a feeling that he still continues to assist us." Next to a photograph of David Walter Ignat, his first grandchild, dressed in a sailor suit, he wrote, "I wonder if, when David reaches maturity, he too will be confronted with the horrible reality of worldwide upheaval and devastating war that those who were the children of a generation ago are facing today."

Glimpses of the family and their special efforts for the war also appear in the booklet. Walter wrote of Virginia, who, despite recovering from an automobile accident and "looking out for a family of three men at home who never seem to have time for anything but work at the shop,"

*Above:* As this advertisement, which appeared in the September 23, 1943 *Amherst News-Times,* shows, the U.S. Automatic Corporation recruited women as part of the war effort.

*Right:* This advertisement for The American Specialty Company's vegetable washer appeared in the April 1943 issue of *Market Growers Journal.* (Reproduced courtesy of Nordson Corporation)

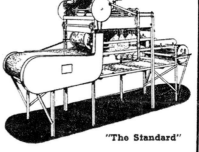

was serving on the library board and was active in the garden club, church societies, and women's clubs. "Never a particle of grease," he remarked, "or a tin can that is not salvaged in her home. At Christmas time Virginia personally selected and packed 83 Christmas boxes for our boys in service." Mary, "very much like her mother," was assisting Joe with *Chips* and "has charge of a group of Girl Scouts, who are sewing for British babies"; Joe had planned and directed the day's celebration. Walter wrote that he would not say much about his two sons, except that "If everyone in our country worked the long hours they do with the same determination, devotion and earnestness, the length of the war would be greatly shortened."[5]

# EFFORTS AND REWARDS

## MORE OPPORTUNITIES

With his businesses on a solid footing and with the active working support of the family, Walter seemed to have recovered much of his energy, and during the remaining war years he widened and diversified his activities to an unprecedented degree. No longer was he struggling along on a tiny salary: With the government contracts and the first U.S. Automatic corporate dividends, he was decently compensated. Among the most important changes he and Virginia made was to move from their small house on Spring Street in Amherst to an attractive, large home with an ample yard at 355 Edgemeer Place in Oberlin. Purchase of the property was completed on June 24, 1944.

Several factors sparked the move. Mary, Joe, and grandson David, who had been born on May 18, 1941, were already living in Oberlin, in a small duplex at 32 North Cedar Street. In September 1943 a second grandson, Joseph Nord "Joe" Ignat, was born. Virginia and Mary were exceptionally close. In addition, Walter and Virginia liked the community: They had made a number of friends in Oberlin since beginning to attend Christ Episcopal Church. Two of their closest friends were a Danish couple, Axel and Ebba Skjerne, he a professor of piano at Oberlin College. The Nords' Oberlin house, so much more comfortable than their smaller Amherst home, made it possible to entertain more. Eric and Evan, now well into their twenties, came with their parents to Oberlin.

Another major step for Walter was to purchase a sizable dairy farm near Wellington, in southwestern Lorain County, in 1943. The property, known as the Starr Farm, was an investment that brought not only financial rewards but also personal ones. As a youth Walter had been immersed in farming, and he enjoyed having a respite from the noise and bustle of the factory. He spent many pleasant hours overseeing the dairy operation. He saw the project as a challenge, as he told writer Alvin

*Samples of Walter Nord's banquet wit:*

*Mr. Fowler is chief librarian of Oberlin College. . . . Strangely enough, Julian's hobby is reading.*

*[On George Frank, editor of the* Amherst News-Times:*] His strong, vibrant voice kept him from being a Secret Service detective but has won for him the nickname of "Whispering George."*

*Seated at my right is my good wife, Virginia. The patch over her eye was not occasioned by a family argument but came about through an automobile accident.*

*[On grandson David Ignat, who wore a sailor outfit:] Commander Maurer remarked that David was the only second-class seaman he had ever seen who refused to pay any attention to a Naval Commander.*

—Walter G. Nord,
*Presenting,* 1943

Silverman of *Case Alumnus* magazine: "So many dairy farmers were selling out and taking factory jobs . . . that I thought I better find out why. So I got myself a 260-acre dairy farm in Penfield Township, Lorain County, to study the problem. It has turned out to be both interesting and a good investment."

At Evan's suggestion and with his help, Walter undertook to develop a second retail frozen food locker plant for U.S. Automatic, in Oberlin.

Walter and Virginia Nord's home on Edgemeer Place, Oberlin, Ohio, photographed ca. 1965. (Reproduced courtesy of Evan and Cindy Nord)

The Oberlin Frozen Food Locker Service Company opened on May 13, 1944 in the old Woodruff Building at 80 South Main Street, with 786 lockers. A *Chips* article noted that "The refrigeration and layout here, as well as in Amherst, was largely the work of Evan Nord." Amherst frozen food plant manager Hollis Reighley was put in charge of this facility as well. Both plants fulfilled a vital role in their communities. The number of lockers grew, with frozen produce from victory gardens replacing much of the meat as wartime shortages increased.

Another new project was the acquisition of an interest in an advertising agency, SuperVision, Inc. of Cleveland. Company advertisements appeared in *Chips* and soon in the pages of trade journals and other periodicals.

With the help of his mechanics at The American Specialty Company, Walter developed a new line of products especially geared to the home-front conservation effort. The first, designed in response to an inquiry from a representative of the U.S. Department of Agriculture, were the Easy Sprayer and Easy Duster, made for spraying pesticides on victory gardens. According to a *Chips* article, "Specialty men, under the guidance of W.G. Nord, developed a sprayer and duster made entirely of non-critical materials. Fibre tubes, dowel rods, leather washers and plastic have been substituted for critical steel." Final assembly took place at a plant in South Amherst. About 500,000 were sold in the first year; triple that in the second. In March 1945 *Chips* featured an illustrated article on the manufacture of "Fly Rocket" sprayers at plants in Amherst and South Amherst. It showed long rows of female workers assembling and packing the sprayers, which were shipped all over the world.[6]

## SERVING COMMUNITY AND COUNTRY

Walter and his companies were now in a position to make charitable contributions, not just to war efforts but also to worthy organizations, while complying with stringent government regulations in regard to excess profits. Hellrigel noted that for the year 1943 the U.S. Automatic board approved more than $35,000 in gifts: $20,000 to the Amherst Hospital Building Fund, $5,000 each to the Amherst Board of Education (used to expand its shop-training facilities) and the Case School of Applied Science, $2,500 to the War Chest Fund, and smaller amounts to the Center for the Sightless and other causes.

Following these contributions, a letter went out on August 18, 1944 to all U.S. Automatic stockholders, declaring that the Board of Directors contemplated making gifts for charitable purposes of up to 5 percent of the company's net earnings. This extraordinary dedication of the full amount of corporate giving allowed by the government (under the Revenue Act of 1935) as a deduction from taxes is an early example of a consistent policy that has continued until the present day. Five percent was a high proportion by all accounts. Studies based on Internal Revenue Service data show that the average annual contribution that year by American businesses was 0.09 percent and that even in 1945, a peak year for corporate contributions responding to high excess-profits taxes, the average was just 1.24 percent.

In these years Walter's community involvement increased. In 1943 he served on the boards of the Outdoor Life Association in Amherst and the Center for the Sightless in Elyria, and on the vestry (governing board) of Christ Church in Oberlin. In line with his position as an industrial leader, he also served on the Lorain County Health Board, becoming vice president; as director of the scrap salvage drive for Lorain County; and as the management member of the Lorain County War Manpower Commission, helping to coordinate the filling of war employee needs. A major contribution to the home-front effort was seeing that a Red Cross blood-donation facility was set up at U.S. Automatic in March 1943; before then, blood donors had needed to make the trip to Lorain. Walter also continued as an active member of the Rotary and Noon Day Clubs.

Furthermore, over the years, following in Herman's footsteps, Walter had become more deeply involved in connecting with others of Scandinavian, especially Swedish, ancestry throughout the Cleveland area and

*Two years ago, a representative of the U.S. Department of Agriculture explained to [Walter] Nord that there was a great scarcity of tin-coated steel for sprayers and dusters. Nord admitted there sure was. The representative said something had to be found to replace tin-coated steel. So Nord worked out a sprayer and duster from wood and paper. The first year his company sold 500,000 of the wartime substitute. Last year sales amounted to 1,250,000. This year more than 2,000,000 sprayers will be sold.*

—Alvin Silverman, "He Must Be an Inventor," *Case Alumnus,* April 1945

# U·S·AUTOMATIC CORPORATION

*Screw Machine Products*

AMHERST·OHIO

THIS IS TO CERTIFY, that I have on this 18th day of August 1944, sent by mail, the following notice to all of the stockholders of record of U. S. Automatic Corporation:

To: Stockholders of U.S.Automatic Corporation.

Your Board of Directors contemplate giving for the purpose of aiding the community growth and development of Amherst and for charitable, educational, philanthropic and benevolent instrumentalities conducive to public welfare including such agencies as War Chest, U. S.O., Red Cross, Salvation Army, Service Mens Organizations, etc., an amount not exceeding five per cent of the net earnings excluding tax ( which amount the Internal Revenue Department will permit as a deduction for income tax purposes).

Since such donations are all for worthy purposes but are not production expenditures, we wish you to know about them and to that end this notice is given.

U. S. AUTOMATIC CORPORATION

(Signed)    W. G. NORD
President.

*Hannah Tompkins*

Sworn to before me and subscribed in my presence this 18th day of August 1944.

*P M Smith*
Notary Public.
My Commission Expires
April 10–1947

beyond. In 1944 he became a director of the American Swedish Historical Foundation, located since the 1920s in a stately museum in Philadelphia. The foundation was—and still is—dedicated to perpetuating the heritage and traditions of Sweden and to celebrating Swedish contributions to American life. The founding spirit of the organization was the historian Amandus Johnson, who researched and wrote of the first Swedish settlers in the United States, the earliest of whom arrived in 1638. The museum was built on the site of a Swedish colony established on land granted to Sven Klute by Queen Christina in 1653.

Eric, too, was giving what time he could spare to his community. In 1941 he ran for a municipal office in Amherst (trustee of public affairs) but was defeated, and the following year he was one of those who spoke against building a municipal electric plant. In 1944 he served on the committee to build a two-story addition to the Amherst Hospital, to which U.S. Automatic contributed. In 1945 he joined Walter as a member of the Amherst Rotary Club. Later, like his father, he served as its president.

Eric was encouraged to continue in the operation of U.S. Automatic rather than serve in the military. Evan, on the other hand, shortly after completing the Oberlin frozen food plant, enlisted in the U.S. Navy. As Eric said, "Evan didn't go into the service until he got everything running." After training at Fort Schuyler in New York and earning a commission as an ensign, Evan served as an engineer on the destroyer USS *Pillsbury 133* in the Atlantic and later put his refrigeration engineering skills to good use on the USS *Lioba,* a refrigerated cargo ship in the Pacific. In all, he served for twenty-five months, returning in the spring of 1946. In 2004 Evan recalled that he had not told anyone he planned to enlist because he was

Walter (left) and Evan Nord standing atop the dam at the Outdoor Life Park in Amherst, ca. 1940–1960. (Reproduced courtesy of Evan and Cindy Nord)

not sure he would be accepted. He went to the recruiting office in Cleveland and was surprised to run into his brother-in-law, Joe, there. Both men enlisted that day. Joe served in New York until the war's end. Mary took over Joe's duties as editor of *Chips,* continuing in that role through August 1946.[7]

## INSIDE U.S. AUTOMATIC

### A Corporate Family

Life was vibrant and purposeful inside the walls of U.S. Automatic and American Specialty as the war progressed. *Chips* and the *Amherst News-Times* offer a window on a company under the management of the Nords that embodied the classic features of a strong corporate culture: a driving sense of purpose and corporate philosophy; a detailed knowledge of requirements and behavior standards on the part of each employee; heroes who could be looked up to; frequent events that offered recognition and celebration of achievements; informal communication networks flourishing in a positive way.

The companies went far beyond this, however. Partly because of Walter's and his sons' personal interest in the employees, partly because of

In the latter part of World War II Evan Nord served in the Pacific Theater of Operations aboard AF-36 USS *Lioba,* an Adria class provision store ship commissioned in 1945. The ship's motto was "Reefer Service to Fleet and Overseas Bases." This photograph was taken on October 19, 1954, probably in the waters off San Diego, California. (Photograph by Oather Morper; reproduced courtesy of San Diego Inbound Tours)

the closeness of the Amherst community, partly because of the war itself, workers at these plants bonded together with a family spirit. They worked together, ate together, read *Chips* together, played sports and danced and picnicked together, celebrated and laughed and grieved together.

In addition to promoting safety, hard work, the purchase of war bonds, and donations of blood, *Chips* helped keep morale high among employees both at home and in the service, with photographs and letters from servicemen as well as pictures of employees and their families. When a serviceman was killed, high tribute was paid. For example, *Chips* featured Harold Morehead's photograph on the cover of the March 1944 issue, described his death off the coast of Greenland, and asked, "What just tribute can the living make to one who has lost his life in performing his duty to his country? Neither statues nor monuments nor great works of art can make payment for one lost life. If there is a fitting tribute to pay these dead show us and we shall do it for this man. Then if tribute is not enough let us expend our every energy in repayment. Work, Produce, Give and Sacrifice should be our watchwords—our hidden medals of war—our tokens of tribute."[8]

Evan Nord served in the U.S. Navy from 1944 until 1946. (Reproduced courtesy of Evan and Cindy Nord)

## EXTRACURRICULAR ACTIVITIES

Each year, a few days before Christmas, employees and their families would gather in the high school gymnasium for a festive holiday party, enjoying entertainment provided by employee musicians and singers. The first year, 1941, a U.S. Automatic Male Chorus was formed, including Evan Nord. A high point came when Walter announced, "To the boys in service, we sent presents of fifty dollars." Another family-like event was the annual employee picnic in August, which grew to involve the entire community of Amherst. Company sports activities included baseball, golf, bowling, and roller skating. As the plant expanded, the baseball field that U.S. Automatic had earlier opened to the community seemed threatened by a road; but in April 1942 *Chips* expressed "a vote of thanks from all the fans to Eric Nord for his efforts in having the road placed around the field instead of cutting through the center."

To help employees and their families cope with restricted wartime diets, the company sponsored a Health for Victory Club. Modeled after a plan used at the Westinghouse Corporation, the club held monthly meetings and supplied nutritionist-approved meal plans, recipes, and other tips to those who were cooking for employees. Marilyn Jenne, who served as secretary to the club, said at the time of its organization in 1942, "Because of shortages and higher prices food buying is a job in itself. A housewife must work harder than ever, especially if the workers in her

Mary Nord Ignat with her sons, Joseph N. (left) and David, ca. 1944. On the piano behind them is a photograph of her husband, Joseph A. Ignat. (Reproduced courtesy of Evan and Cindy Nord)

family are on different shifts. She deserves all the help we can give her. Her health is at stake, too."[9]

## SYSTEMS OF ORGANIZATION

Within this family-like corporate culture, many changes occurred as the war progressed. In the 1930s a visitor would have seen about 100 men, each at his screw machine, turning out parts for automobile factories and other industries. Returning in 1945, the observer would have seen a vastly enlarged plant with several offices and hundreds of uniformed factory employees, about half of them women, watched over by department heads and efficiency officers and engaged in a variety of tasks. A large department was devoted to inspection.

Although the Nords' approach to management remained hands-on and responsive, the expanded organization came to require more structure, structure that came from company management, from the government, and, to a lesser extent, from the labor movement. How it was accomplished once again reflects the good management of the Nords.

Not long after coming to his job Eric found that he needed to select employees for advancement to supervisory positions. As he told the historian Barbara Griffith in a 1995 interview, "I was 23, and I was the engineering/machinist type. I didn't have any training in that sort of thing." At some point Eric contacted Stevenson, Jordan and Harrison, a Chicago-based management consulting firm, and arranged for its industrial psychologist to interview current employees who seemed to have potential for advancement. Bob Kropf was one example of a beginning worker who, through the interview process, was put on a track toward shop management.

The psychologist, Bill Stevens, also interviewed job candidates and advised on hiring them. Eric found his method of screening employees so reliable that he depended on it for the rest of his career. For many years, Eric told Griffith, "He would counsel us against hiring some people because he said, 'They're just not a fit for the organization. They're too aggressive, they aren't careful with the truth sometimes, and I don't think you would want them.' . . . So you build up a culture in a company. . . . If people don't fit the culture they usually don't stay there very long."

Turret lathe operator Cliff Berry was an example of a dedicated machinist who found himself taking on a new job as supervisor. He noted in an interview that he had charge of twenty-five female workers. In fact, being a worker in wartime was never easy, and despite the family atmosphere and the close, harmonious relations with management, many new complexities and pressures were introduced into working life. High productivity, efficiency, accuracy, and safety were goals mandated by the U.S. government.

The pages of *Chips* reveal the almost fanatical focus on precision, carefulness, and efficiency, points that were drilled into every worker, relentlessly, day after day. *Chips* advised workers on everything from calling the foreman ahead of time about a necessary absence to keeping one's hands in good condition. Special accomplishments and useful suggestions were rewarded. In May 1942, as the company geared up to peak production, a labor-management Production Drive formalized some of the company's needs with the establishment of various committees: absences, transportation/carpools, fire prevention / fire brigade, housekeeping, stores, efficiency. Ray Matz won the Slogan Committee's contest with the motto, "Production for Enemy Destruction."

In early 1943, not long after the proud time of receiving the "E" Award, workers and managers began a campaign for wage increases for everyone in the plant. Under government regulations, however, nothing of this kind could be done without a decision by the National Labor Relations Board. A petition was therefore filed by management and employees. That petition was turned down almost totally; and on June 17–18, 1943, workers staged a one-day work stoppage.

Joseph A. Ignat with his wife, Mary, and sons David (left) and Joseph N. (right), ca. 1944. Since 2003 an enlargement of the photograph has graced the foyer of The Nord Family Foundation headquarters in Amherst, Ohio (see p. 180). (Reproduced courtesy of Evan and Cindy Nord)

*CAREFUL
INSPECTION IS
IMPORTANT*

*What makes a good
inspector?*

*Good judgment, an alert
mind and a desire to be
right constitute the simple
requirements.*

*Who are inspectors?*

*Every man in the plant is
an inspector. Every person
who uses any measuring
tool to check parts at any
time is an inspector. The
most harmful thing a
worker can do against
national defense is to make
more than one part wrong.
Not only does he stop
defense wheels but he
causes useless waste of
vital raw materials.*

*Check your parts often.
Examine tools and gages
frequently. Make compari-
sons. Watch for errors. A
careful check in every
department will bring a
perfect piece into the final
inspection room and perfect
pieces find their places
on some machine of
national defense.*

*Read prints carefully. New
men, ask older men to
assist you. See your
foreman if you're not sure.*

*You can't help America if
your work misses the
assembly line and lands in
the scrap heap. Slow down
and take pains to inspect
your piece with care.*

—"Careful Inspection
Is Important," *Chips,*
October 27, 1941

Although the workers had been members of their company union since 1937, organizers from the American Federation of Labor had visited the plant and had put in a bid to represent them. The national union possessed far more power when it came to arguing their case. Both unions were represented at a further meeting with the War Labor Board. On July 20, 1943, workers voted that henceforth the International Association of Machinists, a branch of the American Federation of Labor, would repre- sent them as their union. This union, like the one before it, enjoyed amicable relations with the company's management. Nelson Schieferstein was an early union president, followed by Bob Kropf.[10]

## MORE URGENT MEASURES

As the war progressed, it took its toll on the community. Bond drives became more and more difficult. In July 1944 the *Amherst News-Times* reported that Amherst was the only community in the county to have met its quotas. The Red Cross was busier than ever, collecting blood plasma for injured troops. Almost 20 percent of U.S. Automatic's em- ployees had given blood by September 1944.

So many men had left the community for the war by April 1944 that a committee of the Lorain County Manpower Commission launched a special two-week drive to recruit "every woman not now employed." Several months earlier, in fact, U.S. Automatic had advertised for fifty women to be inspectors, machine operators, and other workers on all three shifts. In recognition of women's wartime efforts, Maria Wheaton Bowers Taft, wife of senior Ohio Senator Robert A. Taft, came to Lorain County in October 1944, as the *Amherst News-Times* wrote, "to observe the part which women in this State are playing in the war effort." At Walter's invitation, she paid a special visit to U.S. Automatic.

By early 1944, production pressures were so great that further for- malization and tightening of work supervision, rules, expectations, and procedures seemed necessary. One step was announced in *Chips* that April: the organization of a Foremen's Club made up of more than thirty supervisors and foremen. They met monthly for a Sunday meal at the Elyria Country Club with top management to discuss "production, safety, employee relations and absenteeism problems" and other matters, in- cluding looking ahead to peacetime. Work safety was a frequent topic at early meetings.

The company also turned again to its management consulting firm. The consultants prepared a job-evaluation system for the plant. Job de- scriptions were prepared in which every job was graded on several fac- tors by a union-management committee. In May 1944 *Chips* informed employees that "these job descriptions and their rates will then be sub- mitted to management and the union for approval, after which they will be sent to the War Labor Board for permission to pay these at the shop." No worker was to receive a cut in wages. Using the manual, however, a worker could look over the requirements of higher-paying positions and apply for one if an opening occurred.

Further explanation of the system came that fall: An incentive plan would pay 1 percent above the base rate for each "one per cent of quality work the employee produces above standard." To define the standard for each job, the union-management committee, now known as the Standards Department, was undergoing training in "time study and standardization" from the industrial consulting firm. Kropf became the company time-study director. Evan told interviewer Griffith, "It was to set standards. Somebody had a target to shoot for, and if they made good pieces and more of them, then they got rewarded."

In her summary Griffith noted, "These measures were viewed in different ways by different people." Some experienced workers like Berry, she stated, at first felt insulted by the studies in which watches were used to time their work. Berry did, however, acknowledge that "when they put this time study in we had more activity at the machines than we had before." And Kropf saw the new production rates as a way of allowing employees to earn more money despite government regulations against raises. Eric continued to employ these basic methods for decades to come.

In January 1945 Walter challenged his workers to better production in a column for *Chips*: "While our showing is nothing to be ashamed of it is nothing to be very proud of either. I am sure we can do better if we try hard enough." Everyone pitched in. *Chips* sent photographs of servicemen's parents at their machines to their sons. Even Powers took his turn running a machine. At the same time, Walter was looking toward the future. Advertisements in *Machine Design, Steel, Purchasing*, and other publications illustrated U.S. Automatic's capacity to make parts for industries in reconverting their machines for peacetime uses.

Also in 1945 one of Eric's special contributions to the company, as a designer of machinery, was officially rewarded. That year, according to his own records, he received his first patent, for a milling machine. In the course of his career he earned more than two dozen patents in the United States, as well as others internationally.[11]

## VICTORY!

With the great push leading to the imminent downfall of the Axis powers in Europe in 1945 came hope for the future. A Veterans' Coordinating Committee in Amherst was formed in March of that year, "to coordinate services for returning veterans." It included representatives of ten agencies, organizations, and businesses. Walter, Eric, Powers, and John Smythe were among the committee's thirteen charter members.

*In my letter to the boys and girls in service I told them about the splendid showing the people at the plant had made in the hospital fund drive. This pleased them very much. I also told them about our receiving an additional star for our Army-Navy "E" flag in July. Many of the letters expressed great satisfaction in learning that we were keeping up our production record. . . . I began to check to see what we really had done and found that while our production had dropped in 1944 compared with 1942 and 1943, . . . this drop was due largely to the fact that the number of employees had shrunk almost in the same proportion as production. I was in hopes that the records would show we had produced more per hour than in 1943 but there was very little difference. . . . I am sure we can do better if we try hard enough. . . . It is difficult to set a standard or to provide a gauge for what each one of us should do. My only solution to this problem is for each one of us to work so that at the end of each day when we reflect on the great sacrifices that are being made by our people all over the world, or when we offer up a prayer for their safety, we can each one of us say to ourselves, "Today I did the best I could to shorten the war and save the lives of our people in service and hasten the day when they can be back home with us again."*

—Walter G. Nord, "Today I Did the Best I Could," *Chips*, January 1945

When victory in Europe was achieved in May 1945, everyone looked forward to the veterans' return. From U.S. Automatic alone, more than 200 male and female employees had served, and 5 men had died: Elmer Leimbach, Harold Morehead, Carl Opfer, Elmer Peabody, and John Szekely.

The *Amherst News-Times* described the town's August 14 celebration of V-J Day (victory of the Allies over Japan), which marked the end of the war. "Participation in the V-J celebration was noisy but friendly and orderly. . . . Cars, with the drivers leaning heavily on the horns, appeared on the streets seconds after the radio announcement [and soon] impromptu parades of cars, decked out with every kind of noise-making apparatus the shortness of time permitted, wound through all the downtown streets." A parade was organized featuring the high school band and the American Legion. The editors wrote a heartfelt editorial on the sacrifices of war and the inevitable changes of peacetime. Just a few days later, more than 2,000 U.S. Automatic employees and people of the community enjoyed their annual picnic at Crystal Beach Park in Vermilion, a lakeside city northwest of Amherst. It was indeed a joyous time for many.

To honor the men and women who had served, especially those who had died, the Amherst community raised funds for new equipment and bleachers for the high school athletic field. Eric served on this committee, and the U.S. Automatic Corporation, U.S. Automatic employees, American Specialty, Walter, Virginia, Eric, and Evan were among the donors. Virginia also took part in a War Fund and Community Chest Committee that raised funds in Amherst and the surrounding area to aid war-ravaged countries, discharged and wounded military personnel and their families, and USO (United Service Organizations) activities in areas where men and women were still serving in the armed forces.

The challenges of the war years were well suited to the particular skills and character traits of the Nord family and those who worked with them. All-out effort, concern for others, technical ingenuity, knowledge of how to minimize failures, all produced major achievements and formed the basis for the future—a nearly seamless transfer of the business from Walter to Eric and Evan.[12]

The end of the war brought a new era of excitement and released energies all over the United States. Families were reunited, service men and women went back to work or to complete their education with government support, production of thousands of peacetime goods resumed, babies were born in record numbers.

## FACING POSTWAR REALITIES

### A TIME OF REJOICING AND WORRY

To some extent the Nords participated in the postwar euphoria. They were certainly happy to welcome Evan, who returned in the spring of 1946 in good health after two years in the navy and was soon putting his skills to work as a products engineer. Before long American Specialty was turning out additional consumer products, such as the Giant Magic Wand Floor Waxer, designed by Walter, and a pavement sealer known as Sealcrete. As the frozen food industry began to develop, the company expanded its sales of vegetable washers to food-processing plants throughout the United States and Canada. At some point, too, it had developed vegetable-packing machines. By early 1948 American Specialty had moved from its old quarters to a space within U.S. Automatic.

At U.S. Automatic, *Chips* enthusiastically greeted each returning worker, and the company family mourned the five employees who had lost their lives in the war. Many others who returned had serious injuries. In July 1946 U.S. Automatic held its first annual open house, inviting the public to view the machines that had helped the Allies to victory. At the annual August picnic, employees who served in the armed forces were asked to wear their uniforms in a group photograph. That October the entire town held a homecoming celebration for its service men and women. The Amherst Chamber of Commerce helped produce an "Amherst War Record," which was published as a double issue of *Chips* in November 1946. The Nords continued to promote a spirit of giving among their employees, from the Blood Donors' Club, to the drive to raise money for lights and bleachers for the high school athletic field in honor of the veterans, to furnishing a new laboratory for the Amherst Hospital.

5

# THE POSTWAR YEARS, 1946–1959

Despite the phasing out of government contracts, manufacturing parts to help industries resume peacetime production appeared to hold promise for U.S. Automatic. In 1946 Walter and his directors secured bank financing to purchase four of the most valued machines from the navy, rather than continuing to lease them, and early in 1947 the board allocated funds for further purchases. In addition, in December 1945 U.S. Automatic's Executive Committee voted to invest up to $40,000 toward the $70,000 purchase price of an iron foundry, the Hagan Foundry in Orrville, Ohio. This was done because the company had been having difficulty obtaining iron castings for production, repairs, and maintenance. Walter became president of this company, which was incorporated on February 1, 1946 with the new name American Cast Products, Inc. The December 1946 issue of *Chips* carried a feature story on Carl Hall, hired early that year as manager of the plant.

To their hundreds of employees the Nords tried to convey a sense of cautious optimism. For example, when Eric spoke to the foremen and supervisors at their monthly meeting in February 1947, *Chips* noted that "his outlook was much more cheerful than was expected." Eric, in fact, had reached a prominent position in the industry as chairman of the Ohio Division of the National Screw Machine Products Association. Yet the fact was that the screw machine products industry, never reliable to begin with, had developed much excess capacity as a result of the war; it was now full of cutthroat competition. This included competition in more routine jobs from very small, low-expense operators. By 1948 U.S. Automatic was losing money, and its loss accelerated greatly in 1949.

Along with their well-developed production team, Eric, Evan, and Walter worked continually to devise strategies to maintain and increase U.S. Automatic's sales. But they also were exploring the idea of decreasing their reliance on screw machine products. In the transformation that followed, it was extremely fortunate that the two younger men, now aged thirty and twenty-eight, were solidly committed to the business and kept working for the best, most innovative solutions. Walter, now in his mid-sixties and deeply involved in the leadership of many businesses and organizations, was ready to let his sons take even more responsibility than they had had during the war. However bleak the sales outlook, one requirement, perhaps not formally stated but always accepted by Evan and Eric, did not change: that, if humanly possible, no employee would be dismissed.[1]

## FINDING A NEW DIRECTION

In the pressured wartime atmosphere the Nords and their mechanics had learned to come up with solutions in a hurry. And as Henry Petrosky, the author of *Invention by Design,* wrote, "Engineers learn a lot by studying how things break and fail." In the new postwar world, the Nords were now considering the possible failure not just of a machine or product but of a business.

Eric, in a 1995 interview with Barbara Griffith, described how he finally became convinced that the Nords should reduce the company's screw machine products business and look beyond it. In 1948 he went to great lengths to redesign parts for an important customer. But despite all his work, within a year they had lost the account to a competitor operating out of a small shop, who offered to make the same parts at a lower price. The experience was disillusioning.

At about the same time, as U.S. Automatic's business declined, banks turned down Walter's request for a much-needed $75,000 loan. Eric recalled in his interview with Jeanne Harrah that "We finally had to borrow the $75,000 from a personal friend of Dad's [Alex Altfeld of Elyria] but we had to put up the whole company as collateral, and that was sort of a wake up call for us. We had had close calls before, we had a lot of them before. This finally moved Evan and me to a firm resolution that we were going to get out of that business one way or another and we talked to Dad about it, and he said, well if that is what you want to do, it will be your work."

The long-term strategy the brothers adopted was to radically reduce their screw machine business by selling half of their equipment, keeping

An aerial view of the U.S. Automatic buildings in the early 1950s. The Amherst frozen food plant is at the lower left, just above the overpass. To the right of the water tower, "Amherst," "N," and arrows, painted on the flat roof of the former Norden bombsight building, are barely visible. For other aerial photographs of the site, see pages 124 and 169. (Reproduced courtesy of Nordson Corporation)

Eric and Evan Nord look ready to welcome workers and visitors to the U.S. Automatic Corporation plant, ca. 1950s. (Reproduced courtesy of Nordson Corporation)

only the best, most loyal, and lucrative customers, and allowing their workforce to drop naturally by attrition. They would use the cash from the sale of equipment to subsidize the business if necessary and also to develop unique proprietary products to lift U.S. Automatic out of its relatively passive job-shop existence and into the realm of entrepreneurship. They envisioned that within ten years the company might be out of the screw machine products business entirely.

The brothers spent more than two years planning the giant sale, utilizing their analytical thinking and calculating skills. Eric found additional help in one of the earliest computing technologies, McBee Keysort punch cards. They used the cards to verify their initial choices of which customers to keep and to select the equipment with which to meet those customers' needs. "We would try and keep the more complicated jobs," Eric recalled. "Anybody that had a screw machine could make the nuts and bolts in their garage."

They took equal care in selecting an auction firm and planning the date of the sale. As the time drew near, many factory employees feared they would lose their jobs, but the Nords assembled all of the workers and assured them that no one would be laid off. The well-publicized auction, described as a turning point by Eric, began on January 22, 1952. It drew manufacturers from throughout the nation and was an impressive success, raising a total of $504,452. Additional proceeds came from the sale of U.S. Automatic's interest in American Cast Products to the Hagan Corporation of Pittsburgh.

The new strategy was a gamble. As Eric said, "We knew where we wanted to be but we didn't know where we wanted to go." And he noted, "I don't recall him [Walter] ever saying, that's pretty risky, let's not do that. It was pretty risky selling half our business at an auction, and not knowing what we were going to do from then on in. People say, well, you like to gamble. No, I don't like to gamble, but I can't say I never have. I like to gamble on sure things if I can."

Evan took over the run-
ning of the plant, a responsibility he retained for the rest
of his career. He willingly
took on the most compli-
cated jobs, and mechanical
improvements were impor-
tant. At one point, with Cliff
Berry's help, he converted
the cutting tools on the machines from high speed to
carbide, which was much
harder and faster. Berry remembered that he and Evan
spent several nights experi-
menting with the carbide
tools. Some of the other
problems Evan had to handle
are revealed in a letter from
his father, traveling in Europe

Eric and Evan Nord at the
door of the main building at
U.S. Automatic, photo-
graphed after the purchase
of the Bede airless spray
process in 1954. The sign
on the door reads, "U.S.
Automatic Corporation /
Bede Products Corporation /
The American Specialty
Company." (Reproduced
courtesy of Nordson
Corporation)

in August 1952: "I was glad to know the roof over the heat treating room
was working out so well . . . [and] that the steel strike had finally ended
and hope that things will settle down now." Evan recalled such annoy-
ances as oil on the wooden floors that came off on everyone's shoes, and
a foreman who was not easy to deal with. Along with Bob Kropf and
legal counsel, Evan handled the plant's union negotiations, work that
he came to enjoy. He remained closely involved with American Specialty
as well.

Eric concentrated his efforts on finding new products, investigating
possibilities in both the United States and Europe. He recently recalled,
"It was a tremendously challenging period and tremendously interesting. I looked under a lot of rocks and found interesting products, but we
weren't positioned either in manufacturing or marketing to make them;
so it involved a lot of looking and sorting." Over the next few years the
company experimented with making some products that had been successful in Europe but turned out to be less so in the United States: ring
springs and grip springs for railroad cars and airplanes, and plastic-bound
magnets. By sheer chance, an opportunity came along that provided the
product the Nords were looking for.[2]

## Birth of Nordson Corporation

In 1950 Walter had become president of SuperVision, a Cleveland advertising agency that furnished advertisements for U.S. Automatic and Ameri-

*Right:* Evan Nord in 1955 with equipment he used in developing the tungsten carbide nozzle for Nordson's earliest airless spray machines. (Reproduced courtesy of Nordson Corporation)

*Below:* Evan (left), Eric, and Walter Nord with early Bede equipment at a trade show in the 1950s. (Reproduced courtesy of Nordson Corporation)

can Specialty, and his son-in-law, Joe, had become the agency's general manager. (Eric recalled that his father helped Joe buy the agency.) Joe visited Eric one Sunday, just a day after Eric had returned from one of his trips to Europe, and told him about a man named James Bede of Cleveland who was making new airless spray equipment to apply heated lacquers and paints, greatly increasing painting efficiency and reducing the use of solvents. Among Bede's customers was the giant DuPont Corporation. The chance nature of this information rested on another odd

circumstance: Joe found out about the Bede devices one day while din-
ing in downtown Cleveland with a friend named "Colonel" Frier.

Joe persuaded the Nords to take a look at Bede's equipment and
operation. When they examined the equipment, Eric and Evan found a
number of serious flaws. It was not properly designed to withstand or
regulate the pressure of heated paints other than lacquers, and Bede was
losing customers as the equipment failed. But after some study, these
resourceful engineers came to believe that the defects could be corrected.
In addition, Bede had in place the beginnings of a well-developed distribution network. Eric and Evan began to see great potential, and after
careful consideration, U.S. Automatic purchased Bede's assets on July 2,
1954 and formed the Bede Products Corporation. On October 11, 1957
the name of the new company was changed to Nordson Corporation.

The name "Nordson" was selected, company lawyer William D. "Bill"
Ginn told Griffith, because "Walter wanted it to have a name that would
signify the efforts that his sons were going to put into it, because Walter
wanted this to be their enterprise. We tried a number of variations and
came up with Nordson." Walter became chairman, Eric president, and
Evan treasurer of the new company.

An initial problem was that Nordson took over from Bede the responsibility of furnishing refunds to Bede's customers for faulty equipment. Eric recalled that although they expected about seven such cases,
within six months they had to make about thirty refunds. Another problem was the fact that Bede held a patent on his equipment and, after the
sale of assets, retained the right to sell his invention abroad, doing business internationally with companies that served as licensees for the products, which still often did not work. Nordson dealt with the resulting
tangle a few years later, after the needed improvements had been made in
the airless system.[3]

## Moving into Production

Over the next five years a great many technical improvements were designed and carried out by Eric, Evan, and the engineers they hired, including two refugees from Poland, Samuel Rosen and Henry Libicki,
who became important in the organization. Frank Ziroe, Ed Hogstrom,
and Reginald Renouf were three experts from the Bede company who
also joined Nordson.

Eric and Evan described to Griffith some of the necessary steps in
perfecting the airless system. Eric replaced a pulsating pump that was
ruining the quality of the applied paint finish with a two-piston pump.
The engineering team used strong, armored, lined hoses that had been
designed by aircraft engineers. Evan tackled the difficult job of designing
a tungsten carbide spray nozzle that produced a smooth, flat spray—as

Eric said, "so you can lay it on like a paint brush." Until Evan and Ziroe, working secretly in rented quarters nearby, perfected the new nozzle, it was believed that making a nozzle from this nearly indestructible metal was impossible. But to the brothers this seemed the only possibility. "For us," Eric told Griffith, "it was life or death: we either made a carbide nozzle or we didn't have anything to sell." To everyone's relief, Evan and his team were successful.

In addition, the spray gun that held the nozzle worked poorly. By the late 1950s Eric and Rosen had perfected a much better spray gun and had taken out a joint patent. By 1959 the entire improved airless system was ready to put on the market. Eric and Rosen continued as a team at Nordson, while Evan and Libicki directed most of their further efforts to U.S. Automatic.

A separate corporation, Baermann-Nord, was formed in April 1955 to produce plastic-bound magnets, carbide nozzles, and spray guns. In 1958 Baermann-Nord was reorganized as the Banor Corporation, limited to the manufacture of nozzles used in the airless spray equipment.

Improvements in the marketing network took place in 1957, when sales subsidiaries known as Nordson Eastern, Inc., Nordson Central, Inc., and Nordson Midwestern, Inc. were established. And in September 1959 the first issue of the *Nordson Newsletter* was published with the aid of SuperVision, "aimed at telling our representatives, customers and friends something about our company and our products." The four-page newsletter with its bright yellow masthead was full of illustrated articles about Nordson products and their applications. Periodically Nordson invited its customers to attend a free, one-week "Nordson School of Spray Painting." The newsletters show that improvements continued to be made and that new applications kept being discovered.

One interesting early application involved spraying the insides and outsides of Coors beer cans with special nozzles. Eric designed a machine that did not need to advance and retract as it painted each can, a simplification that speeded up production considerably. The Coors people, Eric recalled, then wondered whether Nordson could make something to spray pitch in order to seal the sides of concrete storage vats. Ziroe assisted in the development of that equipment—and just a few years later this innovation became important in unforeseen ways.

As the Nordson company stood on the brink of rapid development and U.S. Automatic was holding its own, the Nords discontinued trying to manage the two frozen food locker plants. In company minutes of April 22, 1954 Evan reported "the sale of Oberlin Frozen Foods [the business, not the building in which it was located] to a group of people headed by Hollis Reighley." Two years later, at the annual shareholders' meeting on January 10, Evan noted that the Amherst frozen food busi-

*If the roof leaked [at the plant], they said, "Evan, your roof is leaking!"*

—Evan Nord, interview with Martha Pickrell, June 26, 2003

# NORDSON *Newsletter*

VOL. 1   NO. 1   **NORDSON CORPORATION - AMHERST, OHIO**   SEPTEMBER, 1959

## HELLO!

This is the first of a series of Nordson Newsletters aimed at telling our representatives, customers and friends something about our company and our products.

We want to help our users get more out of their present equipment so will carry tips on usage and maintenance. We will also tell of unusual installations, new equipment and new ideas of every sort.

The size of the newsletter is to be restricted. We will try to be as direct and to-the-point as possibe in all our articles. If for any reason a reader should want more details about a subject covered in the Newsletter we will do our best to provide all the information available.

We solicit stories from our customers and our distributors on unusual installations, useful tips and any other material that will help tell the Nordson Airless story. Of particular interest are case histories with photographic illustrations. This publication is for your benefit. Any comments or suggestions you may have will be welcomed.

## new, complete, portable "spray shop"

### THE NORDSON AP-16000 "PACKAGE" AIRLESS UNIT

"Just plug it in and you are ready to spray". That, in a nutshell, is the story of the new Nordson AP-16000 unit. Designed primarily as a maintenance unit for the Armed Services, institutions and maintenance painting contractors, the new AP-16000 is equally well suited to product spraying where no source of compressed air is readily available.

The unit includes an AP pump, two HA-4000 heaters, a PF-300 filter, a generous capacity two cylinder compressor powered by a 1 1/2 HP motor, mounted on a compact four wheel dolly. A good size air storage tank is mounted on the under side of the dolly.

While spraying capacity depends on the material being sprayed, this unit will easily operate two T-300 guns when spraying materials of average viscosity.

The new AP-16000 is available for either 115 or 230 volt operation. However, it is important that one of these two voltages be specified when equipment is ordered.

This unit opens up an entirely new field to Airless spraying. The unit is well suited for spraying large pieces of equipment right on the shop floor. It is perfect for combination product-maintenance usage. Institutions will find it is perfect for spraying both the inside and outside of buildings, as well as refinishing furniture and equipment – even painting vehicles.

The first page of the *Nordson Newsletter*, aimed at Nordson's customers, prospective customers, and sales representatives. Created by Joseph A. Ignat, it was published until at least 1963. Its successor, launched in 1971, was the *Nordson News*. (Reproduced courtesy of Nordson Corporation)

*Above:* Walter and Virginia Nord at their annual open house, in 1949. (Reproduced courtesy of Evan and Cindy Nord)

*Below:* Virginia and Walter Nord enjoying the cherry blossoms in Washington, D.C., ca. 1946. (Reproduced courtesy of Evan and Cindy Nord)

ness had been sold to former employees. Hellrigel identifies these people as George Vollmer and Boyd Petty, who carried it on until 1965.[4]

## SPREADING ROOTS

With the transformation of their largest business under way, the two generations of Nords cherished the passing years and accepted new challenges. The dairy farm near Wellington continued to provide Walter with much satisfaction as a hobby. He and Virginia enjoyed living in the house on Oberlin's Edgemeer Place. They liked to entertain friends, and a highlight of the year was their annual New Year's Day open house. They also enjoyed traveling occasionally; among their trips were one to the West in 1948 and another to Europe, partly for business, in 1952.

Joe and Mary now lived very close to them. In the early 1950s the Ignats moved from their small Oberlin duplex to a spacious brick-and-stucco house at 251 Forest Street. In that house many spirited discussions took place around the dinner table, often reflecting the diverse politics (Republican and Democrat) and religions (Protestant and Catholic) of Mary and Joe.

A spirit of fun pervaded the Ignats' family life. The younger son, Joe, remembered how his father loved to host baseball games in the back yard for the entire neighborhood and how he organized a soap-making project, having the boys collect bacon grease from neighbors and then, when he had finished making the soap, enlisting them and the neighbors' children to sell it door to door. At one time each bar of soap contained a coin. Before their move, when the first television sets were becoming available, Joe received one as an in-kind payment from a client. He brought it home, and all the neighborhood children crowded into their small living room. Every summer the Ignats and two other families who were close friends spent two weeks in rented cottages at Pentwater, on Lake Michigan.

Mary, small, quiet, calm, soft-spoken, thoughtful, intelligent, a great reader, was remembered by her sons as an excellent mother. Her family, neighbors, and friends often sought her wise counsel. Her children felt they could come to her with any sort of problem and, without being judged harshly, be provided with guidance. Other mothers sought her advice in raising children, and she gave hands-on help as well. In one instance she straightened out an unruly cousin during a few months' stay. Friends turned to her in cases of mental and emotional illness. Son Joe called her a "relationship philosopher." She also was remembered as a good cook and as Virginia's driver, patiently making the rounds of several stores almost daily.

In the Oberlin community, too, Mary contributed frequently, serving as secretary of the Allen Memorial Hospital board and at the hospital's annual bazaar, heading the Visiting Nurse Association, and working as a member of the Parent-Teacher Association and the Oberlin chapter of the League of Women Voters. Her sons recalled that a number of the league's meetings were held in their home.

Evan, for many years a bachelor living with his parents, was extremely close to Mary and Joe and their sons. Their house, not two blocks from the Nords', became his "second home," and each July he would spend a week with them at Pentwater. Evan's influence on the boys was significant. David remembered his "training in golf and tennis, plus memorable effort going into how to behave like a grown-up." In the summers, as the boys grew older, Evan employed them in the shop. David commented, "I think the experience in the shop was quite formative for me, and Joe, too." This even extended to their home. Joe recalled that Evan recruited both boys to work in the Ignats' basement, machining "tungsten carbide recirculating valve seats" on a lathe.

For his part, Eric had found his life's companion. Shortly after the war he had gone to a party in Cleveland given by a former Phi Kappa Psi fraternity brother, "Bud" Body, and his wife. At that party he met Body's wife's sister, a young woman named Jane Baker from Shaker Heights, east of Cleveland. Jane was a person of many accomplishments who brought her own talents and strong interests, especially in art and music, to enrich his life. The granddaughter of Elbert Hall Baker Sr., one of the founders of the Cleveland *Plain Dealer,* Jane was a graduate of both Vassar College and the Pratt Institute, where she also had been a

*Above:* Virginia Nord viewing the exhibit of her fan collection at the Western Reserve Historical Society, Cleveland, October 23, 1957. (Reproduced courtesy of Evan and Cindy Nord)

*Below:* Joe and Mary Ignat in the 1950s. (Reproduced courtesy of Evan and Cindy Nord)

teacher of textile design. By coincidence her father, Elbert Hall Baker Jr., known as "Buck," also ran an automatic screw machine plant, and Eric had known him for a number of years.

On June 19, 1948 Eric and Jane were married at Christ Episcopal Church in Shaker Heights. They set up housekeeping in what Eric remembered as "the tiniest apartment, I think, in Oberlin." Five children were born in the next nine years: Virginia "Gini," Eric "Chip," Emily, Carlotte "Carly," and Richard. With Richard's birth they moved into their fourth and present Oberlin house, which they built in a new neighborhood on what was then the far west side of town. For many years Jane devoted most of her energies to the demanding job of raising her grow-

Jane and Eric Nord at their wedding reception in Shaker Heights, Ohio, on June 19, 1948. (Reproduced courtesy of Eric and Jane Nord)

ing family. She remembered how Walter and Virginia welcomed her into the family like a daughter and how Mary helped her out when it was needed—including coming over one time at 2:00 A.M. to take charge when Jane was ill and Eric was out of town.[5]

## ACHIEVEMENTS AND HONORS

As Walter grew older his interests began to bring him additional board responsibilities and well-deserved honors. For example, not long after moving to Oberlin he joined the board of the Oberlin Savings Bank and was elected chairman, and in 1951 he received a Meritorious Service Award from the Case Alumni Association, which he had served as president.

From 1944 until his death in 1967 Walter served on the Lorain County Tuberculosis and Health Association Board of Trustees, many of those years as board president. He had seen firsthand that many quarry workers developed silicosis, particularly in the early years when little attention was paid to worker safety. He believed strongly in the efforts this organization was making to eradicate tuberculosis and to educate children about the dangers of smoking. Beginning in the late 1930s the association operated a retrofitted Lorain city bus that contained a mobile X-ray unit. The bus traveled to schools, rest homes, the Lorain County Fair, and other places throughout the county to screen people for tuberculosis and other lung ailments. All food-service workers were regularly screened, as were many industrial workers. Walter was instrumental in helping the organization construct its own building—specifically designed by Ralph Silsbee to accommodate the X-ray bus—on Cleveland Avenue in Amherst in the 1940s and was involved in a campaign to replace the aged bus with a newer one in the mid-1960s. The organization's annual report shows that, in 1966, 20,000 X rays were taken. Screening was eventually stopped due to concern over radiation.

Much of the Tuberculosis and Health Association's funding came from the sale of Christmas Seals. The architect John R. "Jack" Clark, who served on the association's board for many years with Walter, recalled that, even when Walter was very old, each year he would bake a cake. He and Virginia would bring the cake with them when they joined a group of volunteers who folded letters and stuffed envelopes for the annual mailing to promote Christmas Seals.

In 1949 Walter was elected president of the American Swedish Historical Foundation, a position he held for the rest of his life. Over the years he helped revitalize and improve the financial health of the struggling foundation, which depended on donations and memorial funds. An especially important contribution was Walter's development of associate chapters in several large American cities. Walter and his family also provided funds for an expanded and specially designed research library at the foundation's Philadelphia museum, named for his oldest brother, Herman, and officially dedicated on September 28, 1957 with many Nord family members in attendance. In addition, Walter contributed informative articles to the foundation's yearbook.

For his work over the years with the foundation and with other Swedish American organizations in Cleveland, Walter received two prestigious awards from the Swedish government. On May 5, 1951 Swedish Ambassador Erik Boheman flew to Cleveland to present to Walter an honorary decoration as a Knight of the Royal Order of Vasa—a medal suspended from a green ribbon—from King Gustav VI Adolf of Sweden. Named for the Vasa kings who united Sweden in the sixteenth and seventeenth centuries, the order was awarded to Swedish citizens and foreigners for their achievements in agriculture, mining, commerce, art, or education, as well as for service to Sweden. The news release commended Walter's "outstanding services performed in fostering better American-Swedish relations between the two nations in civic, cultural, industrial and literary matters here in the United States, and in stimulating deeper interest in a higher standard of citizenship among Americans of Swedish descent." Only three other people in northern Ohio had previously won the award; one was Herman Nord.

Eight years later, after Walter's efforts had produced progress and growth in financial support for the foundation, the Swedish government decorated him a second time, as a Commander of the Royal Order of Vasa. Walter, Virginia, Mary, Evan, Eric, Jane, and others traveled to Philadelphia, where, on December 5, 1959, Swedish ambassador Gunnar Jarring conferred the decoration on Walter in the Herman Nord Library of the American Swedish Historical Museum.

During these years Walter and Virginia also had the privilege of meeting members of the Swedish royal family, who visited America as part of efforts to form closer ties between the United States and Sweden. In May 1958 Sweden's Prince Bertil came to the United States to participate in the Minnesota Centennial. But first he stopped in Washington, where, on May 6, President Dwight D. Eisenhower entertained him, Princess Astrid of Norway, and the Nords, among others. According to Eric, Walter was favorably impressed by "Ike" and "Mamie." Later, on November 11, 1959, Walter visited the Philadelphia museum to meet the young Swedish Princesses Birgitta and Desiree.[6]

## TOWARD BETTER MENTAL HEALTH

Another interest of Walter's that went beyond Amherst and Oberlin was mental health. Eric described how this interest began: "Somebody got him interested in it. And, of course, when you run a plant, and you're

*Back then [in the 1940s], the only way of getting assistance with any mental health problems was if you could afford it. You had to be fairly well off or have a relative who was able to send you to a psychologist or psychiatrist. . . . So W.G. was trying to get it to where everybody who needed mental health care could get some form of help. . . . I remember the time they struggled to get a psychiatrist to come out to Lorain County and help deal with some of the problems!*

—Evan Nord, quoted
in *Leading and Caring
for 40 Years,* 1987

For many years, beginning in the late 1930s, the Lorain County Tuberculosis and Health Association, which Walter Nord served as a trustee and president, operated a mobile x-ray unit known as the "Christmas Seals Bus" to screen people throughout the county for lung diseases. (Reproduced courtesy of John R. Clark)

there on the floor all day, you get all kinds of problems that people bring to you . . . and a lot of them are problems connected with mental health. Somebody's wife was depressed, they've got a kid who is schizophrenic. Sometimes the employees themselves . . . tell you about their problems. There weren't any sources for help in Amherst, or Lorain County. You had to go into Cleveland. Of course, most of these guys couldn't afford it."

This situation, which had been apparent for some years, distressed Walter. He was used to providing help for people in so many ways, both directly and through organizations; yet in this case he felt helpless, so he began to work with others to find a way to bring mental health professionals to Lorain County. At the time, a movement was prevalent throughout the United States to establish associations for the promotion of mental health treatment and awareness. Shortly after the war Walter became active in the newly formed Lorain County Mental Hygiene (later Mental Health) Association and in the establishment of the county's first mental health clinic. Evan recalled that employees made use of the facility and that the fees were on a sliding scale so that all who needed care could afford it. Beginning with a single part-time psychologist, the clinic gradually expanded its staff, services, and facilities. Walter served as president of the organization from 1953 until 1964.

The facilities were funded with public money, requiring special levies voted on by the county's citizens. Marilyn Jenne remembered the many hours spent on the levy campaigns conducted directly from Walter's office at U.S. Automatic. "When the mental health board was running a levy here in the county," she recalled in an interview with Harrah, "we did everything. Our whole office! We did mailings, we took in money, we contacted people for assistance." With his flair for public relations, his

*Thank God for Walter Nord! There are so few who had the foresight that he did. . . . Mr. Nord did things for the clinic because he believed in it—and not to build a monument to himself. It was his great love for humanity, really. I have met very few Walter Nords in my life. He was a completely unselfish person. That was what was unique about him.*

*—Howard Grennell, a psychiatric social worker at the Lorain County Guidance Center, quoted in Leading and Caring for 40 Years, 1987*

Walter Nord and his family with Swedish Ambassador Gunnar Jarring after Walter was named a Commander of the Royal Order of Vasa on December 5, 1959 in the Herman Nord Library of the American Swedish Historical Museum, Philadelphia. Left to right: Evan Nord, Walter Nord, Virginia Nord, Ambassador Jarring, Eric Nord, Jane Nord, Mary Nord Ignat, and Rose Stabe, Mary's cousin. (Reproduced courtesy of the American Swedish Historical Museum)

charm, and his powers of persuasion, Joe played an important part in the levy campaigns. Evan noted, "Whenever W.G. wanted a levy passed, he asked Joe to help"; and Ginn observed that Joe was so persuasive that nobody could ever turn him down.

But Walter's efforts on behalf of mental health did not stop there. He became involved in a statewide association that promoted the cause of mental health awareness and solutions throughout Ohio. The Ohio Mental Health Association, headquartered in Columbus, had been founded in the 1930s. It was active in lobbying the Ohio General Assembly for favorable legislation. As in so many things, Walter was willing to provide quiet but effective leadership, and he was elected president of the association in 1954. He served in this position, too, until his death. Even before this, in 1952, he had attended a meeting of the World Federation for Mental Health in Brussels.[7]

## The U.S. Automatic Foundation

Walter wanted to find a method for his businesses to supplement his own personal philanthropy, to contribute in an ongoing and systematic way to these and other worthwhile causes. From time to time, U.S. Automatic and American Specialty had made donations to the Amherst Hospital, the Amherst High School, the Case School of Applied Science, and the Center for the Sightless in Elyria. But in the early 1950s company profits were very unreliable.

A corporate foundation would be a way of storing up tax-free funds from year to year so that even in an unprofitable year the Nord businesses could provide support. Eric recalled that the company's attorneys suggested to him that "maybe you ought to start a foundation and give a certain percent of your profits, when you have a profitable year, and then don't pay it all out on a year to year basis." He noted that, according to tax regulations, "when you had a good year you could put the money in the foundation and not count it as taxable income up to five per cent."

The establishment of The U.S. Automatic Foundation was part of a massive American philanthropic movement that began with the large, well-known philanthropic organizations of the great nineteenth-century industrialists. The federal government had instituted charitable deductions for businesses in 1935; postwar prosperity had stimulated giving to charities of all kinds; and by the early 1950s families and businesses had established hundreds of foundations.

Jerome Fisher, of the Cleveland law firm Thompson, Hine and Flory, was the company's attorney and a member of the U.S. Automatic board. His assistant, Bill Ginn, a young attorney just beginning his career, also became deeply involved with the Nords and their businesses starting in 1950. The close relationship between Ginn, his law firm, and the Nords has continued to this day.

A foundation may take the form of a trust, rather than a more elaborate nonprofit corporation. Ginn remembered that it was Fisher who did the legal work in setting up The U.S. Automatic Foundation. "The foundation was created in an interesting way," Ginn recalled in a 1992 interview, "because no one wanted to be too formal or too expansive with it, so they created a trust . . . just by

After the Royal Order of Vasa award ceremony in 1959, Virginia and Walter Nord enjoyed a quiet moment in the Herman Nord Library of the American Swedish Historical Museum, Philadelphia. Herman's portrait (see page 47) hangs on the wall behind them. (Reproduced courtesy of Evan and Cindy Nord)

declaring . . . that we were now going to hold funds in trust for charitable purposes in perpetuity and appointing three people as trustees. . . . There wasn't a non-profit corporation with all the members and all the trustees and all that. It was a very simple trust on about three sheets of paper." And it was to have only three trustees, the first of whom were Walter, Paul Warner, president of the Oberlin Savings Bank, and John J. Smythe, Walter's old friend and personal lawyer. Marilyn Jenne handled the secretarial work.

Early records of The U.S. Automatic Foundation, preserved by The Nord Family Foundation, show that to start the fund off, $7,000 was contributed by U.S. Automatic, $1,000 by American Specialty, and $100 by Walter Nord. The agreement of trust, signed on October 16, 1952, pledged the new foundation to "the uplifting and upbuilding of the afflicted and the unfortunate, the extension of knowledge and the encouragement, improvement and betterment of mankind."

The foundation's early contributions reflected these broad goals, and the process of giving reflected its simple structure. Eric recalled that people representing organizations "came over and sat down across from whoever had the authority to write the check and told their story and the chances were they were going to walk out with the check." In its first five years, 1953–1957, the records show gifts of $4,000 to the Ohio Foundation of Independent Colleges, $2,600 to the Ohio Mental Health Association, $2,500 to Community Chests in Amherst and Oberlin (similar to today's United Way), and $1,000 to Case Institute of Technology, with smaller amounts to Upsala College, the Episcopal Diocese of Ohio, the International Rescue Committee, Planned Parenthood, the National Council of Churches, Bluffton College, Wilberforce College, Kenyon College, the American Swedish Historical Foundation, Christ Church of Oberlin, the Ohio Public Health Association, the Red Cross, the American Friends Service Committee, the Heart Fund, and the American Foundation for the Blind. The three original trustees served into the early 1960s, and the foundation and its disbursements remained modest.

An important step in regard to the foundation, and to the future of philanthropy within the Nord businesses, was taken in 1954 when the Bede Products Corporation, which became Nordson Corporation, was established. Ginn recounted that, at the meeting to determine whether to proceed, the Nord family decided that, for the life of the new enterprise, 5 percent of all pretax domestic profits would be dedicated to public charitable purposes. This practice had been initiated by the parent company, U.S. Automatic, in 1944 (see page 62)—a rare commitment, then and now, among American businesses. The Dayton Hudson Corporation of Minneapolis had adopted the 5 percent standard in 1946 and is frequently credited with being one of the first to do so among public companies. Thus U.S. Automatic was clearly a pioneer in 1944; and, more

*When he [Walter Nord] came into a room, he took over. I mean, he didn't push himself, or force himself, but you knew he was there. He went ahead and got things done. He'd say, "Well, we're going to have to do this today, let's do it, right now, let's get at it." He didn't fool around.*

—Marilyn Jenne, interview with Jeanne Harrah, August 12, 1992

than a decade later, the 5 percent requirement became, and remains, an underlying precept of Nordson Corporation.

In the 1950s Walter was rewarded for his philanthropy and other good works with three honorary degrees: in 1953, from Upsala College in East Orange, New Jersey, a college of Swedish American origins; in 1958, from Oberlin College; and in 1959, from Wilberforce University in Wilberforce, Ohio, an African American institution on whose board he served. At Oberlin, Walter was one of the honorary degree recipients feted at a special ceremony on October 18, 1958, celebrating the 125th anniversary of the college. His citation, from Donald M. Love, secretary of the college, read, "Neighborly resident of the City of Oberlin, long interested in the problems of education, able business executive, thoughtful and warm-hearted social servant, recognized at home and abroad as one whose wise altruism can be relied upon in any movement to ease the lot of man or to promote international friendship." And from Oberlin College President William E. Stevenson: "Practical idealist, true citizen of the civilization of brotherly men."[8]

# 6

# NEW CHALLENGES, 1960–1973

In the 1960s and early 1970s the United States was jolted out of its postwar complacency. Beginning with the reaction to the Russian Sputnik spacecraft, continuing with the invigorating call to public service by President John F. Kennedy, the campaigns of the civil rights movement to remedy long-standing injustices, the demands of youth to be heard in protest against fighting in Vietnam and elsewhere in Southeast Asia, and the emergence of the feminist and environmental movements, it was a time of taking action, of grappling with change. These years produced the Civil Rights Act, Medicare/Medicaid, the Occupational Safety and Health Act and the Environmental Protection Act, growing automation in industry, and intensified awareness of our neighbors around the world, especially the Third World.

## HOME VALUES

For the Nord family these were years of great loss, new beginnings, solid building, and dynamic change, years in which Eric and Evan more than ever became the family standard-bearers, each in his own distinctive way: Eric, developing and transforming a business and stepping into the role of community leader in Oberlin; Evan, keeping the plant on an even keel and finding a mission in harmonizing the old and the new.

### Harvest of a Fulfilling Life

In the early and mid-1960s Walter, as he neared and entered his eighties, continued to follow a demanding schedule. After decades of attending to each task with a combination of practical intelligence and an appealing, respectful, and caring approach to the people involved, he was widely appreciated and beloved.

Still central in his life was his orderly desk in a large corner office at U.S. Automatic on Jackson Street in Amherst, where he presided while letting Eric and Evan largely run the business. James "Jim" Doughman, brought in by Eric as part of the Nordson team in 1966, remembered that Walter came to him every payday to personally deliver his check and in the process would ask him how things were going and whether he needed anything. Friendly faces always awaited Walter at the company, including some people who had started with him in the 1920s and 1930s and Marilyn Jenne, his secretary since 1941.

In Oberlin Walter spent a good deal of time at the Oberlin Savings Bank, where he continued to serve as chairman of the board, and at Christ Episcopal Church, attending to various practical matters as longtime senior warden of the vestry (chairman of the church board). He visited from time to time with his son-in-law, Joe Ignat, who had purchased the old railroad passenger station on South Street to serve as the headquarters of SuperVision.

Particularly satisfying were his visits to the new Oberlin Community Center at 80 South Main Street, dedicated in 1964, which had been created out of the former Oberlin frozen food locker plant. The frozen food storage business had become unprofitable as customers bought their own freezers, and U.S. Automatic had found itself with an empty building. Walter and Evan developed a plan to convert it for community use.

The U.S. Automatic plant a few years before new construction, ca. 1960–1965. (Reproduced courtesy of Nordson Corporation)

Under Evan's primary direction, with help from Eric, the old plant was remodeled by volunteers from the company and from the Oberlin Historical and Improvement Organization (O.H.I.O.), created in July 1964 when the Oberlin Historical Society and the Oberlin Village Improvement Society merged. Because O.H.I.O. had not yet received its tax exemption as a 501(c)(3) nonprofit organization, U.S. Automatic donated the building to Oberlin College, and O.H.I.O. undertook to manage it for the community. When O.H.I.O. received its exemption, the college quit-claimed the property to it.

At a meeting of the O.H.I.O. board, when Walter, a trustee, was absent, the other trustees named the building the Nordson Center. Walter did not wish such recognition, however, and, the name was soon changed to the Oberlin Community Center. On the first floor were offices and meeting rooms for the new Head Start program—the first federally funded preschool for disadvantaged children in Lorain County—and other social service organizations. Upstairs, the City of Oberlin Recreation Commission used the multipurpose room for youth activities, such as dances.

The land behind the new Community Center was also owned by Oberlin College. The brick, Italianate-style Monroe House, built in 1866, originally stood about 100 yards to the north, on what was then College Place. The house was moved to its present site on that college land in 1960 to prevent its demolition to make way for the new Oberlin Conservatory of Music complex. Oberlin College transferred ownership of the Monroe House to O.H.I.O. in 1982, and extensive renovations were completed under Evan's leadership in time for Oberlin's sesquicentennial in 1983. Originally the residence of Gen. Giles W. Shurtleff, leader of Ohio's first African American regiment to serve in the Civil War, it was subsequently the longtime home of James and Julia Monroe. Monroe was an Oberlin College professor, abolitionist, congressman, and one of the founders of the Republican Party in Ohio; his wife Julia was a daughter of Oberlin's famed religious leader, Charles Grandison Finney, who also served as the college's president from 1851 to 1865.

Walter and Evan Nord, Frank Chapman Van Cleef, and other founders of O.H.I.O. envisioned a historical park, including the Monroe House, in part of the block bounded by the conservatory parking lot on the north, South Main Street on the east, West Vine Street on the south, and South

The Nord family, ca. 1961. Front row: Eric "Chip," Emily, Carlotte "Carly," and Virginia "Gini" Nord. Middle row: Mary Nord Ignat, Virginia Grieve Nord, Walter Nord, Jane Nord, holding Richard Nord. Back row: Joseph A. Ignat, David Ignat, Evan Nord, Joseph N. Ignat, Eric Nord. (Reproduced courtesy of Evan and Cindy Nord)

Professor Street on the west. Their hope was realized, though not until many years later and under Evan's leadership.

Another integral part of that park, which became the Oberlin Heritage Center in 1998, was the property at 73 South Professor Street. From 1884, when it was built, until 1923 the brick Victorian house and the nearby barn had belonged to Frank Fanning Jewett, an Oberlin College professor of chemistry, and his wife, Sarah Frances Gulick Jewett, a noted author of textbooks on public health and hygiene. For nearly four decades thereafter, the property was owned by Pliny Deane Hubbard, a civil engineer, and his wife, Laura. In 1966, after the Hubbards had passed away, O.H.I.O. purchased it from their son.

Evan was instrumental in renovating the Jewett House and barn for use by O.H.I.O., and in 1997 another hope of the organization's founders was realized: an exhibit, in the woodshed attached to the house, commemorating the work of one of Jewett's students, the aluminum pioneer Charles Martin Hall, who discovered the electrochemical process for separating aluminum metal from its oxide ore on February 23, 1886. Hall's work led to the production of aluminum on a large scale and made it affordable for industrial uses.

The third main feature to be added to the Oberlin Heritage Center was the one-room "Little Red Schoolhouse." Oberlin's first public school building, it had been constructed in 1836–1837 for $215 at a spot just north of where The First Church in Oberlin, UCC, is today, at the corner of Main and Lorain Streets. When the schoolhouse could no longer accommodate all of the town's children, it was moved to other sites and adapted to other uses. In 1968 it was positioned adjacent to the Monroe House, and in 1997 it was relocated to its present site, southeast of the Jewett House barn.

Walter's interests also took him beyond Oberlin. He might head south to the Wellington area to see how farm manager Stanley Sooy and his family and the animals at his dairy farm were and also to pay a call on his older brother Frank, who was blind and lived in a nearby nursing home. Or he might head northeast to Elyria, to visit the Center for the Sightless's Skills Division, the sheltered workshop sponsored by the organization he had chaired since 1938. Occasionally he made longer jaunts: to Columbus, for meetings of the Ohio Mental Health Association; to Wilberforce, Ohio, for meetings of the university board; or to Philadelphia, for annual meetings of the American Swedish Historical Foundation.

Over the years Walter and Virginia had been intimately involved in issues of education, from his twenty years on the Amherst Board of Education and his sponsorship of improvements at Amherst High School, to alumni activities at Case, to serving Wilberforce and the United Negro College Fund, to making donations to schools and colleges through The

*My first memory of W.G. Nord was in his office at U.S. Automatic Company. . . . Walter was a gentle, quiet person. I don't know that he ever raised his voice. He was very gracious, the most gracious person I ever met. He would be genuinely concerned with your feelings —it would be a total projection over to you, no matter who you were. I don't know that Walter would ever tell you that you did something wrong, but he would demand a very high level of performance and you would want to perform on that level. You'd want to do a top notch job for Walter.*

—Ray Muzilla, president, Lorain County Mental Health Association, 1966–1967, quoted in *Learning and Caring for 40 Years,* 1987

The Monroe House, built in 1866 and moved to its present site in 1960, was first occupied by the Civil War Gen. Giles W. Shurtleff and his family. It is better known, however, as the home of the politician and Oberlin College Professor James Monroe and his wife, Julia Finney Monroe. Now part of O.H.I.O.'s Oberlin Heritage Center, the building houses the organization's offices and resource center; and several of its rooms, furnished with nineteenth-century artifacts, are part of the center's historic-sites tour. (Photograph by Richard Holsworth)

U.S. Automatic Foundation. Earlier, Virginia also had been active in the Parent–Teacher Association. Now, at a time of renewed focus on education throughout the United States and with the baby-boom generation filling the high schools, the Nords saw a need to bring postsecondary education within the grasp of more young people in Lorain County. In 1961 they established the Walter and Virginia Nord Scholarship Fund for graduates of the county's high schools.

Walter also played an important role in the establishment and growth of Lorain County Community College, chartered by the state of Ohio in 1963. In September of that year he accepted the chairmanship of a citizens' committee to secure a local tax levy for the new college campus. After a hard-fought, countywide campaign, the levy passed by a close vote. Next, according to Eric, Walter headed the site-selection committee. Eric remembered that this was a difficult job and that Walter could

The 1884 Jewett House is also part of the Oberlin Heritage Center. Its first owners were Frank Fanning Jewett, a chemistry professor, and his wife, a textbook author. After their deaths it became the home of Pliny Deane Hubbard, a civil enginer, and his wife. O.H.I.O. purchased the house from the Hubbards' son in 1966. Many of its rooms, like those in the Monroe House, are furnished with nineteenth-century artifacts, and its kitchen has been restored to resemble an early-twentieth-century kitchen that reflects the principles advocated by Mrs. Jewett. In the connected woodshed is an exhibit showing the work of one of Professor Jewett's chemistry students, the aluminum pioneer Charles Martin Hall. (Photograph by Richard Holsworth)

not and did not please everyone on the committee—but he had the advantage of having learned from the county commissioners where major new roads were planned.

The college's location, in Elyria (the county seat) and within easy reach of Interstate 90, has been a factor in its rapid growth and success. The expanding role of the college, with its spacious campus dotted with low, interconnected buildings, has continued to be of interest to the Nord family. In 2003 an Ohio Historical Marker was placed on the campus to underscore its importance as the first community college in Ohio to have its own permanent campus.

In yet another educational project, one of national scope, Walter worked with the American Swedish Historical Foundation and the Swedish Labor Board to establish a student trainee program that found temporary positions in business and agriculture in the United States for fifteen

The Oberlin Heritage Center was not the original location of the town's first public school building, now known as the Little Red Schoolhouse. Constructed in 1836–1837 on North Main Street near the intersection with Lorain Street, it was moved to a series of other sites and adapted to other uses when larger school quarters were needed. It is a popular stop on O.H.I.O.'s historic-sites tours, and every June Oberlin's third-graders, in appropriate costumes, spend a day in the schoolhouse, following the routines of their nineteenth-century predecessors. (Photograph by Richard Holsworth)

or more Swedish students each year. By 1967, when Evan took over the program from his father, twenty-seven students were trainees.

Much progress was taking place in Walter's other major field of philanthropy, mental health. In 1961 the Lorain County Guidance Center was officially incorporated, with Walter as its president. In 1963 its professional staff made 5,220 client appointments, 300 of which were with clients new to the center. At its annual meeting in 1964 the Lorain County Mental Health Association, which Walter continued to lead, was praised by a speaker as one of the pioneer mental health organizations in the state. The next year Walter chaired the annual meeting of the Ohio Mental Health Association, which included addresses by government officials on the state of mental health treatment in Ohio and the nation.

In the late 1950s and 1960s, as their newly shaped company was growing, Eric and Evan also found time to reach out in various forms of service. The community of Oberlin honored the entire Nord family at a banquet on December 8, 1965 at the Oberlin Community Center. To further honor Walter, in 1966 the Small Business Administration named him "Ohio Small Businessman of the Year." On May 26, 1966 more than 100 business leaders, government officials, and old friends gathered at a luncheon at the Oberlin Community Center to pay tribute. The award plaque, presented by officials of the state office of the Small Business Administration, praised Walter "for best exemplifying the imagination, initiative, independence and integrity characteristic of America's millions of small businessmen who make a vital contribution to our growing economy."[1]

## DIFFICULTIES AND CHANGES

The period was far from entirely positive for the Nord family, however. After suffering from breast cancer for almost three years, Mary Nord Ignat died in Oberlin on May 8, 1965, at the age of fifty-one. Her funeral was held at Christ Church, where she had been a member, and she was buried in Oberlin's Westwood Cemetery. In her memory, the Nords purchased the spacious house at 158 Elm Street and presented it to Christ Church for use as a rectory.

Losing Mary was a great blow to all the family, and to the community as well. Evan felt the loss keenly, for he and Mary had always been especially close. To help fill the void, he spent some of his spare time at the plant, some in sports—golfing, boating in his cabin cruiser, *The Hawk,* and, especially, playing tennis. One day a spirited young woman, Cynthia "Cindy" Whitehead Tinker, appeared on the court, and before long a friendship developed. On May 28, 1966 Evan and Cindy were married at Christ Church. Cindy, divorced from a former Oberlin College art instructor, had three children, Eric, Bruce, and Kathleen "Katie," whom Evan shortly adopted. Within a little more than two years, Evan and Cindy were the parents of Ethan and Allyson, and Evan found himself the father of five. Very quickly, Evan's life had been transformed. As he said to an article writer, "How do I feel about my family of five? Great, just great." He was a loving, attentive father. To accommodate their expansive family, Evan and Cindy purchased Joe's large home at 251 Forest Street, where Evan had spent many happy hours with the Ignats and their children.

On May 15, 1967 Walter suffered a sudden, severe stroke; and just a few hours later, on May 16, he died at Allen Memorial Hospital in Oberlin. He was eighty-three. To quote from his obituary in the *Lorain Journal,* "There are few individuals in private life whose lives have touched so many people either directly or indirectly as did Walter Nord's." Just the week before, the *Journal* noted, he had been making arrangements to host the next meeting of the Ohio Mental Health Association at the Oberlin Community Center.

O.H.I.O.'s annual meeting the next day began with a moment of silence, and a committee was appointed to write Virginia Nord about that silent moment and its significance. The letter stated that "every person in the room said his private prayer of thanksgiving for what Walter Nord had meant to him or her." On Friday afternoon, May 19, a simple funeral service was held at Christ Church. Hundreds of friends, associates, and employees packed the church as well as the Parish Hall, where the overflow crowd joined in the service through loudspeakers. Walter was laid to rest in Westwood Cemetery, near Mary. A brief eulogy published in the order of service read in part: "Walter Nord showed forth in life the enduring Christian virtues of humility, courtesy, and service." Soon afterward the Ohio Senate passed a resolution in his memory, enumerating his volunteer activities and achievements and expressing sorrow for his death. It was adopted by the Ohio General Assembly on May 22, 1967.

Walter's Wellington farm was sold about a year later. His estate, which went largely to Virginia, included more than 3,000 shares of company stock. In 1968 the new Nordson headquarters in Amherst was dedicated to Walter's memory. In 1970 the Lorain County Guidance Center was renamed the Walter G. Nord Community Mental Health Center, and the Walter G. Nord Junior High School—now the Walter G. Nord Middle School—was dedicated in Amherst.

Joe Ignat remarried a few years after Mary's death, to Lee Blackman, but he too died in the prime of life, on May 23, 1969, at the age of fifty-four. He was buried next to Mary in Westwood Cemetery.

Although Virginia's health was declining, she survived Walter by six years, the last three of them at Welcome Nursing Home in Oberlin. She passed away on October 31, 1973. Following a service at Christ Church, she joined Walter, Mary, and Joe in Westwood Cemetery.[2]

# MEETING THE CHALLENGES OF LEADERSHIP

## POLITICS

In 1960 Eric was forty-two years old, the father of five young, active children, president of the six-year-old Nordson Corporation as well as secretary of the U.S. Automatic Corporation, and a newly elected member of the Oberlin City Council. A Republican like his father, Eric was not a politician, but he had been drawn into running for election by a group of liberal local leaders who enlisted his help, as a respected, moderate businessman, in making major city improvements. Of special interest were the issues of bettering city utilities and finances, developing an industrial park, implementing a new code with the power to condemn substandard

*ABOLITIONISM IN OBERLIN*

*Oberlin became an abolitionist hotbed and a major stopover on the Underground Railroad before the Civil War. Abolitionists here held a range of opinions; some believed prayer could end slavery; others pursued political measures; and a few embraced violence. Oberlin also was active in reform movements, including women's rights, suffrage, temperance, and village improvement. Behind this marker is the home of Giles Shurtleff, an abolitionist, professor, and army general who led the first African American regiment from Ohio to serve in the Civil War. The home's second owner was James Monroe, Oberlin's best-known political abolitionist. Monroe was a professor, a U.S. Congressman, and the U.S. consul in Brazil during the Civil War. He lived here with his wife, Julia, a daughter of Oberlin's great religious leader, Charles Grandison Finney.*

—Ohio Historical Marker, southwest-facing side, at the brick crossroads of the Oberlin Heritage Center, dedicated on April 12, 2003

housing, and creating fair-housing opportunities for Oberlin's low-in-
come residents, including a substantial African American community.

Soon after coming to the City Council, Eric was elected its chairman.
The council worked closely with the paid staff headed by the salaried city
manager and with commissions of volunteers called in to study and ad-
vise. Analyzing problems of water supply and sewage had first brought
Eric into the political process. According to the political scientist Aaron
Wildavsky in his book about Oberlin, *Leadership in a Small Town* (1964),
Oberlin's system of governance worked reasonably well, but progress in
many areas had been slow due to the conservatism of some Oberlin businessmen.

Cindy and Evan Nord
come down the aisle
after their marriage
ceremony on
May 28, 1966 at Christ
Episcopal Church,
Oberlin. (Reproduced
courtesy of Evan and
Cindy Nord)

Evan Nord poses with three members of his new family on his wedding day. Left to right: Cindy's daughter, Katie, and sons, Eric and Bruce. (Photograph by Andrew Stofan, Oberlin, Ohio; reproduced courtesy of Evan and Cindy Nord)

Evan and Cindy Nord's children Ethan (left) and Allyson, ca. 1969. (Reproduced courtesy of Evan and Cindy Nord)

Virginia Nord with her
granddaughter Carlotte
"Carly" Nord, in the 1960s.
(Reproduced courtesy of
Eric and Jane Nord)

Enactment of the housing code by the council had come the year before, after a hard-fought
battle. But not much was done until a tragic event
turned a vivid spotlight on housing conditions
for Oberlin's African American community. On
February 21, 1960 a fire in a substandard, im-
properly heated house took the lives of seven
children. The community was stunned, and many
who had ignored issues of race and poverty became deeply involved in addressing Oberlin's
substandard housing.

Right away, Eric and the other council members took a number of actions. Detailed inspec-
tions of suspected substandard dwellings began.
A Housing Renewal Commission was formed
to study the whole subject of improving housing standards. Eric and others on the council
created a nonprofit corporation, the Oberlin
Housing Foundation, which collected private
contributions and dozens of pledges of volunteer labor, hoping to make it possible for poor
residents to improve the condition of their
homes. And a major drive began for the enactment of a fair-housing ordinance for Oberlin.

Segregated housing patterns and barriers for African Americans in
purchasing houses had long been the practice in Oberlin, as in most
other communities. A citizens' committee, which began to meet in May
1960, drew up a petition urging the City Council to draft a housing ordinance. After gathering more than 500 signatures, the committee presented
the petition to the council on January 16, 1961. Opinion was divided on
the council as well as in the town, but the council appointed a committee
to study how to draft such a law. That committee recommended a basic
ordinance modeled on a Cleveland law. After hot debate at a large public
hearing, followed by votes and revisions at three City Council meetings,
"An Ordinance of the City of Oberlin Relating to Fair Housing Practices" passed, four votes to two, on November 20, 1961. Eric was very
much in favor of the new ordinance, voted for it, and worked closely
with the council on it at each stage. Aimed especially at subdivisions and
large landlords, it prohibited racial discrimination in the sale or rental by
owners of five or more "dwelling units, apartments, or building lots."

Those opposed to the ordinance were adamant, however, and in January 1962 the Oberlin City Council and government were successfully
sued for exceeding their authority in the Lorain County Common Pleas

Court by Ira Porter, an influential Oberlin citizen. The council appealed the case to the Ohio District Court of Appeals. The ordinance question and related issues brought Eric strong opposition. In an interview with the historian Marlene Merrill, Eric said, "I was really unpopular at that time. . . . For a couple of years, I would get these telephone calls, at my home . . . one o'clock, three o'clock [A.M.]."

But the results were positive. Eric noted that the Oberlin Housing Foundation, though it ran into financial problems and eventually disbanded, did complete some projects. The Housing Renewal Commission's work eventually resulted in a federal public housing development of fifty-four units built in scattered locations in 1965 and 1966.

Oberlin's Fair Housing Ordinance eventually survived the appeal process, partly because Eric rewrote its preamble. It became the first fair-housing law in Ohio to be declared constitutional by the state Supreme Court. Although its effect on changing Oberlin's segregated housing patterns is unclear, it provided a major stimulus for passage of a statewide law. Only one week after the Oberlin law was declared constitutional, Ohio Governor James Rhodes announced that he would be willing to sign a statewide fair-housing law. And just five months later such a law was indeed passed, signed, and put into effect.

Another difficult issue Eric faced was the matter of how to pay for capital improvements in an industry-poor city. For one thing, he agreed with those who wanted Oberlin to attract more environmentally clean industry. When land was set aside for an industrial park, he helped bring in a new company, the Muller Packaging Company. More significantly, during his second two-year term the City Council enacted a municipal income tax. Afterward, a group of people who were opposed to the tax called for a referendum, which repealed the tax. Eric felt so strongly about the need for the tax that he announced he would not run for a third term. The next council eventually had the tax reinstated.

Presiding over the City Council was not easy. But according to Eric, when a group persuaded him to head the Oberlin Board of Education in 1965, he found an even more difficult task. He told Merrill, "That was really a traumatic job." Now he had to deal with the strong feelings and opinions of not a few but hundreds of involved residents, most of them parents. Eric served in this position for four years.

The school population was growing rapidly, and new facilities were needed. When he first joined the board, he recalled in another interview, he found that its members were working toward putting up temporary buildings to reduce overcrowding. He was strongly opposed to this. After a great deal of debate, the board decided to ask the citizens to vote on a levy to put up permanent buildings. The levies passed, and additions were built to the two grade schools. "I wasn't inclined," Eric said, "to spend money on temporary things when the need was permanent." Difficult disciplinary issues concerning certain students also came to the board. These were agonizing to deal with, for every move the board made ran into strenuous opposition from someone.

One of Eric's tasks as a member of the school board was to serve on a regional group to plan a vocational training center for high school students. He recalled that eleven school districts went together to seek a bond issue for the school's construction, which would bring in state funds as well. Eric was instrumental in the success of the bond issue for Oberlin. But it was difficult to obtain approval for the bond issue in all of the districts, and finally the project went ahead with just a few school districts participating. Built 2 miles south of downtown Oberlin, the Lorain County Vocational Center opened in September 1971. Known today as the Lorain County Joint Vocational School, it has subsequently attracted much more support and has grown considerably. In addition to high school students, it now reaches more than 4,000 adults with training classes.

At about the same time as he served on the City Council, Eric also served on the Allen Memorial Hospital board and was active in the process of expanding the hospital. Like his father, Eric eventually learned that working as a private citizen could sometimes be more effective than taking formal part in politics.[3]

## BOLD STEPS IN MANAGEMENT

In addition to entering town politics, Eric made another decisive move as the 1960s dawned: to make Nordson Corporation more competitive in an ever-more-demanding business environment. Eric was well suited to this challenge. Carrying on the service orientation, inventiveness, and decisiveness of his father, in business he was more competitive, highly motivated toward success, and concentrated in his efforts than his father. He had read much of the new literature on the science and philosophy of business management. And he was fully supported by his father, as long as he lived, and by Evan, both on the shop floor, with his expertise in manufacturing and human relations, and on the Board of Directors. At every step the brothers also had the invaluable collaboration and advice of their attorney, Bill Ginn of Thompson, Hine and Flory in Cleveland.

Developing its own products had clearly been a big step in the right direction for Nordson, but Eric saw the need to build a stronger organization to improve and market those products. As he had done before, he looked for expert help from outside. This time he went even further, bringing in the first non-family executive at the management level. In early 1960 Nordson's Board of Directors hired as vice president of the company an acquaintance of Eric's, Kenneth H. "Ken" Daly, who held a master's degree in business administration from the Wharton School of Business and had been vice president of a larger screw machine plant nearby.

Eric made a presentation entitled "A Look at the Future of Nordson" to his assembled department heads soon afterward. "We have survived the first five years," he began, "and have seen our equipment and the airless process gain substantial acceptance." Now, he continued, Nordson was on the threshold of a "new era" in which its success would inspire "strong competition."

"Nordson is at a crossroad," he said. "On the one hand, we can stay small. . . . On the other hand, we can work toward transforming our organization so as to be adapted to the expanding market. . . . Nordson's board of directors has chosen to pursue the larger field." To begin an orderly transition, Eric announced that he would give up some of his duties "and concentrate my efforts on product development, production, process research and policy matters." The board had selected Daly to take over some of Eric's duties and build "a good sales organization." Eric concluded by asking employees to give Daly "the kind of all-out cooperation you have always given me."

In some family-run organizations, bringing in the first non-family executive could be highly problematical. But in this organization, aside from developing products, the family had never taken a narrowly proprietary attitude. Coming in, after all, to an existing company, the family had

Eric and Jane Nord with their family, ca. 1963–1964. The children, left to right, are Richard, Virginia "Gini," Eric "Chip," Carlotte "Carly," and Emily. (Reproduced courtesy of Eric and Jane Nord)

seen itself as serving the organization, rather than the other way around. The family had taken out little in the way of profits or dividends over the years, and, in fact, viewed profits as an opportunity to give aid to the community. This impressed Daly from the beginning, and he fit in well with the Nordson corporate culture. An article announcing his appointment in the *Nordson Newsletter* described his service with the Boy Scouts and the United Fund of Greater Cleveland. Eric felt fortunate to have found him at just the right time.[4]

Kenneth Daly, Nordson Corporation vice president, as pictured in a 1970 Nordson brochure. (Reproduced courtesy of Nordson Corporation)

## Strengthening the Sales Organization

Daly's first task, as Eric had noted in his address, was to improve marketing and sales. The *Nordson Newsletter* shows that some good marketing techniques were already in place when Daly arrived. Detailed, illustrated articles showed airless equipment being used to paint everything from railroad cars, airplanes, immense walls of buildings, and a flood-control dam to garage doors, furniture, cans, and salad bowls. Frank Ziroe, director of the "Nordson School of Spray Painting," was shown teaching. Lists of students and their companies included Boeing, Procter & Gamble, and other familiar names. Products were also showcased at trade shows.

When it came to a sales organization, however, Nordson had only a few of its own sales offices and was working primarily through distributors. Eric and Daly agreed that full-service Nordson sales organizations were needed, to provide knowledgeable salesmen, training, service, and parts for customers.

In another stroke of luck, a young salesman named James "Jim" Taylor came in one day shortly after Daly had started. Eric and Daly were so impressed with Taylor that they hired him away from his company. Before long, company lawyers helped form a number of additional subsidiaries to provide full sales and service. Nordson Southern, Inc., in Charlotte, North Carolina, and Nordson Pacific, Inc., in Fullerton, California, were the first, and Taylor was sent to Charlotte to take charge of Nordson Southern. Over the next few years, more subsidiaries opened.

According to Daly in his interview with the historian Barbara Griffith, Bill Stevens, Nordson's consulting industrial psychologist, suggested that the company's salesmen be given professional instruction. Daly brought in Reg McHue, who taught the salesmen that what they were selling was not just a product but a package of values, or benefits. Salesmen, for instance, were taught the value of using case histories of similar, successful applications by other customers. Among Daly's goals were offering all their customers analyses of their needs, test facilities to simulate customer operations, readily available parts and service, and comprehensive training services and manuals.

A 1966 article in *Western Manufacturing* describes a typical sales office: Nordson Pacific's headquarters in Buena Vista, California. More than just an office, the facility included a classroom and a demonstration room that was "equipped with a complete paint spray booth, an overhead trolley conveyor, and an exhaust system and baking oven," as well as space for stocking service parts and making repairs.[5]

## INTERNATIONAL BEGINNINGS

Eric considered the hiring of Daly and Taylor as turning points, along with another significant event of 1960: the opportunity to take over the foreign business of the airless painting equipment inventor James Bede. Eric went to Europe to examine the situation closely and found each foreign company selling slightly different equipment. Much of it was purchased from Nordson, but the Germans, Italians, French, and English licensees had each substituted some of their own designs.

Eric was most impressed with the French company and gave it a license to manufacture certain parts. He also made the bold request of asking the French licensee to convene a meeting in Paris of all the European licensees. That seemed impossible, for few even spoke the same language. "Well," Eric told Griffith, "we got them all in one room, and we eventually got them all to agree that they would stop fussing around. All I could offer them was . . . that Nordson would be their licenser, that we would furnish equipment that would do the job, and we would send technical people over there to help them."

The strategy worked, and within a few years foreign sales became a significant factor in Nordson's growth. The next step was to develop coordination of the foreign business. In 1965 Taylor and Eric went to Brussels to set up a European headquarters. When possible, as their licenses expired, Nordson replaced the licensee companies with Nordson subsidiaries staffed by foreign nationals. Bob Thayer was sent to assist Taylor, who remained in charge in Europe and later headed all international sales. New subsidiaries opened in Belgium in 1966, West Germany in 1967, Mexico in 1968, the Netherlands and Japan in 1969, France and Australia in 1971, and England in 1972. Foreign salesmen received the same package of values training as did those in the United States.

In October 1969 James T. Lynn, general counsel for the U.S. Department of Commerce, presented the "President's 'E' Award for Excellence in Export Expansion" to Nordson Corporation. Daly accepted the "E" flag, which honored the company for its "imaginative international marketing efforts" promoting a positive image of American business abroad.

*To our small, technically oriented company he [Ken Daly] brought new insights into marketing, financial and strategic planning. He also brought a wealth of good common sense supplemented by a high level of energy. Ken's character and personality made him thoroughly and universally liked both as a team player and as a leader. Adjectives such as objective, analytical, personable, honest and dependable come immediately to mind when describing him.*

—Eric Nord, *Nordson Corporation Annual Report*, 1980

All employees received "E" pins as well. A few of the old-timers must have added them to their "E" pins from the war years.[6]

## Formalizing the Organization

In the meantime, Daly had begun a process of bringing greater formality to the growing organization. Griffith, summarizing a number of interviews, described how Nordson's non-hierarchical structure, in which everyone pitched in as needed, helped the company attain lightning-fast speed in its product innovations. Yet Daly saw the need for such measures as putting objectives on paper, coordinating the development of products with the preparation of service literature, and instituting inventory controls. Nordson's first five-year plan was completed in 1963.

Eric remembered that, around 1964, Daly persuaded him to write down the philosophy and objectives of the company as he saw them. In his interview with Griffith, Eric noted that writing did not come easily to him, and he described spending several hours one night trying to express the company's basic philosophy in a short paragraph. His statement reads as follows:

> CORPORATE PURPOSE. Nordson shall strive to be a vital, self-renewing organization which, within the framework of ethical behavior and enlightened citizenship, produces wealth for its customers, employees, stockholders and the community in which it exists.

The mission statement reflects not only the values that Eric first learned from his father but also his own vision of society. In forming that developing vision, he was influenced by the writings of John W. Gardner, head of the Carnegie Corporation and author of the popular books *Excellence* (1961) and *Self-Renewal* (1964). Gardner brought an energizing view of a society that aimed for the highest possible accomplishment at all levels and in every field. He believed in fostering a culture of "continuous innovation, renewal and rebirth" through individual creativity and self-fulfillment. The philosophy was well suited to the current corporate climate, which tended to reject earlier, more authoritarian models.

Eric became acquainted with Gardner at meetings of the American Management Association, which he frequently attended, and bought multiple copies of Gardner's books to give to Daly and other key people at Nordson. He remembered that the process of writing corporate policy documents emerged from a weeklong American Management Association seminar for a dozen Nordson managers.

In order to attract and keep top-level talent, Eric explained, it was determined that ownership of Nordson should be shared with its employees. At Ginn's suggestion, the initial step was to issue to key employees debentures that were convertible into stock. The plan worked so well

Eric and Evan Nord enjoying a moment of relaxation together, ca. 1970. (Reproduced courtesy of Nordson Corporation)

that it was duplicated over several years. As a prime example of the talent Eric wished to keep at Nordson, Daly was promoted to executive vice president in 1969 after nearly a decade of successful innovations in the company.[7]

## NEW PRODUCT DEVELOPMENTS

Despite being a busy executive and traveling to Europe about twice a year, Eric managed to spend a good share of his time on product research and development, along with his engineers and toolmakers. The airless equipment was continually being improved: In 1960 the *Nordson Newsletter* announced a faster spray gun; in 1961, a Continuous Lath Coater consisting of a self-contained paint chamber and recovery tank; and in 1962, a smaller Versa/Spray unit, electrostatic equipment to spray hard-to-reach recesses and grooves, as well as the first Hot Melt Airless Spray unit, which applied "paraffin, waxes, starches, pitch and certain solid plastics."

The electrostatic equipment was an important addition, but its production was delayed because of patents held by another company. Hot-melt technology, on the other hand, involved major innovations by Nordson that in just a few years surpassed airless spray in Nordson sales.

By a stroke of luck, one day in the early 1960s Taylor sat next to an adhesives salesman, Robert Crowell, on a flight home from Charlotte and learned that the adhesives industry, in developing new types of molten adhesives, was looking for new types of devices to apply them. Crowell believed that Nordson ought to be able to develop this equipment, and when Taylor conveyed his comments to Eric, Eric agreed. As he told Griffith, their earlier experience in making machines for spraying Coors reservoirs and other projects gave them a head start. "We developed a piece of equipment fairly quickly," Eric said.

Eric designed his first hot-melt unit based on Crowell's suggestions, but he soon found that they were not truly representative of what the market demanded. As he told Griffith, his machine was too large and was designed for a "relatively low performance adhesive. . . . The market was in a *small* unit that would handle higher performance adhesives." Seeing his mistake, Eric came up with a new design and solved another problem, that of keeping an adhesive hot without damaging it, by persuading an adhesive manufacturer to modify its product.

By 1964 the system was fully developed, and by 1967 hot-melt equipment sales were excellent. That adhesives salesmen also became, in effect, salesmen for Nordson was extremely helpful. In Europe, however, acceptance of the new technology took somewhat longer. Daly recalled to Griffith that in 1966–1967 Thayer was sent to develop the hot-melt business in Europe and settled in Dusseldorf, Germany. He had great success: Hot-melt equipment sales came to surpass airless equipment sales in Europe. In opening its business in Japan, the company focused solely on hot-melt technology because this field was entirely untapped.

With its new and improved products and maturing organization, Nordson's sales began to soar. Graphs and statistics showed an increase in net sales from less than $3 million in 1960 to more than $14 million in 1969. Nordson's star was rising.

Marilyn Pietch Jenne with Evan Nord (right) and Amherst Mayor Marvin Davis, ca. 1970. (Reproduced courtesy of Nordson Corporation)

As sales grew, however, some major problems arose. A number of competitors began to challenge Nordson's products and technology. An important example was the Ransburg Corporation of Indianapolis (now part of ITW), which filed suit in 1965 to bar Nordson from using electrostatic technology as a part of airless spraying. Ginn remembered, "Ransburg had successfully developed a patent position around electrostatic spraying. Nordson defended itself well but lost the case in the trial court. We were able on appeal, however, to negotiate a cost effective exchange of licenses allowing Nordson to continue its electrostatic business unimpeded." Several other companies also sued Nordson, but, Ginn noted, "Nordson was successful in every instance, either by defeating the challenges, or by negotiating appropriate settlements."

These lessons were well learned: Obtaining protection through patents became an important part of Nordson's business strategy. The company took an implementing step by hiring patent attorney Thomas L. Moorhead in 1969 to establish a legal department and to work alongside Ginn and others at Thompson, Hine and Flory.[8]

## MERGERS AND A NEW HEADQUARTERS

In the 1960s U.S. Automatic had entered a period of transition. Some of its machinery was now devoted to making parts for Nordson equipment, in addition to its remaining specialized contract work in screw machine parts. Evan, who as vice president of production headed shop operations and union negotiations, worked with engineer Henry Libicki to meet customers' special, often difficult, requirements and to make improvements in manufacturing technology. An illustrated brochure from that period, titled *Imagineering*, promised "modern men and machines," "tomorrow's methods today," "electronic cost control," "job lot automation," and "customer minded management" to parts customers. But the intent to phase out the contract business that had built up U.S. Automatic was clear. For its part, American Specialty was near the end of its operations. Its primary business, that of making vegetable washing and packaging equipment, was sold to the Nabakowski firm of Amherst in 1960.

In 1965–1966 a series of legal changes took place. First, American Specialty and Banor were merged into U.S. Automatic; then Nordson and its sales subsidiaries were merged into U.S. Automatic; and finally, on November 14, 1966, the name "U.S. Automatic" was officially changed to "Nordson."

So U.S. Automatic was no more. Redesign and expansion of Nordson Corporation headquarters at 555 Jackson Street began in 1966 and was completed early in 1968, just a few months after Walter's death. Eric recalled that a corner office had been reserved for his father. An article in the February 1968 issue of *Automatic Machining* featured a photograph of the building's dedicatory plaque to the memory of Walter Nord. The author noted that "The name has changed, as has the product mix, but the influence of the elder Nord continues in slogans, seen in and around the modern 86,000-square-foot, 470-employee plant. Slogans such as, '*We like to make it here, then the responsibility is ours,*' '*The best engineering is done by those who listen to the sounds of the marketplace,*' '*A Nordson sale is more than getting a name on a dotted line.*' "

*Evan was the guidepost as far as human resources were concerned. He was sensitive to the needs of the employees. He handled union negotiations, interfacing with the union and the workers on behalf of the company. Because he was a hands-on type of guy, he knew every job in the plant and how it should be performed with expertise.*

—William Ginn,
interview with
Martha Pickrell,
June 23, 2003

*Evan was never a man to stand idle. Whenever he saw something that needed to be done, he got it done or he did it himself. . . . The job had to be done right, or he wasn't satisfied. His motto was, "If it's not done right, don't do it at all." Evan was there all the time. If you needed something, all you had to do was phone him and he'd be right down there to help.*

—Clifford Berry,
interview with
Martha Pickrell,
June 24, 2003

Turning to technical matters, the author noted that the screw machines were now down to eight, with the same number of major customers. In later interviews Evan and Libicki described the process of gradually phasing out their remaining contract business, a process that was almost complete by 1972. Many of the customers were reluctant to change suppliers, so Evan and Libicki worked diligently to find new ones for them. They also took steps to train former contract employees for absorption into Nordson.

Not long after the headquarters building was completed, the company published a detailed marketing brochure to show how far Nordson had come and to display all of its services. The text, organized around Walter's plant mottoes and liberally illustrated, described engineers at work, factory people at their machines, and technical-service people advising customers and included case histories of applications by major customers such as General Electric. It ended with statements by Eric and Daly and with Eric's "Corporate Purpose." Throughout, the brochure stressed the depth of Nordson's commitment to innovative engineering, customer service, and ethical values.

On a page that featured a photograph of Evan, standing, slim and tanned, in shirt sleeves and necktie next to a screw machine, the company's "We like to make it here" philosophy was elaborated: "Evan Nord, manufacturing vice president, has concentrated his business life on contract metalworking, accepting many 'impossible' projects turned down by other manufacturers. Intricate work is a challenge to the Nords and to the technicians and craftsmen who share with them the rare quality of 'making things right.'"

Among the employees pictured in the brochure were a small number of African American workers. For the past several years, U.S. Automatic and Nordson had tried to diversify its workforce. Evan recalled how he began to integrate the labor force by hiring two Oberlin men who had been working in a barber shop. George Goodson, one of the two, stayed for many years and became a much-valued employee, active in the union. Evan described Goodson as "our first black ambassador" to the plant's workers, many of whom had never known an African American. Joe Ignat confirmed that the process began in about 1959 or 1960.[9]

## THE EARLY 1970S: NEW DEVELOPMENTS

The early 1970s offered more new challenges. The national economy and the federal government exerted an important influence on Nordson's products and sales. In 1970 and 1971 sales were somewhat hampered by a flat economy with rising inflation. By 1972, however, the economy had rebounded, and Nordson took advantage of the situation to expand its sales force.

The prospect of new federal environmental regulations prompted an editorial by Eric, who now occupied Walter's corner office. Writing in the new *Nordson News* in the spring of 1971, he described the company's goals of reducing pollution by maintaining a clean plant and reducing waste for the customer. As an example, he pointed to perfecting an electrostatic process of applying powder coatings that greatly reduced the amount of wasted paint and the use of solvents. Eric and his engineers put much emphasis now on their new dry powder process, which offered yet another major technology to Nordson's customers. The fall 1971 issue described the process of first coating, then baking, to produce "an extremely durable finish." In 1972 *Nordson News* announced the "first day's run of our new automatic powder system."

The company paid heightened attention to product safety after passage of the Occupational Safety and Health Act of 1970. In 1971 Eric created a product safety and liability department headed by Don Scarbrough. When a customer had an accident a nearby Nordson technician was sent to the site, wherever it might be, and reported back to Scarbrough immediately. Information on what caused the accident became part of Nordson's records and was incorporated into future manuals. In 1972 *Nordson News* announced a new product safety department, a customer's advocate with a wide variety of functions, with Samuel Rosen heading it as vice president of quality assurance.

The Nordson Corporation office building at 555 Jackson Street, Amherst, pictured some years after its completion in 1968. (Reproduced courtesy of Nordson Corporation)

*Just as the smooth inter-action of the components of a fine machine is necessary to satisfactory performance, so, too, is the harmonious interaction between a corporation, its employees, suppliers, customers and the community in which it resides, necessary to the mutual profit of all.*

—From 1973 Nordson Corporation open-house literature, quoted in D. J. Pease, "Pease Porridge," *Oberlin News-Tribune,* September 20, 1973

The company was certainly growing, and its technology was becoming more complex. In 1971 *Nordson News* described another large new building project: two additional structures, totaling 91,500 square feet, to house the expanding engineering department, offices, and physical distribution facilities and, they hoped, to meet requirements for the next five to ten years. The *Lorain Journal* had captioned a photograph of the groundbreaking on May 24, 1970 thus: "With little pomp Nordson Corporation of Amherst broke ground recently for its $900,000 engineering building. . . . Nordson's total expenditures for expansion and modernization projects over the past five years amount to nearly $2 million." On May 20, 1970 the *Elyria Chronicle-Telegram* had reported that the new engineering building would be completed later that year and that "The new building, which will contain 46,000 square feet, is being built behind the main Nordson plant, Jackson and Franklin Streets. Engineering, research and development are primarily responsible for Nordson's continuing growth during a period when industry is tightening its collective belt. 'Innovation is both easier and more profitable than trying to outrun, outshoot and out-claim the competition,' said Eric Nord, president, in expressing his company's business philosophy."

In the fall of 1973, when the new facilities were complete, the company held an open house to celebrate Nordson's continuing growth and development. A newspaper account pictured Eric greeting visitors, Jim Doughman speaking with a local senior citizens group, John Juniker talking about computer processing, Harold Nell explaining how equipment was repaired and rebuilt for customers, and Cathy Siegfried of quality assurance welcoming visitors. The front page of a special open-house edition of *Nordson News* showed a group of smiling, waving employees and gave some impressive statistics: 920 employees, 575 of them in Amherst and the rest staffing thirty-eight sales offices and distributorships around the world. Foreign sales accounted for about one-third of all Nordson business.

Eric looked back on the past thirteen years with great satisfaction and looked ahead with anticipation. Much planning, in fact, was going on that year. Eric had decided to elevate Daly to the presidency of the company and to step into the role of chairman, though retaining the title of chief executive officer. On March 2, 1973, at a special meeting, Nordson shareholders voted to increase the number of shares from 1.2 million to 6 million and to inaugurate an employees' stock-option plan open to all full-time employees.

The plan proved to be of great significance. Ginn, who had worked with Eric and Evan in designing it, noted that Nordson's way of calculating each employee's number of shares of stock was based on length of employment, regardless of the employee's rank. He characterized this plan, along with the convertible-debenture plan for key executives, as "a deter-mined effort to spread ownership of the company among the employees, particularly those who had built the company to its present eminence and were likely to be important to its future." And he further commented, "That took the same philosophy that had been developed by Walter Nord, that success be shared with the community through philanthropy, and implemented it for all employees by sharing ownership." Even though no market existed for Nordson shares in those early days, Ginn noted that someone was always available to buy employees' shares, "so that no one was prevented from cashing in on their investment in the company and its future."

Equally important, the March 1973 shareholders' meeting adopted a modified version of Eric's mission statement and wrote officially into the legal requirements of the company that it "contribute approximately 5% of the annual pretax earnings of the Corporation to the support of edu-cational, charitable, and community activities, and that the Corporation encourage its employees, and particularly its executives, to take active roles in such undertakings."[10]

## "ENLIGHTENED CITIZENSHIP"

The last statement in the 1973 official policy formally recommended what had been happening for a long time: company and employee involve-ment in the community. For example, the 1968 *Automatic Machining* article noted that some of the company's work was farmed out to what it called "Dept. 6½"—the Skills Division of the Center for the Sightless, a ma-chine shop in Elyria for the blind and other disabled persons. A Nordson foreman volunteered his expertise, and the organization's history noted that Evan was closely involved as well.

In fact, by the late 1960s one Nordson employee was devoting all of his time to community issues. Jim Doughman first came to Nordson in 1966 as sales office manager. However, he was given a new job a few years later, when Eric accepted an appeal from President Richard M. Nixon through the National Alliance of Businessmen to take charge of Lorain County's JOBS program, finding work for the chronically unemployed. Eric loaned Doughman to the U.S. Department of Labor for a year and noted that, under Doughman's direction, about 500 people were placed in jobs, including a few at Nordson—an enviable record. When he re-turned to the company, Doughman became Eric's community affairs di-rector, working full time on community projects.

Among the many causes supported by Nordson employees were blood donation, Junior Achievement, and the United Way. Doughman was to spend much time with the unified county United Way, organized

*We feel very definitely that management has an obligation to themselves, to stockholders, employees and customers to be successful. An obligation to put out good products and create wealth for the entire group. There's no room for not being successful, but beyond that we feel success isn't just a matter of serving stockholders, customers and employees. We also have an obligation to make the community a better place in which to live. . . . Excellence in anything turns me on. A lot of things turn me on such as an individual progressing up to maxi-mum capacity.*

—Eric Nord, quoted in Bob Cotleur, "Eric and Evan Nord: They Have a Philosophy," *Lorain Journal,* January 26, 1970

to avoid duplication in fund-raising efforts. In 1972, when a job realignment temporarily displaced a group of Nordson employees, instead of layoffs the company devised special assignments. With the approval of their union, Nordson offered employees the choice of working for reduced pay on several community projects, such as sprucing up the nearby Lucy Idol School, now the Lucy Idol Center for the Handicapped, in Vermilion. The program was a pronounced success.[11]

## The Second Generation Takes Charge

As company profits increased, The U.S. Automatic Foundation had built up its funds and its level of contributions, from six grants totaling about $2,400 in 1960 to fifty-one grants totaling more than $51,000 in 1972. In the early 1960s, grants to educational institutions, including those by the Nord scholarship fund, remained the largest area of giving. In 1972, education still represented almost half of the awards, with mental health second.

Important changes had been made, however. The mid-1960s brought a complete turnover in the foundation's three-man Board of Trustees. First, in 1964, longtime trustee Paul Warner resigned, and Eric was elected to take his place. In 1966, upon the death of John Smythe, Ginn, who had been closely involved with the foundation since its beginning, was invited to become a trustee. And finally, in June 1967, shortly after Walter's death, Evan became the third trustee and was immediately elected president and treasurer, with Eric as vice president and Ginn as secretary. This threesome remained in charge of the foundation for more than twenty years. In January 1967 The U.S. Automatic Foundation officially became Nordson Foundation.

The house at 251 Forest Street, Oberlin, was owned by Mary and Joseph Ignat and later by Evan and Cindy Nord. It was the scene of much innovative planning and community organizing in the late 1960s and 1970s. (Photograph by Geoffrey Blodgett; reproduced courtesy of Jane Blodgett)

Ginn, in his 1992 interview with Jeanne Harrah, discussed the way the three men worked together: "We never had, that I can recall, any kind of fundamental disagreements. . . . It was a labor of love for the three of us. We respected each other's views and judgments and we brought different perspectives." He added that, as a Cleveland resident, he often played the role of devil's advocate, bringing up questions that occurred to him with his greater detachment from Lorain County.

For Evan, the foundation and other community opportunities were especially welcome. Like Walter and Eric, he had always wanted much more out of life than designing machinery and managing industrial production. That desire had grown as Eric's role in the family business became more predominant and the contract work, in which Evan had become so expert, diminished. Like Walter and Eric, he had an appetite for work and for hatching projects that knew no bounds. This was evident in the way he took on the challenging task of transforming older buildings, beginning with his conception and design for remodeling the Amherst cold storage plant in 1941, through several other projects, including virtually rebuilding what became the Oberlin Community Center. In 1967 he succeeded his father on the O.H.I.O. board and in 1969 was elected junior warden and chair of the properties commission at Christ Church, where he had previously supervised renovation projects.

Evan's marriage to Cindy in 1966 and his becoming president of Nordson Foundation in 1967 were empowering events, all the more so because he and Cindy shared deep concerns and worked together on many projects. At the most basic level, this longtime bachelor was now a husband and father, with a house full of children and pets. And Cindy provided Evan with a new perspective on life. Coming from a background of childhood emotional trauma and having weathered a divorce, she was a woman of strong character and opinions, determined to raise her children, further her own education in child psychology, and make a positive impact on the world. Coming together with Evan was a great boon for her as well.

In a 2002 interview Cindy described how their Forest Street home had become a center for the development of community projects. In about 1968, for example, Evan followed his father in becoming deeply involved in the cause of mental health. As part of a nationwide movement to deinstitutionalize the mentally ill and provide more services in communities, the Ohio General Assembly created county oversight boards. The Lorain County Board of Mental Health and Mental Retardation, as it was known in its first years, contracted with the previously established Lorain County Guidance Center and provided a vehicle for its expansion and for the development of satellite centers, including one in Oberlin. Because Evan was a charter member of this new board, much planning took place at the Nords' house, and mental health experts were frequent overnight guests.

Evan and another Nord relative, Joe Ignat's widow, Lee, were both involved, along with O.H.I.O., in an innovative project to improve the lives of people with mental retardation. Following passage of an Ohio law supporting the establishment of schools for children with mental retardation, the Murray Ridge School opened in Elyria in 1968. In the early 1970s, after a further advance in Ohio law supporting services for adults, a work facility, known as the Murray Ridge Production Center, and group residences were established by the supervising agency, the Lorain County Board of Mental Retardation, now the Lorain County Board of Mental Retardation and Developmental Disabilities.

Funds for creating group-home facilities were limited, however, and neighborhood opposition was an issue in some cases. O.H.I.O. made it possible to create the first group home in Lorain County—the first group home in Ohio, according to Dr. Ellen Payner, then superintendent of the county board. In 1972 Evan, O.H.I.O. Board President Stephen Johnson Jr., and former Board Presidents Frank Chapman Van Cleef and John A. Cochrane enabled O.H.I.O. to purchase the Ferguson House at 89 South Professor Street, two doors south of the Jewett house, to be leased for $1 a year to the Board of Mental Retardation as a group home for eight women—and now men as well—employed by the Murray Ridge Production Center. Lee Ignat, administrator for the board, oversaw the entire project, which included extensive renovation efforts by many Oberlin volunteers. The house has been in use as a group home since 1973, part of the thriving, countywide program that includes the school, adult training and counseling, and three work facilities employing 650 persons.[12]

## THE FOUNDATION EXPANDS ITS IMPACT

With the two brothers' leadership and Cindy's influence, the board of Nordson Foundation entered a more activist phase, not just supporting causes but also initiating projects. Two of the first centered on educating young children from poor families. Cindy had been volunteering for the Head Start program in Oberlin, which was expanding and badly needed its own building. Eric recalled that, as school board president, he also was strongly committed to the Head Start program. He added, "Evan found the building and made it happen."

Some years earlier, before Mary died, Joe had purchased the former Oberlin passenger station, built in 1866, and had it converted into an office so that he could run SuperVision, the advertising agency, close to home. Since Mary's death, however, Joe had been gradually pulling out of the business and no longer needed the building. A lease of the old

*[The newly constructed Oberlin passenger depot has] solid brackets of a very tasteful pattern . . . door and window caps which are of a similarly neat and heavy design. . . . The floor is of double thickness and, in short, every part of the work in the building is of the best character. . . . [It] is the finest of any intermediate station on the [rail]road, and the location is the roomiest and the pleasantest of any station—intermediate or terminal.*

—"The New Depot: All About It," *Lorain County News,* November 21, 1866

The former Ferguson House, near the Oberlin Heritage Center, is now the 89 South Professor Street Group Home. (Photograph by Sarah MacLennan Kerr, August 2004)

depot to Head Start was arranged. Then, in April 1969, just a month before Joe's death, the Nordson Foundation board approved the purchase of the building for $35,000—a major expenditure—and later that year leased it to the Oberlin Board of Education for $1 a year. Cindy and Evan spent a great many hours working on the building's purchase, renovation, and remodeling, and soon fresh paint revealed the charming, Victorian wooden exterior. The new Head Start center opened in the fall of 1969, and by 1971 some sixty children filled two classrooms originally used as men's and women's waiting rooms. A kitchen and an office occupied the old baggage room. A well-equipped, spacious playground was built in the park in front of the building, and an old caboose, purchased in another Ohio town, was placed near the former railroad track bed for the children to enjoy.

Renovated and adapted for a creative new use at a time when beautiful historic train stations throughout the country were being demolished at an alarming rate, the Oberlin Depot soon attracted national attention. It was featured in *Reusing Railroad Stations* (1974), and Evan, Cindy, and others enjoyed traveling to Indianapolis to receive a national award for the project.

A second project on which Evan and Cindy worked together was the development of the Oberlin Early Childhood Center. Concern about the problems of Oberlin's young children, especially those of working parents, led a group of community activists in 1968 to take an additional step by establishing an all-day, sliding-fee day-care center, which met that summer at Christ Church and that fall at The First Church in Oberlin, United Church of Christ. The community group that Evan and Cindy worked with obtained temporary financial support from the short-lived Oberlin Community Foundation (founded in 1967 and on whose board Eric served). The group researched similar day-care operations elsewhere and looked for a permanent home. Much of the planning for the center, again, took place at Cindy and Evan's house.

When appeals to various community agencies failed, the group turned to Nordson Foundation. Consideration was given to expanding the Oberlin Depot to accommodate a child-care facility, but this plan was abandoned after some neighborhood opposition was encountered. An imposing Greek Revival home, built in 1852 on a spacious lot at 315 East College Street, was for sale. It had been the home of Jabez Lyman Burrell, a charter trustee of the Oberlin Collegiate Institute, as Oberlin College was called in its early years, and later of Henry Churchill King, a president of the college. More recently, Walter and Virginia's close friends, Axel and Ebba Skjerne, had owned the house. In December 1973 the foundation's trustees authorized its purchase for $75,000, and Evan and Cindy became deeply involved in planning and constructing a state-of-the-art facility for the Oberlin Early Childhood Center on the back portion of the property, as well as in restoring the house itself, with the intention that it would be used as the residence for the center's executive director and as a gathering place for parents. This was a major commit-

Oberlin's former passenger depot, on South Main Street, was renovated in the late 1960s under the leadership of Evan and Cindy Nord for use by the Head Start program. It again underwent extensive renovations and opened in 2004 as a community meeting facility operated by The Nord Family Foundation. In June 2004 the caboose shown here on the right was moved to the Sandstone Museum Center in Amherst.

Evan Nord and Jean McElya, director of the Head Start program, hung the program's sign on Oberlin's renovated passenger depot in Oberlin in 1969. (Reproduced courtesy of Eric and Jane Nord)

ment for the foundation, which took the unprecedented step of borrowing the necessary cash against its assets. It took two years for the day-care center to be completed.

Evan remained deeply loyal to Amherst, and among other foundation actions during this period was acquisition of property next to the Amherst Public Library in April 1972. The land was turned over to the library, enabling it to expand later. The following year the foundation was given the former Tuberculosis and Health Association building at 621 Cleveland Avenue in Amherst, which was no longer needed because the association had merged with other organizations in nearby counties. Evan assured the association's board president, Harrison Comstock, that "The Foundation will attempt to make the building available to organizations with programs serving the health and welfare needs of Lorain County." The building was indeed remodeled and made available to community groups, and ownership of it was eventually transferred to the city of Amherst. Evan's continuing commitment to education, mental health, and historic preservation led to many other community-enriching projects.

Change was inevitable, however; and in the foundation world change arrived with the Federal Tax Reform Act of 1969. The reform came about in response to growing dissatisfaction with the way in which some founders exploited "their" charitable foundation for their own personal benefit or the benefit of their closely held corporation. Although this was far from the situation with the Nords, the reform applied to all foundations and included minimum annual payouts of 5 percent of asset value, more numerous reporting requirements, and penalties on making grants to certain types of beneficiaries.

None of the provisions in the new act presented any real problem for the Nords, because the culture of giving back to constituent communities that characterized Nordson Corporation, as expressed in part through Nordson Foundation, gave both entities a sure and steady underpinning. The most relevant of the limitations was a requirement that a foundation not hold a dominant interest in a corporation controlled by the foundation's grantors. Because Virginia Nord's shares had been gifted to Nordson Foundation, those shares arguably represented a prohibitive degree of ownership and control over Nordson Corporation. Due to some adroit planning by Eric, Evan, and Ginn on the eve of the effective date of the Tax Reform Act, however, Nordson Foundation had fifteen years in which to divest itself of any excess shares.

The historic Burrell-King House, purchased by Nordson Foundation in 1975, became the property of the Oberlin Historical and Improvement Organization in 1989. Built in 1852 by Jabez Lyman Burrell (1806–1900), a cattleman and farmer who was also an ardent abolitionist and believed in equal education for all, the house was the home of Oberlin College President Henry Churchill King from 1884 to 1934. It is listed on the National Register of Historic Places and is a City of Oberlin Historic Landmark. (Photograph by Richard Holsworth)

Thus there was more than enough time to reorganize Nordson Foundation in such a way as to comply with all legal niceties and provide it with an asset base appropriate for the new generation of leaders. Thanks to the success of Nordson Corporation, shares of Nordson stock in the foundation that had been worth about $400,000 at Walter's death were partially redeemed in 1988 by Nordson Corporation for $38 million, leaving the foundation with $2 million of Nordson shares. The foundation continues to hold, quite properly, up to 2 percent of the corporation's outstanding stock.[13]

# 7

# TEAMWORK AND BROADENING, 1974–1988

The Nords had always depended on their employees, friends, and neighbors. They had sought the most competent professional help available for their companies and, in the early 1960s, had taken the bold step of bringing high-level executives into Nordson Corporation from outside the family. Moving into the 1970s and 1980s, with all the economic and technological changes those years brought, the Nords' philosophy of teamwork was applied to an even greater extent, both to the company and to the foundation.

## AN ENLARGING VISION

### NORDSON IN THE STORMY 1970S

In many businesses dominated by a family, an owner hangs on to control for too long. Eric and Evan, however, were determined to arrange matters so that they could progressively let go of their day-to-day involvement in the company. At the same time, it was crucial to them that Nordson Corporation be properly managed, that it grow, and that it maintain its integrity and not be absorbed by some other business entity.

Eric and Ken Daly were approximately the same age, complemented each other's strengths, and had worked compatibly together for more than a decade. Eric had great confidence in Daly and now decided to let him assume the presidency of Nordson, while Eric retained the titles of chief executive officer and chairman. These changes took effect on January 15, 1974.

The management team faced major challenges as the U.S. economy reeled under the impact of the Middle East oil crisis. In the company annual report dated December 18, 1974, Eric and Daly addressed the changes in coating and sealing materials forced by the worldwide oil shortage, resulting inflation, and governmental pollution regulations. Nordson was responding, they wrote, by making many changes in its equipment.

That same month *Nordson News* featured the Engineering Department, which had grown from just four men in 1963 to more than fifty in 1974. Fred Powers, in his narrative "An Industry Grows in Amherst," written that year, described the four stages of product innovation: project planning, concept development, project development, and production development. Evan continued in general charge of the plant, assisted by Henry Libicki. Eric expressed his enthusiasm about the company's culture of growth to a writer from the *Lorain Journal* in an article published on January 6, 1974: "We've been [attracting] young executives. We have a lot of people brought in from the outside. We go to some pains to attract people capable of doing work at our present level of production and with the growth capacity to handle expanding work."

For his part, Daly was satisfied to see that the computerized, coordinated systems of planning, production, sales, and marketing he had advocated and developed were at last falling into place. As he described it some years later, the basic principle behind these refinements was to achieve the quickest possible availability of products with the lowest possible investment in inventory. Nordson's expansion was paying off, and sales figures for 1974 were heartening.

A favorable report from Citicorp Venture Capital in October praised Nordson for its "superior product reliability and sales and service capability" and sound financial management. The report pointed out that Nordson was almost unique in its direct foreign sales capabilities and that its products were relatively inexpensive for capital goods (less than $10,000), tended to be bought for purposes of cost reduction, fulfilled new antipollution requirements, and paid for themselves within a year. Nordson had captured a large share of the market in its hot-melt and drink-can-coating equipment.

The inflation that was gripping the economy continued to be a problem, however. That same October, Nordson's workers voted to reject the two-year contract offered by management and went on strike. More than three weeks later their union, the International Association of Machinists and Aerospace Workers, won a three-year contract with improved wage increases and benefits and—importantly—with the removal of restrictions on cost-of-living increases.

Only the second work stoppage in the memory of Eric and Evan, it was a difficult time. Evan was deeply involved in the negotiations. Speaking to the historian Barbara Griffith, he recalled, "The union president then, with whom I was good friends, was Stanley Lewis. . . . He came up and reported that they voted to strike. . . . I said, 'Fine, Stanley. We're going to operate the plant. And we don't expect you to give us any trouble, and we'll remain good friends.'"

The December issue of *Nordson News* reported that the salaried employees had kept operations running until the hourly workers returned. It noted that Eric and Daly had welcomed the workers back to work with a letter in which they emphasized the workers' "importance to the welfare and growth of the company." The letter ended with this statement:

*I felt it was a mistake to stay in the saddle too long. It's no way to build a team. You need to get some young, ambitious people in and make room for them. One thing [John W.] Gardner said that always impressed me was that with the young officers in the army, their ambition was not to get a larger tent, but a command.*

—Eric Nord, interview with Martha Pickrell, January 28, 2003

*We weren't really up and going until the mid '70s, in other words, totally computerized and having a sequential record of everything before it happened and forecast ahead of time what people are going to buy.*

—Kenneth Daly, interview with Barbara Griffith, June 8, 1995

An aerial view of the Nordson Corporation plant in Amherst in the early 1970s. Compare this photograph with the earlier view on page 73 and the later one on page 169. (Reproduced courtesy of Nordson Corporation)

"The challenge is clear. There is not the slightest doubt that we can meet it and regain our momentum. It is simply a matter of each one of us trying to do the job a little better, looking for more efficient ways to work, and most important, pulling together to get the job done." Longtime employees must have remembered Walter's similar exhortations during World War II.

Difficulties continued in 1975. Demand for Nordson's products did not live up to expectations, and the company was forced to cut its expenses. But 1976 was much better. In their annual report for that year Daly and Eric credited the internal changes made in the past few years. In addition to their production control system, a 1975 plan of Daly's had been implemented that split Nordson's engineering, sales, and marketing operations into two divisions: the Nordson Packaging and Assembly Division (adhesives), and the Nordson Finishing Equipment Division (coatings). "Our ability to respond promptly to customer requirements," they wrote, "has been substantially improved." The company also developed two additional international sales outlets, in Hong Kong and Switzerland. By 1977 sales had climbed to more than $58 million, and the company celebrated "the most outstanding year in Nordson Corporation's history."

## AN IMPORTANT DOCUMENT

Early in 1978 a statement of the company's business philosophy, entitled "Nordson's Approach to Management," reached stockholders as part of the 1977 annual report. This statement, still repeated and refined each year, committed Nordson to a number of corporate goals and strategies. The company aimed to double its sales every four years (later adjusted to five years) and to earn an average of 18 percent on shareholders' equity. It strengthened and expanded its organization with on-the-job training and growth, teamwork, and "delegation of planning and implementation to the lowest possible levels of authority," with managers as team leaders.

Setting long-term goals involved all levels of management; flexible short-term goals were established that allowed for minimum and optimum productivity. The statement raised the possibility that the company would look for new opportunities "outside of its traditional fields" and affirmed Nordson's commitment to its employees' well-being, "creating an environment which provides the opportunity for employee self-fulfillment and growth, security, recognition and equitable compensation." Finally, it affirmed the long-standing policy of "contributing an average 5 percent of pretax earnings to the educational, charitable and other similar activities in those communities where Nordson has a presence."[1]

## HONORING LONGEVITY, HISTORY, AND AMHERST

In June 1976 the *Lorain Journal* interviewed Jim Doughman, Nordson's community affairs director. After describing levy campaigns he had conducted on behalf of the mental health clinic, the Lorain County Health Department, and the Amherst Public Library, he listed his favorite projects. One was the transformation of the Amherst railroad freight depot near the Nordson plant, built in 1905 and closed in 1963, into the Nordson Depot, a site dedicated to use as meeting space by local nonprofit organizations.

The project had been Evan's idea. A few years after the depot was closed he suggested that the company, which was looking for parking space, buy the depot and the land surrounding it. He recalled that the property, which included railroad siding, was not easy to obtain from the railroad and that the purchase took some time. Renovation started soon afterward and took about three years. The initial plan had been to convert the building into a performing arts center to be operated by the city; later, however, it was decided that the facility would be owned and operated by Nordson Corporation. Jack Clark, of the firm of Clark and Post, Doughman, and Nordson workers participated in the renovation. Evan noted, "I [even] had my son Eric pulling nails out of boards."

James Doughman, Nordson Corporation's first community relations director, ca. 1980s. (Reproduced courtesy of The Nordson Corporation Foundation)

Workmen painstakingly wire brushed the interior brick walls and rafters, installed a hardwood floor, replaced the freight and loading doors with large windows, and added a kitchen, an office, and restrooms. Round tables covered with red-checked cloths were brought in, as were an immense hanging freight scale, a potbellied stove, and other attractive curiosities. Some consideration was given to developing a railroad museum on the adjoining property, but the museum did not come to fruition. Evan, Doughman, and Clark did, however, make an extensive search throughout Ohio and West Virginia and acquired three vintage railroad cars to display adjacent to the depot: a passenger car, a Pullman sleeper, and a red caboose dating from 1924. They also tried to, but could not, secure an elegant parlor car.

Today the Nordson Depot is in high demand: In 2003, for example, it was used for more than 260 community functions by groups such as

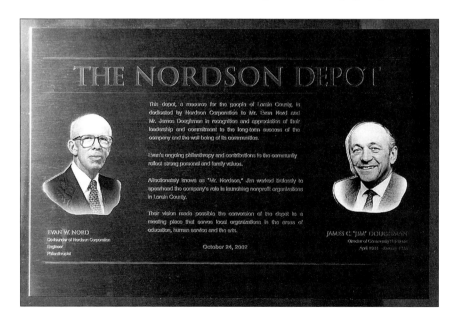

Evan Nord (right) presenting a thirty-five-year service pin to Eric Nord at the first Nordson Old Timers Dinner, held in the Nordson Depot in November 1975. (Reproduced courtesy of Nordson Corporation)

scouts, political organizations, sports associations, nonprofit organizations, ethnic organizations, and labor unions. On November 21, 1978 the old depot was officially listed on the National Register of Historic Places. The building underwent some extensive additional renovations in 2002, including the installation of wheelchair-accessible restrooms, repainting and refinishing woodwork, and site improvements, and on October 24, 2002 it was officially dedicated to Evan Nord and the late Jim Doughman.

Work on the building reaffirmed the close connection of first U.S. Automatic and then Nordson to the Amherst community. The depot served as a bricks-and-mortar statement of the company's gratitude to the town. Just as important, Nordson made a special effort to begin to honor the

Clifford Berry, a longtime Nordson worker, photographed in 1976 at the Nordson Depot in Amherst with two vintage automobiles, a 1925 Flint (left) and a 1931 Ford Model A, that he rebuilt for Evan Nord. (Reproduced courtesy of Clifford Berry)

employees and families who had given many years to the company. In June 1975 *Nordson News* featured interviews with forty-year workers Cliff Berry, Elton Schibley, Walter Smith, and John Belden. Referring to the company's growth over a period of four decades, Evan concluded that none of Nordson's growth would have been possible without the help of such loyal employees.

Around the same time, Nordson, at Doughman's initiative and with aid from his new assistant, Nancy Scott, established an Old Timers Club for its employees and retirees. The club held its first awards dinner, recognizing company service of fifteen years or more, in the Nordson Depot in November 1975. The banquets have continued to be a highlight for employees and retirees alike, so much so that they long since outgrew the depot.[2]

## PHILANTHROPIC FLOWERING

During the period 1974–1979 Nordson Foundation's grants to community organizations grew tenfold, from about $49,000 to more than $450,000 per year. This was possible because of the foundation's mounting assets, including the growing value of Nordson stock given by Virginia Nord and ever-increasing annual contributions by the company. Beginning in 1976 all contributions became a permanent part of assets, and all grants were satisfied out of earnings on the invested funds. With the high interest rates of those years, meeting federal requirements that the foundation give away at least 5 percent of its assets posed no problem. Doughman devoted about half of his time to foundation work.

Grants for bricks-and-mortar projects figured prominently in this period. To realize Cindy and Evan's dream for the Oberlin Early Childhood Center without partially liquidating its assets, Evan and Clark drew up site plans, and the foundation borrowed $600,000 from a bank. The loan was repaid over time through contributions made to the foundation by Nordson Corporation. The preschool moved into its new facility in April 1976.

Delivery of a caboose and its installation on the grounds of the Oberlin Early Childhood Center was quite an undertaking. Here the trucks that brought the caboose to Oberlin are parked in front of the Burrell-King House on East College Street. (Reproduced courtesy of the Oberlin Early Childhood Center)

In addition, the founda-
tion was continuing to support Head Start by paying
utilities and maintenance for
the Oberlin Depot, and the
remodeling of the former
Tuberculosis Association
building in Amherst for use
by community agencies was
being completed. By 1979
the foundation had committed itself to providing the
land for the new Walter
G. Nord Community Men-

tal Health Center at 6140 South Broadway, in Lorain (now The Nord
Center), designed by Clark and Post. The center was completed in 1982
and later expanded.

Nordson Foundation and Nordson Corporation worked closely together in their philanthropic efforts. A committee of employees was
formed to make recommendations for foundation gifts. And the corporation took a leadership role in a project to help the Neighborhood
House Association of Lorain (a longtime "settlement house" with many
innovative programs) construct a community center at 3806 Clifton Avenue in Cityview, an impoverished area of small houses located just south
of 36th Street, then the southern city limit of Lorain. Doughman worked
closely with Neighborhood House officials, area residents, the architect
Jack Clark, and former resident John Corrigan of Lake Erie Electric on
this project, which took six years of planning before construction could
begin, Clark recalled. This was another of Doughman's favorites, and it
involved the foundation as well. Financial and in-kind donations were
obtained, and Nordson employees, including labor-union members,
donated their time to help in the construction. The May 1, 1973 *Lorain
Morning Journal* reported that the Neighborhood House's annual meeting and banquet had been held in the unfinished building. It also quoted
Clark, who, as one of the speakers, had paid tribute to the union members who donated their services to help on the building. "In essence," he
stated, "what we're doing here is building a $200,000 facility with $30,000
cash." Eric noted that the center has made a big difference in the Cityview
area.

The company also took pride in the many employees who had moved
into community leadership roles. An article in the *Amherst News-Times* in
June 1977 publicly honored seven Nordson employees: Andrew Cirbus,
for leading the county mental health board; Frank J. Kovach, president of

The Oberlin Early Childhood
Center was completed in
1976 with the aid of grants
from Nordson Foundation.
The facility was built directly
behind the Burrell-King
House, which was originally
incorporated into the project
to serve as the residence for
the center's executive
director. It serves up to 135
children each year. (Reproduced courtesy of the Oberlin
Early Childhood Center)

*The way we chose the
community groups we
serviced was basically
determined by Eric and
Evan's approach to enlight-
ened citizenship: in the
communities where Nordson
had major facilities, we
searched out problems of those
groups and individuals who
were disadvantaged and
sought ways to strengthen
and better their circumstances,
whether by direct help or by
strengthening other groups
which could help them
directly.*

—Nancy Scott, Nordson
Corporation community
affairs manager, 1975–1995

Henry Libicki, Nordson
Corporation's vice president
of operations, in 1978.
(Reproduced courtesy of
Nordson Corporation)

the Amherst Hospital board; Reinhold H. Koch, former president of the board of the Lorain County Rehabilitation Center; Raymond E. Murphy, prominent in the Boy Scouts organization; and Joseph E. Jarosz, Wayne J. Pakan, and John E. Dunn, all leaders in Junior Achievement. In 1978 Nordson Vice President Sam Rosen served as chairman of United Way; and in 1979–1980 Vice President Henry Libicki chaired the mental health center board. Many other employees were involved in volunteer work as well, and continue to be. Nordson's service and financial aid to community agencies was a closely coordinated effort under the direction of Doughman and Scott. All were carrying on the Walter Nord tradition.[3]

## ERIC AND EVAN: HONORS AND CHANGES

Oberlin College honored the Nord brothers with Distinguished Community Service Awards at its commencement ceremony on May 26, 1974. In addition to describing both men's roles in the company and the foundation, the presentation mentioned Eric's service on the Oberlin City Council, the Oberlin Board of Education, and the board of the Lorain County Joint Vocational School and his upcoming chairmanship of United Way. Later, in 1977, Eric was elected a trustee of Oberlin College. The college recognized Evan for his work on the Lorain County Board of Mental Health and Mental Retardation and on the boards of the Center for the Sightless, United Way, and the Oberlin Heritage Center / Oberlin Historical and Improvement Organization (O.H.I.O.), as well as for his service on the Ohio Citizens' Council. It especially stressed his preservation work in Oberlin.

In 1976 Eric became involved in another of his father's favorite institutions, Lorain County Community College. He served on the college's foundation and chaired its campaign to raise funds for construction of the Stocker Humanities and Fine Arts Center. The building, with its 984-seat, state-of-the-art auditorium, was dedicated in 1980 with a concert by the Cleveland Orchestra as its first program. Eric, influenced by his wife, Jane, an artist and musician, had widened his horizons and had been drawn increasingly to the arts.

In fact, now that their children were of college and young adult age, Jane spent a great deal more time with her art and her music. In 1976 she earned a master's degree in art education from Case Western Reserve University and became an art teacher, instructing students at Lorain County Community College in drawing and painting techniques. She entered her own paintings in juried exhibitions, and in the fall of 1977 she and other Oberlin artists began to discuss an organization that came to be known as the Firelands Association for the Visual Arts (FAVA). The following year Bill Ginn helped the group draw up organizational plans; the state of Ohio soon granted FAVA a charter to operate as a nonprofit corporation, and the Internal Revenue Service granted it tax-exempt status as a 501(c)(3) organization. Aided by Nordson Foundation, galleries, classrooms, and offices were created out of a former recreation area on the second floor of the Oberlin Community Center, in what was once the food-locker plant operated by the U.S. Automatic Corporation. Within a short time FAVA was offering exhibits of note and providing various kinds of art instruction, both for adults and for children. The facility met an important need for Oberlinians, both artists and nonartists, who were not part of the college's art community. Musically, Jane became an active member of the Oberlin Friday Music Club.

Samuel Rosen, vice president of quality assurance, in his office at Nordson Corporation in 1978. (Reproduced courtesy of Nordson Corporation)

During this time tragedy struck Eric and Jane and their family. In April 1980 their second-oldest child, Chip, was killed in a go-cart racing accident in Talladega, Alabama, at the age of twenty-nine. The blow was devastating to the entire family.

Evan and Cindy were still in the midst of raising their children, and, in addition, Cindy was pursuing demanding studies in psychology—first at the Gestalt Institute in Cleveland and then at Oberlin College, from which she graduated in 1978—and had begun to train as a counselor. Evan had taken on additional volunteer responsibilities since the death of his father, including serving as president of the Walter and Virginia Nord Scholarship Fund and completing numerous projects as junior warden and chair of the properties commission of Oberlin's Christ Episcopal Church. Carrying on Walter's interest in Oberlin history, Evan had continued to take an active part in O.H.I.O. projects. For example, he oversaw the renovation of the Jewett House and the Monroe House, which had been badly damaged by a storm in 1976.

By the late 1970s both Cindy and Evan were ready for a lifestyle change. In 1978 Evan decided to retire from active employment at Nordson after more than thirty-five years, although he remained on the board of the company until 2002 and served on the board of the foundation for many years. He dreamed of being able to play tennis outdoors year-round. Cindy had developed a love of horses and wanted a congenial climate for breeding, raising, training, and showing them competitively. So they and their family made up their minds to head south. During an exploratory trip in a camper, Evan and Cindy discovered the Columbia, South Carolina, area and decided to look no further. First settling at a planned commu-

The Stocker Humanities and Fine Arts Center at Lorain County Community College, Elyria, was dedicated in 1980. (Reproduced courtesy of Lorain County Community College)

nity, Reflections, in 1978, they later built a home in Blythewood, north of Columbia. Their Meadow Ridge Farm is large and scenic, with ample room for horses, tennis, and other outdoor enjoyments.

In South Carolina Evan and Cindy spread the family mission into a new area. Evan soon became deeply involved in community organizations, among the first of which was the Central Caro-

lina Community Foundation, a small, struggling effort incorporated in 1984. The founders asked Evan to join the board, and shortly thereafter he offered a challenge of $25,000 to the other board members, which they matched, raising a total of $250,000. Somewhat later he and Cindy made a contribution of $1 million. The foundation was on its way.

Unfortunately, not long after settling in South Carolina, Cindy sustained serious injuries in a horseback-riding accident. They remain part of her life to this day.[4]

## COMPANY TRANSITIONS

### "OUTSIDE OF ITS TRADITIONAL FIELDS"

These words in the "Approach to Management" statement in Nordson Corporation's 1977 annual report revealed that some new thinking had been going on about ways in which the company might grow. With its increasing success, maintaining a high profit level had become a possibility, a primary goal, and, in an inflationary environment, a necessity. Many companies were achieving greater growth and profitability by diversifying into new lines of business, purchasing smaller companies to enhance their capabilities.

In Nordson's case, innovation and embracing change had always been a key to growth. From the very beginning, Walter, Eric, and Evan had been willing to go out on a limb to find new ways for their company to survive and thrive. Now the company was in a good capital position to expand. So it is not surprising that, from 1978 to 1985, Nordson launched a significant effort in product diversification. In 1979 the company purchased the packaging machinery segment of Domain Industries of New Richmond, Wisconsin, and the American Packaging Corporation of Hudson,

Ohio. In 1978 Nordson also bought manufacturing rights from an Italian company, Basfer SRL, that had begun to develop industrial robots. With these new resources Nordson almost simultaneously entered two new businesses: making packaging machinery, and designing robots specifically to do some of the more physically taxing jobs involved in applying paint and other coatings.

Expansion into packaging machinery seemed natural, because Nordson was already making adhesive-applying equipment that was purchased by customers for their packaging assembly lines. Robots were a popular idea in the late 1970s, but, as Eric later told Griffith, the Nordson robotic project was mostly his own idea, not especially favored by Daly or the other top managers. Perhaps one can hear a reflection of Walter's earlier desire to make things easier for the quarrymen in Eric's statement that "I never thought that replacing human beings was the main motivation. . . . I did think robots could have done a lot of really dirty jobs a lot better than human beings and relieved the human beings from those onerous positions." Operators of spray-painting equipment, for example, often developed carpal tunnel problems. Coming up with workable designs for the coating-applying robots required sophisticated knowledge of electronics, so a whole new group of electronic systems engineers had to be hired.

By the end of 1979 the company truly reflected a growth mode. With its new acquisitions, sales had jumped to almost $130 million. The number of employees had doubled, from 1,208 in 1978 to 2,260 in 1979. Satellite facilities were up and running, or nearly so, in Norcross, Georgia (at Technology Park, near Atlanta), New Richmond, Wisconsin, and Anderson, South Carolina, and, by 1980, in North Ridgeville, Ohio. In addition to producing machinery that made film-wrap packaging and designing robots, much progress was being made in Nordson's traditional products. The company now offered equipment to apply a new type of adhesive known as FoamMelt, a foamed adhesive with many uses in assembly operations. Sales were booming.

A robot manufactured by Nordson Corporation applies coating. (Reproduced courtesy of Nordson Corporation)

In their opening message in the 1979 annual report Eric and Daly made another important announcement: "Nordson shares are now traded in the Over the Counter (OTC) market. We are pleased with this development because it provides a service to our shareholders. . . . However[,] . . . we would hate to see ease of trading result in ease of speculating. . . .

In 1979 Nordson completed this Norcross, Georgia, building, which served as the headquarters for its adhesive applications group. It housed the engineering, sales, and marketing departments. (Reproduced courtesy of Nordson Corporation)

As a step toward preventing unwarranted expectations or fears, we call attention to our corporate objectives. . . . We do not operate for the sole purpose of maximizing earnings per share. We operate for the purpose of creating benefits for all of our constituencies: customers, employees, shareholders and the communities in which we exist."

That year, 1979, Nordson celebrated its twenty-fifth anniversary. In July, at a community banquet at the Nordson Depot, the Amherst Historical Society honored the company for its restoration efforts. Local historian Valerie Jenkins presented a memorable essay entitled "The Past Is Not Forgotten." And in late September the company held a series of open houses. At least 5,000 people attended the festivities in the plant, the depot, and a tent next to it, and many received a sixteen-page illustrated publication, *Nordson . . . The First Twenty-Five Years.*

At the new divisional headquarters in Norcross, Eric gave a press-conference address in October on "The Nordson Commitment to Growth through Service." He introduced Nordson and its products to the Atlanta community, describing the company's history and values and giving its rationale in building the new Packaging and Product Assembly Division offices there. "Although we are an integral part of our community in Amherst," Eric said, "we decided that our continuing health depended on fast response to market needs and on high levels of innovation and that these characteristics could best be fostered in several small, autonomous units rather than in one large operating group. We also felt that while it is not impossible to emphasize human aspects in a large organization, it is much easier in a smaller setting."

Evan had an important role in planning the Atlanta-area facilities and, indeed, was involved with virtually all Nordson building projects up to the late 1970s. Clark had vivid memories of the trip he and Evan made to Norcross, Georgia, to determine exactly the best placement of the new office and engineering building on its site in Technology Park. They took surveying instruments with them and put stakes in the ground to mark the corners. In building projects at Amherst in the 1970s, in which his firm was usually involved, Clark remembered that either Evan, Libicki, or Rosen represented the company at regular meetings with the contractors to oversee every detail.[5]

## LESSONS LEARNED

After a long and successful tenure at Nordson, Daly retired from the presidency of Nordson when he turned sixty-five in June 1980. Eric wrote a tribute to him for the 1980 annual report, praising him for all he had brought to the company and for being instrumental in increasing sales from $3 million in 1960 to $149 million in 1980. He praised Daly's intelligence, business knowledge, honesty, objectivity, ability to work with and inspire others, and "wealth of good common sense supplemented by a high level of energy." Daly remained a director until 1989.

Jim Taylor, who had worked closely with Daly and with Eric for some years, was selected for the presidency. In their first annual report, Taylor and Eric noted that a nationwide economic slowdown, continued inflation, and the great expense of making so many changes had limited the growth of profits that year. More warning signs appeared the next year, when "the 1981 demand for industrial coating robots was much weaker than market predictions." By 1982 Taylor was instituting some measures designed to cut costs and improve productivity.

*Left:* Valerie Jenkins Gerstenberger, here recalling memories of her girlhood friend, Mary Elizabeth Nord, during the dedication of The Nord Family Foundation headquarters on June 19, 2003, also spoke at the twenty-fifth anniversary celebration of Nordson Corporation. (Reproduced courtesy of The Nord Family Foundation)

*Below:* Kenneth Daly (left) and Eric Nord, enjoying Nordson Corporation's twenty-fifth anniversary festivities in September 1979. (Reproduced courtesy of Eric and Jane Nord)

James Taylor, president (1980–1985) and chief executive officer (1982–1985) of Nordson Corporation. (Reproduced courtesy of Nordson Corporation)

At the end of October that year, Taylor became chief executive officer. Eric, then sixty-five, remained as chairman and as an employee who engaged in the company's long-term planning. Eric had made the announcement on August 26, 1982 in a speech to the Nordson Management and Professional Club, detailing his reasons for stepping down and putting into words for future managers his vision of the company (see Appendix 2). It was time, he said, to exit from management—to allow others to move up, to remove a possible brake on the company's ability to take risks, and simply because he had served for forty-two years!

Eric reaffirmed the values learned from his parents: not to put wealth first but, rather, "to make the business highly productive" and "to see to it that the fruits of that productivity were shared." "We are," he said, "to an increasing extent, leaving the future success and internal harmony of Nordson to you—our extended family." After describing some of the risks taken and difficulties surmounted over the years, he expressed his hope that "we continue to be a venturesome company operating somewhere out on the leading edge."

This was an era of increasing merger mania in American business. Having been asked often whether Nordson might be vulnerable to takeover by another company, Eric reassured his listeners that it would not happen, because the stock held by the family, the foundation, company directors, and large investors among employees and retirees amounted to about 70 percent of the total. In a final word, he emphasized paying attention to the dimension of "heart," quoting Pascal: "The heart has reasons that reason may never know." David Ignat recalled hearing Libicki comment that when Eric finished his speech, no eyes in the room were dry. A little more than a year later Eric officially retired as a company employee, although he retained the chairmanship.

The next three years were basically a time of caution, despite continued forward movement in some areas. In 1983 the company dedicated the first building in what Taylor envisioned as a new headquarters complex in Westlake, half an hour closer to Cleveland and all its business advantages. The new three-story building, designed by Clark and Post, was devoted entirely to research, engineering, information systems, and financial functions. The attractive, 27-acre site was chosen carefully, and offices were situated so that, according to a tour brochure, they afforded employees "a maximum opportunity to enjoy the scenic wooded area surrounding the building." The company also opened new international branches in Taiwan, Spain, and the Virgin Islands.

But stress in the economy continued, international sales were hurting because the value of the dollar rose, and both of the product-diversification experiments were proving to be costly failures. As Eric later explained to Griffith, making packaging machinery put Nordson into competition with some of the best customers of its adhesive-applying machinery. And

as for robots, it turned out that few, if any, of the increasing number of U.S. robot manufacturers could compete with those in Japan, which dominated the market.

In its 1983 annual report Nordson announced the sale of one packaging division and the expected sale of the other (which was, indeed, completed within two years). The following year the company announced that a decision had been made to withdraw from the robotics business and to limit any further diversification to areas more closely related to Nordson's core business. The company was using some of the proceeds of sales of the assets to repurchase shares of Nordson stock.

At the time, Eric was disappointed at giving up his dreams for the robotics business, but later he realized that the electronic capabilities Nordson acquired in designing robots had proved to be extremely important to the company's later development. Loss of the robot business had another positive outcome: The corporation donated six robots to Lorain County Community College to help train students in robotics.

Nineteen eighty-five signaled a radical change in the company's management. Taylor resigned in midyear, and, for six months, Eric returned as president and chief executive officer. Despite his appreciation for Taylor's competence, important differences had arisen between them about how to move the company forward. Once again rumors flew that Nordson was for sale, but the company squelched them quickly. "Nordson has absolutely no plans to merge," a spokesman told the *Elyria Chronicle-Telegram*. And in remarks to the Nordson board on June 3, 1985 Eric affirmed that, far from wanting to sell the business, the family would retain its ownership of controlling shares. "Evan and I," he said, "are more interested in continuing our ownership in Nordson than we are in making a lot of

Nordson's Westlake, Ohio building, photographed around the time of its dedication in 1983. The transition of the corporate headquarters to Westlake was completed in 1986. (Reproduced courtesy of Nordson Corporation)

*Looking back on it from the vantage point of 13 or 14 years, Evans Kostas [vice president, technology] was absolutely right when he said the money you put into the robots, although it's down the drain when you pull the plug on the robot program, is some of the best money you've ever spent. It did move us into an altogether different business and now our electronics department — I'd put them against anybody. But it started back then.*

—Eric Nord, interviews with Barbara Griffith, February 3 and March 20, 1995

money. We feel that Nordson has done many of the things we want to see done. We want to see it continue in its philosophy."[6]

## A SHOT IN THE ARM

Eric had no intention of remaining in his leadership role. Through business connections one of Eric's board members had learned of a dynamic, forty-six-year-old Standard Oil of Ohio vice president with a brilliant reputation named William P. "Bill" Madar. A graduate of Purdue University with a master's degree in business administration from Stanford University and more than twenty years of management experience in the petroleum and chemical industries, Madar also had a strong record in community service. The Nordson board was looking for new members who could contribute useful experience. And so, in 1985, Madar was asked to join the board. He soon impressed Eric and the other board members so favorably that he was named president and chief executive officer in January 1986. Eric noted, "When you look for a CEO you first look inside."

Madar proved to be a most creative chief executive. He was known for his questioning, "professorial" style of discourse and for his "lily pad" theory of imagining and developing new products and applications based on Nordson's existing competencies. Lily pads are in a "pond" of potential markets for Nordson products. Nordson's growth strategy was to stay in the pond of potential markets but to go from one lily pad to another, responding to additional opportunities on adjacent lily pads. This was conceived of as a strategy that exploited Nordson's strengths in application know-how and international sales and service, rather than having Nordson grow by jumping out of the pond with which it was familiar and into adjacent ponds where market challenges and products were entirely different.

As Doughman noted, Madar was "a very exciting person to be with." And as Libicki recalled, "He sees things . . . the same as an artist looks at a picture." His vision soon inspired the entire company.

Madar's approach to Nordson's employees reaffirmed Eric's and Daly's and could be summed up in one word, "empowerment"—letting people come up as much as possible with their own ideas and solutions and finding ways to release their creativity. He also belonged to a new generation of manag-

*Our relationship with our employees is one that is based on trust, and the word people now use is "empowerment," but we've been doing this for a long time. Our manager acts as a coach and . . . [removes] the barriers that might inhibit any employee from applying their full creativity, energy and brainpower to solve the customer's problem.*

—William Madar, quoted in Nordson Corporation, *They Mean Business,* 1994

Nordson KK (Japan) headquarters occupies part of this building in Tokyo, pictured ca. 1993. (Reproduced courtesy of Nordson Corporation)

ers who were taking a close look at management structure and sometimes finding that it contained too many layers. Not long after joining the company Madar asked Libicki, who was soon to retire, and selected members of the management team to join him in a study of the organization.

Madar decided on two basic organizational strategies: to do some streamlining of management, and to further reorganize the operating divisions based on geography. Four sales and service divisions were created in November 1986: North America, Europe, Japan, and Pacific South (Asia, Australia, and Latin America), along with a core Application Equipment Division to handle most of the manufacturing. Each geographical division had the responsibility of developing new markets, and, in some cases, new products. The corporate offices moved to the building in the woods at Westlake. Although a second office building that Taylor planned for administrative staff had not been built, arrangements were made to move the offices into the second floor of the existing building. According to Clark, the arrangement worked nicely, with ample space and with state-of-the-art infrastructure for computers.

From 1986 to 1988 Madar's changes and innovations were solidly implemented, and the company regained its momentum. New sales branches opened in Singapore, Korea, Norway, Finland, and Brazil. The 1987 annual report revealed the company's advance into the "nonwoven" market, applying powders, fibers, and sizing as well as adhesives to various textile and paper products, such as bedding and disposable diapers. Nordson machines could now also apply tomato sauce to pizza, lubricants to dies, and static-preventing coatings to automotive lenses and instrument panels. In 1988 came even more exciting news. The Japanese subsidiary had developed machinery to apply adhesives and coatings to miniaturized electronic equipment, and a worldwide development effort had produced a machine, called Select Coat™, which applied a protective coating to circuit boards.

With increasing business and decreasing dollar valuation, worldwide sales increased nearly $40 million a year, from $168 million in 1986, to $205 million in 1987, to $245 million in 1988. *Forbes Magazine* listed Nordson as one of the "200 best small companies" in the United States in 1987 and again in 1988. That year the company broke ground for a new 100,000-square-foot Engineered Systems Center in Amherst. It was part and parcel of Madar's heavy commitment to research and development, to plant more lily pads and see them propagate.[7]

A photographic representation of Nordson President William Madar's "lily pad" philosophy of product development. (Reproduced courtesy of Nordson Corporation)

## THE FOUNDATION FINDS A WIDER SCOPE

Working for both the company and Nordson Foundation had become a demanding task for Doughman. In fact, by 1979 Eric, Evan, and Ginn, the foundation's three trustees, had decided that the growing organization really needed, and could afford, full-time staff of its own. That fall, fifty-six-year-old Jeptha "Jep" Carrell, an ex–Marine, former city manager, college consortium president, author, researcher, and teacher, became the foundation's first full-time executive director.

Jeptha Carrell, executive director of Nordson Foundation and its successor, The Nord Family Foundation, 1979–1989, in his office, ca. 1984. (Reproduced courtesy of Jeptha Carrell)

In yet another example of the power of chance in this history, Carrell heard of the opening because Ginn. happened to be riding in an elevator with Carrell's old friend Homer Wadsworth, president of the Cleveland Foundation, with which Ginn was also involved. Ginn casually mentioned the Nordson Foundation opening to Wadsworth, not knowing that Carrell, wanting to leave his job with an educational consortium in southern Ohio, had recently written Wadsworth asking him to be on the lookout for job possibilities. Wadsworth immediately suggested that Carrell be contacted.

When they hired Carrell the trustees may not have known just what an energetic, dynamic person they had found, but soon they did. Not content with the grant-making, bricks-and-mortar, and educational ventures that had been the foundation's primary focus since the 1960s, Carrell wanted to see it initiate a number of larger projects that could have a major impact on the entire Lorain County area. Even before he arrived, he had become interested in the idea of a community foundation.

## THE COMMUNITY FOUNDATION OF GREATER LORAIN COUNTY

*I would put my money on community foundations . . . being most concerned with community problems that are really painful.*

—Jeptha Carrell, interview with Jeanne Harrah, March 19, 1993

Community foundations had grown up in numerous areas around the nation (Cleveland's was the pioneer) and were proving successful in tapping previously untapped sources of philanthropy. Unlike family foundations, which are usually based on one family's assets, community foundations normally include money pooled from hundreds of sources. Evan recalled that Daly had earlier suggested they look into starting a community foundation. Eric and Ginn remembered that for several years they had attended meetings of local businessmen to discuss the possibility.

Fortunately, along with his desire to develop such a foundation, Carrell brought knowledge of the virtues and complexities of community foundations, gained in the course of his earlier work. In a later interview with Jeanne Harrah, he expressed his conviction that because they tended to be controlled by people with close community interests, such foundations could be especially effective in responding to serious problems. On the negative side, he noted the complexity of administering community foundations because they typically comprise a number of separate funds and because, unlike private foundations, they depend on raising money.

Eric credited Evan with providing the turning point in Nordson Foundation's decision to go forward with the idea. And with Carrell on board, it now seemed possible. Much of 1980 was spent putting together a framework for the new organization. Eric recruited potential board members, Ginn drew up the legal documents, and Evan aided the effort by a donation of stock. At its first meeting, on November 1, 1980, the board of the new Greater Lorain County Community Foundation (its initial name) accepted the first installment of a $500,000 challenge grant from Nordson Foundation and its offer of a part-time executive director "to staff the Community Foundation in [its] early stages": Jep Carrell.

Funds were raised with extraordinary speed, and by October 1981 the new foundation had acquired its first million dollars and awarded its first grants. Carrell's position turned into a six-year commitment. Operating out of an office in Elyria starting in 1981, he did double duty as executive director of both foundations. By the end of 1986 the new foundation, whose name had been changed the year before to the Community Foundation of Greater Lorain County, was well launched with assets of $6 million. Among the funds the foundation came to include was the Walter and Virginia Nord Scholarship Fund.

Carrell kept the two organizations separate, but they cooperated on occasion, as in 1982 when a local recession created a desperate need for emergency assistance. Nordson Foundation, through its initial grant, made it possible for Carrell and the new Community Foundation to start the county's first food bank, known as the County Cupboard. It served more than 5,000 people in its first year. After operating for a while through United Way, by 1986 it had developed into a regional food-bank operation serving three counties. It is now known as the Second Harvest Food Bank.[8]

Attorney William Ginn of Cleveland, shown here at Nordson's Westlake headquarters in the 1980s, has been very important in the affairs of the Nord family and its associated corporations and foundations since 1950. (Reproduced courtesy of Nordson Corporation)

## Handling Two Foundations

Other Carrell initiatives included the Neighborhood Concepts Company, a separate corporation established in 1983, with the backing of Nordson Foundation, to rehabilitate older vacant housing in Lorain and Elyria, and the Oberlin Cable Co-op, organized to provide cable service to Oberlin television viewers. The Neighborhood Concepts Company, which had only limited success, was an instructive lesson for the foundation; from then on it did not try to undertake large projects of this type. The Oberlin Cable Co-op, in contrast, is still thriving and now also offers cable Internet and digital service. Leadership Lorain County began in 1984 as a joint project between the two foundations, "designed to identify, motivate and develop community leaders." Up to thirty "students" met monthly to study various nonprofit and government agencies. At least twenty classes have participated since then in a successful ongoing program.

In handling Nordson Foundation's many other grants, Carrell pursued some distinct strategies. For the benefit of prospective grantees, in 1979 the foundation published its first annual report. Specific guidelines were developed: For example, the foundation avoided most religious organizations, many national campaigns of organizations, organizations with high fund-raising costs, and agencies in the Cleveland area. (This policy was changed in 1983 when the Westlake headquarters opened.) In addition, he aimed to award fewer but larger grants. These and other principles were discussed at trustees' meetings during 1982, and a Policy Advisory Committee, including younger Nord family representatives, was formed the following year.

By 1983 Nordson Foundation and the Community Foundation were receiving about 360 requests for grants annually. Carrell badly needed help. Anne Marie Cronin, an experienced social worker with degrees from Baldwin-Wallace College and Case Western Reserve University, joined Nordson Foundation as an assistant administrator that year. As she later told Harrah, her duties came to include reviewing all of the programs, preparing the annual reports for both foundations, and doing administrative work for Leadership Lorain County and the Neighborhood Concepts Company. Office support was added, as were, starting in 1985, interns from Oberlin College.

The annual reports of Nordson Foundation showed ingenuity in grant making and increasingly gave potential recipients some of the details of grant-winning programs. Because of continuing financial support of the Community Foundation, Nordson Foundation limited its other grants to a total of about $600,000 per year through 1986, but some of these were fairly substantial. Among major beneficiaries were United Way, the Oberlin Early Childhood Center, the Neighborhood House Association in Lorain,

*We've done an annual report since 1979. Very few family foundations do an annual report. So, it has always been that attitude that we are accountable to the public for what we do.*

—Anne Marie Cronin, interview with Jeanne Harrah, November 16, 1992

the Lucy Idol Center for the Handicapped in Vermilion, the South Amherst schools, and the Lorain County Joint Vocational School. In the 1980s the greatest share of grant dollars shifted from education to health and social services, much in keeping with a general national trend.

The Lucy Idol Center for the Handicapped is an example of an institution that benefited from various types of support from Nordson Foundation. Begun by Lucy Idol as a small school for handicapped children in 1954, the program came to include mentally and physically handicapped youth and adults, with strong continuity of management and staff. Among services the foundation provided for the center were grants for physical therapy, guidance in starting an endowment fund, and litigation to secure Medicaid funds for the center as a private agency. Carol Peck, associate director and daughter of the founder, noted that the legal advocacy work by Ginn and his colleagues at Thompson, Hine and Flory enabled not just the Lucy Idol Center, but other private nonprofit agencies in Ohio as well, to qualify for these government funds.

The launching of the Community Foundation of Greater Lorain County and the increasing public recognition of Nordson Foundation helped stimulate a greater interest in philanthropy in the county. Carrell took the initiative in forming a local round table of philanthropic organizations, bringing their staffs together for meetings and encouraging joint projects.[9]

Anne Marie Cronin, assistant director of Nordson Foundation and The Nord Family Foundation in 1983–1995, at her desk, ca. 1993. From May to December 1994 she served as acting executive director of The Nord Family Foundation. (Reproduced courtesy of The Nord Family Foundation)

## EXPANDED GIVING, FUTURE PLANNING

In early 1987 the Community Foundation of Greater Lorain County became independent in its staffing and operations with the help of a large, multiyear donation from Nordson Foundation. Freed from Community Foundation work, which had come to occupy nearly 70 percent of their efforts, Carrell and Cronin now had much more time, and more money, available for grants: a total of $1,270,109 in 1987. With its growing resources, by 1988 Nordson Foundation had become one of Ohio's ten largest private foundations.

The staff and trustees saw an opportunity for new initiatives. Three major ones emerged right away. Out of concern for the quality of local government and nonprofit organizations grew the Public Services Institute of Lorain County Community College. Fortunately, while developing this idea Carrell happened to meet Roy Church, the new president of the college, and quickly interested him in the idea. Moreover, Carrell's contacts with executive directors of neighboring foundations helped lead

*[On obtaining approval from Lorain County Community College for the Public Services Institute:] I really thought going into that meeting that I wouldn't get them to agree to it. But I really pushed and because I was so anxious to do it . . . Eric said immediately, "OK, let's do it." . . . He was willing to [take a] risk because what you do with a CEO is support him.*

—Jeptha Carrell, interview with Jeanne Harrah, March 19, 1993

Linden School, a nationally accredited day-care facility for disadvantaged children in Elyria, is among the many programs supported by The Nord Family Foundation. This image appeared on the front cover of the foundation's 1993 annual report. (Reproduced courtesy of The Nord Family Foundation)

to cosponsorship from the much larger George Gund Foundation, based in Cleveland, and the Stocker Foundation, based in Lorain. With Nordson Foundation pledging $335,000 over four years toward a $523,000 start-up budget, the Public Services Institute opened in the fall of 1988. Its first projects involved market research and strategic planning and training for several local educational and governmental agencies.

The second and third initiatives, the Child Care Resource Center of Lorain County and Linden School, were closely related. They grew out of a study by the Michigan-based High/Scope Educational Research Foundation on the value of early childhood educational experiences, especially for disadvantaged children. Nordson Foundation had already committed itself to the cause of young children, so these initiatives were a natural extension of its mission. It gave several hundred thousand dollars to fund them.

Cronin did the lion's share of the work in developing these two initiatives. The Child Care Resource Center, located in Lorain and run

with the cooperation of six community agencies, provided basic information on child care and on how to choose a child-care provider, offered
assistance to people involved in day care, ran a toy-loan program, and
started a teen parent cooperative called "Teen Moms Together." Linden
School, located in Elyria, filled a gap in quality day care for disadvantaged children. The Child Care Resource Center opened in February
1988; Linden School, which became Lorain County's first nationally accredited child-care center, in March 1989.

In addition, Carrell recalled, Nordson Foundation played an important part in strengthening the board, staff, and programs of the Oberlin
Early Childhood Center. Concerned for the other end of life, at about
the same time the foundation helped a group of Oberlin residents plan a
continuing-care retirement community. In this instance Eric played a crucial role by arranging to guarantee a $6 million loan that enabled the
nonprofit Kendal at Oberlin to open in 1993. Three years later it was featured in *New Choices* magazine as one of the twenty leading retirement
communities in the United States.

Along with sponsoring its new initiatives and making other grants,
the trustees of Nordson Foundation continued to look toward its future.
Evan and Eric were in their mid-sixties, and between their families and
the Ignat family, several adult children were now scattered in various
parts of the United States. The two brothers hoped to interest the younger
generation in taking part in the work of the foundation before too long.
In 1983–1984 three of the younger family members—the oldest in each
of the three families—had participated in the Policy Advisory Committee, which, after seven study sessions, completed a report suggesting future granting policies. And in August 1986 family members gathered in
Oberlin "to hear about Foundation policies and practices and to discuss
its future." To David, the oldest of the new generation, the planning meetings offered "quite an education." Many issues, new to him, needed to
be considered in determining the wisest use of philanthropic dollars.
Very soon, the younger generation did indeed become involved.[10]

*The Nordson Foundation
is especially interested in
programs assisting disad-
vantaged persons, minorities
and the mentally or
physically disabled, and in
projects which attack root
causes of problems.*

—Mission statement,
*Nordson Foundation
Annual Report*, 1987

# 8

# INTO THE NEW MILLENNIUM, 1989–2004

**W**hen they held their planning sessions in the early and mid-1980s and chose to involve younger members of the family, Evan and Eric Nord, Bill Ginn, and Jep Carrell were preparing to take a series of bold and creative steps to transform Nordson Foundation, a trust conceived in 1952 by Walter Nord, into an organization dramatically responsive to the needs of another generation. The chrysalis was about to evolve as two butterflies.

In thinking about the future of their stewardship, the trustees kept coming back to one theme: how best to pass on the foundation's mission and direction. In the words of a later report, "If the Foundation were to continue on the mission begun by Walter and Virginia Nord, it was felt the Foundation needed to begin nurturing a new generation of Trustees. Moreover, since the Corporation had evolved into new leadership, the time had come for it to establish its own direct grantmaking programs."

And so, after a great deal of preparatory work by Ginn, two separate organizations were created: The Nord Family Foundation, to be responsible for the stewardship of assets linked directly to the Nord family; and The Nordson Corporation Foundation, to administer the commitment of the corporation to see that at least 5 percent of its domestic pretax profits went for community purposes. On November 30, 1988, at a festive breakfast at the Nordson Depot in Amherst, Eric and Evan announced the change to a group of more than fifty civic leaders and heads of charitable organizations.

The Nord Family Foundation, launched with about $51 million in assets from the predecessor foundation, had as its membership all adult lineal descendants of Walter and Virginia, along with their spouses. Adopted children were included. The members were empowered to elect a twelve-person Board of Trustees—nine family members and three "community trustees," people from outside the family—for three-year terms. The now-separate Nordson Corporation Foundation (at first called simply by its former name, Nordson Foundation) was to be run by a four-member Board of Trustees elected annually by the corporation's Board of Directors. Its primary source of funds was the pretax profits of Nordson Corporation; the focus of the grants was to include not only northeast Ohio but also other locations where Nordson had extensive operations.[1]

# THE NORD FAMILY FOUNDATION

When the new foundation's incorporation papers were filed with the Ohio Secretary of State on August 31, 1988, Evan, Eric, and Ginn served as its first trustees and officers. The official changeover came at the end of the Nordson fiscal year, October 31, 1988, and the first membership meeting of The Nord Family Foundation was planned for April 1989.

## THE EARLY YEARS

The newly organized Nord Family Foundation soon had its first project, reflecting Evan's passion for local history. On November 30, 1988 the *Amherst News-Times* announced that the foundation's trustees would purchase a sandstone former one-room schoolhouse on Milan Avenue, on the west side of Amherst. The Hickory Tree Grange, which owned the building, had been struggling financially, and transfer to the foundation of the hall's ownership and maintenance would bring the grange secu-

rity. Moreover, it would provide the centerpiece for a larger project. It was, Evan said, "the first step in creating a small, informal historic district." The foundation acquired a sandstone house and vacant land across Milan Avenue from the grange hall. That building, the Quigley House, became the museum of the Amherst Historical Society.

In another part of the plan, the Amherst Hospital, looking for space for parking, had recently donated to the Amherst Historical Society a small sandstone building it owned on Spring Street, with the condition that it be moved. Originally a one-room schoolhouse, the structure had served as St. George's, the next-door Episcopal mission church of Eric and Evan's boyhood. A group of volunteers had carefully dismantled it, stone by stone, and Evan planned to have it reassembled on the purchased land. If not for Evan's efforts, this might not have happened. Ginn remembered when Evan first spotted the old church on a drive by the Amherst Hospital "and saw them about to demolish the original building. He succeeded in stopping the demolition."

The Amherst Historical Society was thus given its first quarters in the Hickory Tree Grange building and Quigley Museum. Evan had kept his promise to his father that the society would have a home.

On April 8–9, 1989, members of The Nord Family Foundation from far and wide assembled at the Oberlin Inn for the foundation's first membership meeting and retreat. With guidance from Carrell, Eric, Evan, Ginn, and others, the group, in the words of the first annual report, "met for two days to discuss organizational issues and begin its education in

The Quigley House, built in 1832 here at the corner of Milan Avenue and Lake Street by Joseph Quigley, an early quarry owner, is one of the oldest sandstone structures in the Amherst area. It was purchased in 1988 by The Nord Family Foundation and became the main museum of the Amherst Historical Society. Ownership of the house was transferred by the foundation to the society in 1999. Since the time of this early photograph the porch has been enlarged and the grounds have been landscaped. (Reproduced courtesy of The Nord Family Foundation)

*I think it's really important that other people of means acquire a similar ethic, because the needs have grown so much and the opportunities for them to make a difference are there.*

—Henry Doll, quoted in Glenn Gamboa, "Nord Family Legacy Makes a Difference," *Lorain Morning Journal,* December 20, 1992

St. George's Chapel (left) and the Hickory Tree Grange are among the historic buildings in the Amherst Historical Society's Sandstone Museum Center. (Photograph by Sarah MacLennan Kerr, March 2004)

grantmaking." Paul N. Ylvisaker, formerly with the Ford Foundation and a noted authority on family foundations, spoke to the group on "The Role of Foundation Trustees." According to Ylvisaker's own brief notes, he outlined their responsibilities to their family's traditions, to the public, and to the historic functions of philanthropy. He advised them on legal concepts pertaining to foundations. Peter Davis, an expert on family-owned companies, then at the Wharton School of the University of Pennsylvania, also worked with the group to explore generational issues. An important concept reflected upon at the retreat and taken to heart by the attendees was that family foundation funds truly belong not to the donor but, because tax benefits are involved, to the public domain.

That meeting resulted in the election of the first fully constituted Board of Trustees of The Nord Family Foundation and produced, according to the 1989 annual report, a "restatement of the Foundation's mission and granting guidelines." The foundation adopted this goal: "to impact the effectiveness with which social, cultural, educational, health and civic organizations deal with human needs and aspirations." The first officers were Evan Nord (president), Eric Nord (vice president and treasurer), and Bill Ginn (secretary). The other initial family trustees were Jane Nord, Cindy Nord, David Ignat, Joseph N. Ignat, Virginia Nord Barbato, Bruce Nord, and Ethan Nord. The community trustees, in addition to Ginn, were longtime Nordson employees Marilyn Jenne and Henry Libicki, then retired.

One of the earliest actions of the new foundation board was the decision to divest itself of the Burrell-King House in Oberlin. In 1989

THE NORD FAMILY FOUNDATION

The Nord Family Foundation officially turned the house over to the Oberlin Historical and Improvement Organization (O.H.I.O.) and provided for its maintenance through a $100,000 endowment fund at the Community Foundation of Greater Lorain County.

In June 1989 Carrell, then sixty-six years old, announced his decision to retire after a most successful ten-year career with the Nords. In a news release from The Nord Family Foundation, Eric paid tribute to Carrell's "enormous contribution to the Foundation community and particularly to the citizens of Lorain County." That September, in a smooth transition, Henry C. "Hank" Doll, a fifty-two-year-old executive formerly with Cleveland's George Gund Foundation, became the new executive director.

Immediately after Carrell's retirement Evan recruited him to serve as his own successor on the O.H.I.O. Board of Trustees, beginning in 1990. Carrell played major roles in encouraging the organization to hire a professional director, build its endowment, and establish a strategic planning process, all with the active support of Evan. Today Carrell is an honorary O.H.I.O. trustee.[2]

Henry Doll, executive director of The Nord Family Foundation, 1989–1992, shown ca. 1989. (Reproduced courtesy of The Nord Family Foundation)

## THE DOLL YEARS

The Nords had found another highly resourceful person in Doll. A graduate of Princeton University and Yale Divinity School and an ordained Presbyterian minister, he was analytically inclined, had a broad vision of the possibilities of philanthropy, and was skilled at bringing people together to define their goals. He also had a history of personal philanthropy that was congenial to the Nord family. "Our task as Board and staff," he wrote in his first annual report, "in addition to becoming better acquainted, is to forge a consensus about direction and grantmaking priorities." During 1990 Doll focused the energies of the foundation on reaching that consensus and on planning for the future.

This was a period of challenge for all foundations. Many people were experiencing increasing hardships, yet government support of helping agencies was decreasing. As Assistant Director Anne Marie Cronin told Jeanne Harrah in 1992, "The climate has changed for non-profits. . . . [It] has forced all foundations, but especially in Lorain County where there are only three general grantmaking foundations, to take a broader role." Cronin mentioned specifically "the reduction in government support for basic programs and reentry into the workforce for women with young children, and increased demand for day care" and noted that "Lorain County has never come back full strength from the early '80s."

After surveying the foundation's members to determine their concerns, Doll and his staff organized a productive three-day retreat for the foundation in Charleston, South Carolina, in April 1990. The members

*The trick of the foundation— a family foundation—is to continually try to reach those points of consensus where everybody can feel good about what you do.*

—Henry Doll, interview with Jeanne Harrah, August 21, 1992

Cindy Nord doing play therapy with children at the Nurturing Center in Columbia, South Carolina, ca. 1980s. The Nurturing Center was one of the first agencies outside northeast Ohio to be supported by The Nord Family Foundation. (Reproduced courtesy of Evan and Cindy Nord)

*I think a lot of it [strengthening families] has to do with education . . . formal or informal education, or whatever, to try and promote the family as a unit to strengthen the values that the kids grow up with, with good examples from their parents, and proper discipline and respect for others.*

—Evan Nord, interview with Jeanne Harrah, August 25, 1992

decided to continue as a general purpose foundation in Lorain County and to make northeast Ohio their primary granting area but to begin to make some grants in other areas where foundation members lived. For the latter, they concentrated on two primary goals: "strengthening the family and strengthening the public service." In a further step, trustees met with experts in various fields to begin to develop program priorities. Reflecting information presented by Cronin, programs were developed to meet the needs of diverse families, such as those headed by single mothers. Cronin, as program officer and assistant director, worked with grants that addressed these issues. To strengthen their focus on public service, housing, and economic development, the foundation hired a second program officer, Jeffrey M. Glebocki.

One of the earliest awards made to a program outside Ohio, carrying out the mandate to strengthen the family, was a $31,500 grant to the Nurturing Center, a facility for the treatment and prevention of child abuse being established in Columbia, South Carolina, by Cindy Nord. After extensively researching other programs, Cindy designed a three-day-a-week dual curriculum for children and their parents. Play therapy, led by Cindy herself, became one of the therapeutic services offered to the children, who were referred to the center by various local agencies.

Extending his planning goal to all of Lorain County, under the mandate to strengthen the public service, Doll developed a multiyear community initiative known as "Lorain County 2020." He described it in the

1990 annual report thus: "County and municipal officials, representatives of business and agriculture, social service providers, and religious leaders embarked upon a process to establish a common agenda designed to address factors which inhibit social and economic progress within the County." A second initiative Doll designed was assisting selected family-service agencies with their planning and administration over a three-year period, identifying areas that needed improvement and then aiding them in making those improvements.

Innovation continued during the early 1990s, in terms of both leadership and programs. After serving as vice president of The Nord Family Foundation for a year, in June 1991 the fifty-year-old physicist David Ignat became the first of Walter and Virginia's grandchildren to be elected president. Doll described the progress of Lorain County 2020 in the 1991 annual report: One hundred community leaders, aided by expert planner Peter Szanton of Baltimore, had developed a list of priorities for county action, focusing on goals of "improving the County's leadership, education, and physical appearance." The foundation applied its theme of strengthening the family to all of its grant areas. Under education, it began a new scholarship program, Lorain County Access to Higher Education, as well as a new program of grants to schools to support "special projects to enhance the partnership between school and home."

The 1992 annual report stressed the theme of working together with all of the foundation's nonprofit partners. A major example was aid given to the Community Foundation of Greater Lorain County for its new initiative, the Center for Leadership in Education, in Elyria, designed "to revitalize elementary and secondary education in the county." The foundation's own new initiatives included a Grassroots Leadership Program, supporting neighborhood leadership and projects, and a Family Investment Fund to make small loans to single parents.

In September 1992, after three years at the helm of the foundation, Doll announced that he would resign the following January to return to the ministry. In an article in the *Lorain Morning Journal* Eric noted, "Hank has been a wonderfully imaginative and effective executive director." Cronin told Harrah later that year, "He has been our transitional leader and we could not have done it without him." Doll, in turn, praised the foundation's trustees and the way they worked together for the common good despite inevitable differences of opinion.

The second retreat, held in 1993, reconsidered the goals of 1990 and discussed goals for the future. Good preparation for this, as well as a fitting celebration of the fortieth anniversary of the establishment of Nordson Foundation, took place in 1992, when, following up on a suggestion by Evan, Jeanne Harrah, an expert in folklore and oral history, was hired through the Western Reserve Historical Society. Starting in

*The government has the ability to tax, and the foundation exists because our government has seen it fit to allow people to make donations to a foundation in lieu of taxation (well, to a certain level), and the contract, really, is, the government says, "We will let you start a foundation and we will allow people to put some of the money that would otherwise go in taxation into the foundation," and thereby they allow an accumulation of wealth in a foundation, and that's a public trust. In no way is [it] money that the foundation can use at their own discretion for whatever they want to use it for . . . and a lot of people new to the foundation world are very confused about that. . . . They say, well, it is our money funding it. Well, no, it isn't their money; it's really government money, but you have the privilege and responsibility of seeing that that money is used for the purposes for which your foundation was set up. And the minute you stray from that, the government has the right and the obligation to cancel the foundation's charter.*

—Eric Nord, in The Nord Family Foundation, *Nord Family Foundation Member Retreat, June 25–27, 1999*

July of that year, she interviewed eleven people who had played an important part in the foundation's history since 1952.[3]

## NEW GENERATIONS, REINVIGORATED MISSION STATEMENT

The years since 1993 have been a continual learning experience for the foundation. Four third-generation family members, David and Joe Ignat, and Eric and Jane's children Gini Barbato and Richard Nord, have served as president, always backed up by Evan and Eric. The first fourth-generation trustee, Elizabeth Ignat Bausch, a daughter of David and Eleanor Ignat, was elected to the board in 1995; the second, Elizabeth's sister Emily Ignat Porter, in 2001; and the third, Erin Ignat, Joe and Pamela Ignat's daughter, in 2003. With three trustees' meetings and one membership meeting each year, and with membership retreats every three years, the generations have learned to work together. Divergent viewpoints have been aired, issues discussed, and differences resolved with growing openness.

Many of its members, who numbered more than forty by 2003, see their roles in The Nord Family Foundation as an important part of their lives, expanding their knowledge, stimulating them with worthwhile challenges, and helping to keep the extended family in close contact. Trustees and staff have continued to work productively together since Doll's departure, even through several changes in leadership. Sandra L. Pyer served as executive director from April 1993 to May 1994. Anne Marie Cronin then served as acting executive director from May to December 1994. David R. Ashenhurst became the executive director in January 1995 and served until February 1997, followed by Rickie Weiss, who was interim director from May 1997 until April 1998, when John J. Mullaney assumed the executive directorship. Mullaney, a native of New York City and a graduate of Boston College and Georgetown University, has extensive experience in working with impoverished areas of the world. He remains at the helm of the foundation.

The foundation has extended, broadened, and, in some cases, re-evaluated its major commitments. Support for innovative programs of organizations in Ohio, South Carolina, Colorado, and Massachusetts has continued. Despite growing affluence in the economy up until 2001, public funding has declined in most of the foundation's granting categories, making its support more vital than ever. Each year Mullaney and two program officers, Joy Anderson and Karen Cook, investigate an increasing number of grant requests to determine whether they meet the foundation's criteria. The foundation awarded more than 150 grants in 2003 in the areas of education, health and social services, civic affairs, and the arts and culture. The number of grants made outside Ohio is now almost 25 percent, but the emphasis on northeast Ohio remains strong.

*I would say that the [Nord Family] Foundation is an instrument for bringing the family together.*

—Henry Doll, interview with Jeanne Harrah, August 21, 1992

*I have a lot of faith in these young people [the younger generations of Nords]. I know every one of them personally.... I have a lot of confidence in the fact that this is going to be one of the real success stories in terms of later generational foundation developments. If it doesn't happen that way, Eric, Evan and I have failed in our mission.*

—William Ginn, interview with Jeanne Harrah, September 16, 1992

In 1993 the trustees again restated the foundation's mission statement: "The Nord Family Foundation, in the tradition of its founders Walter and Virginia Nord, strives to build community through support of projects that bring opportunity to the disadvantaged, strengthen the bond of families and improve the quality of people's lives." That mission, that statement, remains. The need for direct aid in health, welfare, and equal-opportunity education has never been greater. As president Gini Barbato wrote in the 1996 annual report, "The Foundation's task becomes more difficult with each year. The number of community residents who confront poverty, minimal family support, and limited opportunity for meaningful employment continues to grow." And as Mullaney wrote in 1998, "The real impact of welfare reform upon the lives of people, particularly those with dependent children, has yet to unfold." He wrote, too, of the impact of violence in the home and of measures designed to counteract it.

## PROJECTS AND GRANTS SINCE 1993

Just a few of the hundreds of agencies The Nord Family Foundation has supported since 1993 are: City Year, Inc., a youth service program in Boston and Columbia; El Centro de Servicios Sociales, a multifaceted Hispanic agency in Lorain; Sistercare, Inc., a Columbia-based agency that aids victims of domestic violence; Echoing Hills Village, a group home for disabled adults in Warsaw, Ohio; the Florence Crittendon School in Denver, for teen-aged parents; the Women's Development Center of Elyria, with programs of self-sufficiency for women; Cleveland Public Radio; educational television; the Great Lakes Science Center in Cleveland; and distance learning through the Lorain County Community College Foundation. Support has continued for the Center for Leadership in Edu-

The headquarters of the Center for Leadership in Education, designed by Clark and Post and opened in June 1998, is in Elyria, Ohio, adjacent to the campus of Lorain County Community College. The center is an independent, community-supported organization that promotes and evaluates successful approaches to educating children and provides educators with effective tools that help students achieve. The Nord Family Foundation has supported the center since its establishment in 1992. (Reproduced courtesy of the Center for Leadership in Education)

The Nord Center, in Lorain, is one of the largest mental health providers in northeast Ohio. This photograph was taken after the completion of a major addition in 1993. (Reproduced courtesy of The Nord Center)

*At The Nord Family Foundation, grants represent an investment in our society's future. Each grant carries with it the hope that the program it supports will reach beyond the initial constituency to enlighten and influence many others. We believe a grant placed in the hands of a few forward-thinking citizens can advance an entire community.*

—Virginia Nord Barbato, *The Nord Family Foundation Annual Report, 1996*

cation, the Lorain County Access to Higher Education program, the Child Care Resource Center, Linden School, and Vocational Guidance Services.

The Oberlin Early Childhood Center is another of the many organizations that have benefited from the foundation's support. In recent years, particularly under the leadership of the current executive director, Nancy Sabath, the center has received much recognition for its excellent programs and its outstanding teachers. It attained accreditation from the National Association for the Education of Young Children in 1996. In 2000 it received the Irene Bandy-Hedden Award from the Ohio Department of Education Office of Early Childhood, and its nature trail led to recognition by the Ohio Department of Wildlife as a "Wild School Site," the first early childhood program in Ohio to receive this designation.

The Nord Center, in Lorain, realizes the dreams of Walter, Evan, Eric, and others for an effective mental health facility to serve Lorain County. One of the largest mental health providers in northeast Ohio, the center now serves about 5,000 clients annually, through 250 employees and with a $13 million budget.

Common Ground: The Cindy Nord Center for Renewal, a 20-acre retreat and conference center 6 miles west of Oberlin, reflects the special vision of its founder and president, Rose Bator of the Sisters of Humility of Mary. It was established in 1994 on the beautiful, wooded site of the former Oberlin Country Day Camp. Thanks to the support of Cindy Nord and the Community Foundation of Greater Lorain County, Common Gound purchased the property in 1997. The center is a place of natural beauty where people who work together can come to revitalize their spirits and renew their sense of purpose. To quote from its bro-chure: "Common Ground values the lessons of Earth as a basis for orga-nizational work, sustainability, global mindfulness, thoughtful leadership and commitment to the community."

Support of the arts and culture has grown, too. A major highlight was the development of the New Union Center for the Arts. The distinctive Victorian Gothic–style, three-story brick-and-sandstone building on South Main Street in downtown Oberlin was designed by the Cleveland archi-tect Walter Blythe and constructed in 1874 as the town's Union School. It ceased serving as a schoolhouse in the early 1920s, when the new high school on North Main Street—now Langston Middle School—opened. In 1927 the building was purchased by a local businessman, Edmund Westervelt, who transferred ownership to Oberlin College. Renamed Westervelt Hall, the structure was used as a "temporary" college class-room building until 1961. At various points the building was threatened with demolition, to make way for either a parking lot or a gas station. At other points it was considered for use as a city hall with jail cells in the basement, as the public library, or as apartments.

Jane Nord provided the crucial leadership in the adaptation of Wes-tervelt Hall as a center for the visual and performing arts. The Nord Family Foundation purchased the historic building in 1995. The renova-tion, planned by Clark and Post, included all new mechanical systems, installation of an elevator, updated safety features, and a landscape plan by Eric and Jane's son Richard, a landscape architect. Dedicated on June 21, 1996, the center became home to seven arts organizations.

When the renovation was complete, O.H.I.O. took on, as a commu-nity project, the reconstruction of the lofty original bell tower, which had

*I would like to have the foundation remain very approachable. My impres-sion is that some founda-tions get to the point where they think they are sort of the reason for the existence of the foundation, and they become unapproachable, or at least very difficult to approach, and I think that's a hazard that every foundation and every person who has the wherewithal to be of help runs. It's easy to get arrogant, and I think that's a real hazard for wealthy people and for foundations.*

—Eric Nord, in The Nord Family Foundation, *Nord Family Foundation Member Retreat, June 25–27, 1999*

The log lodge at Common Ground: The Cindy Nord Center for Renewal is a quiet and peaceful retreat surrounded by woods, gardens, and other facili-ties. (Photograph by Sarah MacLennan Kerr, March 2004)

The New Union Center for the Arts, in Oberlin, was renovated by The Nord Family Foundation and dedicated in 1996. The original bell tower was replicated as a project of the Oberlin Historical and Improvement Organization and completed in 1997. (Left-hand photograph taken in the late 1970s, when then owner Arthur H. "Kenny" Clark was replacing the windows and cleaning the brickwork; right-hand photograph by Richard Holsworth)

*The joists [of the Union School] are three inches thick and fourteen wide, are being laid twelve inches apart from center to center and look as though the combined intellect of Oberlin could not break them through.*

— *The [Oberlin] News,*
October 23, 1873

been removed in 1940. The new tower replicates the details of the original tower but is constructed of modern materials. Manufactured in Campbellsville, Kentucky, sections of the tower were transported on flatbed trucks to Oberlin, partially assembled on the ground, and then hoisted to the roof of the building. The entire community celebrated the completion of the tower with a series of events, including a Crazy Hat Parade and bell-tower dedication ceremony on May 17, 1997. The bell was cast by McShane Bell Foundry of Glen Burnie, Maryland, established in 1856. The tower has become a beloved landmark that dominates Oberlin's skyline, and its bell rings daily to announce the noon hour to downtown visitors, workers, and shoppers.

In the New Union Center for the Arts are the gallery, office, and gift shop of the Firelands Association for the Visual Arts (FAVA), along with offices, rehearsal space, and studios for several other nonprofit performing and visual arts organizations, most of which are partially funded by the foundation. These currently include Choral Spectrum, The M.A.D.★ Factory, the Northern Ohio Youth Orchestra, Oberlin Choristers, and the Ohio Dance Theatre. The building, like the renovated depots in Oberlin

Not even the chill of a March day could keep Betsy Manderen, executive director of the Firelands Association for the Visual Arts (above, left), Jane Nord (above, middle), Pat Murphy, executive director of the Oberlin Historical and Improvement Organization (above, right), and Eric and Evan Nord (below, left and right, respectively) from joining the throng who waited for the new tower to be hoisted onto Oberlin's New Union Center for the Arts in late March 1997. (Photographs by Richard Holsworth)

*[The Union School] is a fine edifice and will be a credit to the town and a lasting testimonial to the liberality of the citizens and to their devotion to educational interests.*

— *The Lorain Constitution,*
May 20, 1874

and Amherst, O.H.I.O.'s Jewett and Burrell-King Houses, and Christ Church in Oberlin, is listed on the National Register of Historic Places. The New Union Center for the Arts, the Oberlin Depot, and the Jewett and Burrell-King Houses are also City of Oberlin Historic Landmarks.

The Nord Family Foundation has continued to support the Oberlin Heritage Center / O.H.I.O. It provided a two-year grant in 1992–1993 that enabled the organization to hire its first paid professional staff. With the help of The Nord Family Foundation, other area foundations, and the community, O.H.I.O. has undergone a remarkable transformation under the leadership of Board Presidents Marianne Cochrane, Pat Holsworth, Roberta Garcia, and Cathe Radabaugh, working together with the organization's first—and present—executive director, Patricia Murphy, who was hired in 1993. Extensive site improvements and modifications to make the Oberlin Heritage Center more accessible to the community were planned, adopted by the O.H.I.O. board, and implemented through a Historic Landscape Master Plan designed by Richard Nord in the mid-1990s.

Evan provided much behind-the-scenes guidance, encouragement, support, and enthusiasm over the years. He also masterminded the creation of a new exhibit at the Jewett House, "Aluminum: The Oberlin Connection," which opened in September 1997 in conjunction with the designation of Oberlin as a National Chemical Historic Landmark. It includes a re-creation of Charles Martin Hall's woodshed experiment station and a restoration of the Jewett House kitchen, which had been modernized in the 1970s, to a circa 1910 time period that evokes the public health and hygienic kitchen standards advocated by Sarah Frances Gulick Jewett in her textbooks.

Today O.H.I.O. offers historic-site tours and public programs, children's summer camps, and many community activities year-round. More than 18,000 residents and visitors attended its tours and programs in 2003. The organization has received much recognition for its programs and publications, including the Cleveland Restoration Society's Trustees Honor Award for Preservation Organization Excellence (presented on July 24, 2003), several awards from the Ohio Association of Historical Societies and Museums, and Heritage Ohio / Downtown Ohio's "Preservation Hero" award (presented on May 20, 2004). O.H.I.O. succeeded in designating downtown Oberlin as a National Register Historic District in 2003 and in having the City of Oberlin named one of the National Trust for Historic Preservation's Dozen Distinctive Destinations for 2004.

By the mid-1990s the Oberlin Community Center building at 80 South Main Street was inadequate to meet the needs of the three agencies it then housed, and it had serious structural and maintenance problems. The tenants found other quarters nearby, and the much-used structure was demolished in January 1997. FAVA moved to the New Union Center for the Arts;

*Above:* Implementation of Richard Nord's landscape master plan for the Oberlin Heritage Center / O.H.I.O. is ongoing. In the 1990s some 27,000 century-old paving bricks were salvaged from a street in Elyria and individually cleaned by volunteers. Here O.H.I.O. Honorary Trustee Glenn Hobbs (with suspenders) confers with Zach Glime (left), Richard Nord, and Clint DeWorth about their installation in 1998. (Photograph by Richard Holsworth)

*Left:* Among the many celebrants at the July 15, 1995 kickoff for the installation of the landscape master plan at the Oberlin Heritage Center were Jane Nord, her granddaughter Rebecca Nord, and Rebecca's father, Richard, who developed the plan. The center's Little Red Schoolhouse is in the background. (Photograph by Patricia Murphy)

*Above:* This re-creation in the Jewett House woodshed depicts Charles Martin Hall and his sister Julia working on their 1886 aluminum-reduction experiment. Evan Nord and Oberlin College chemistry Professor Norman Craig were instrumental in planning the exhibit, which opened in 1997 in conjunction with the dedication of Oberlin as a National Chemical Historic Landmark by the American Chemical Society. (Photograph by Richard Holsworth)

*Right:* Evan Nord enjoyed traveling around Lorain County with his friend and former Nord Family Foundation Trustee John Clark. Here, ca. 1998, they were visiting the Little Red Schoolhouse at the Oberlin Heritage Center. (Photograph by Patricia Murphy)

Oberlin Seniors of Neighborhood House, Inc., to 90 East College Street. Oberlin Community Services moved first to leased space on South Main Street and then, in 2001, to its own attractive new building on South Professor Street next to the Oberlin Depot. In making the new headquarters a reality, Oberlin Community Services worked closely with Eric, The Nord Family Foundation, and Clark and Post, which designed the spacious frame building to harmonize with the nearby depot. The agency provides a wide range of services, including emergency assistance of many types, a food bank, academic assistance for public school students, and Meals on Wheels.

Under Evan's leadership the Oberlin Depot, which had long served as a home for Head Start, was extensively renovated by The Nord Family Foundation for the second time. It was refurbished according to plans by Clark and Post and opened in February 2004 as a meeting facility that is available free of charge for use by nonprofit community groups, following the model provided by the Nordson Depot in Amherst.

With help from The Nord Family Foundation, the Amherst Historical Society has further developed the Sandstone Museum Center, in accordance with a master plan prepared by Richard Nord. After having been dismantled stone by stone and re-erected on its new site, St. George's Chapel was dedicated on May 17, 1998. Evan and Jack Clark recalled that a large sandstone roundel with a carving of the cross was dropped by one of the quarrymen during the reconstruction but, amazingly enough, did not break. The chapel was equipped with interior furnishings from several churches in Amherst. In addition to the chapel and the Hickory Tree Grange, the complex also now includes the circa-1840s Harris-Dute House. The house, originally located on Oberlin Road, had been scheduled for demolition, but the Amherst Historical Society intervened, and the owner donated it to the society if it could be moved—which it was. The Octagonal Barn, moved from Middle Ridge Road, had also been slated for demolition to make room for a housing development. A new blacksmith's shop was constructed using materials salvaged from other buildings. And in June 2004 the caboose beside the Oberlin Depot, which Evan had donated to the society in December 2003, was moved to the Sandstone Museum Center to commemorate the "Great Amherst Train Wreck" of 1916. Across Milan Avenue from the main complex are the society's Quigley Museum and offices, the latter in a former church building.

## POLICIES FOR A NEW CENTURY

At the foundation's June 1999 retreat in Colorado Springs, an interview with Evan and Eric was videotaped to record in their own words some of the values and goals they wanted to pass along. Evan stressed the importance of supporting the foundation's core missions: mental health, help-

*CHARLES M. HALL AND FRANK F. JEWETT*

*Aluminum pioneer Charles Martin Hall was born in 1863 in Thompson, Ohio (Geauga County), and moved with his family to Oberlin in 1873. Hall graduated from Oberlin College in 1885, studying chemistry under Professor Frank Fanning Jewett (1844–1926). Jewett, who lived in this house from 1884 to 1923, encouraged Hall's interest in chemistry and aluminum, then a semiprecious metal. Hall discovered an electrochemical reduction process for producing metallic aluminum from aluminum oxide dissolved in molten cryolite in his woodshed laboratory at his family's home at 64 East College Street on February 23, 1886. This process, the culmination of research with Jewett, became the basis for the aluminum industry in America. In 1888 Hall cofounded the Pittsburgh Reduction Company, later the Aluminum Company of America (ALCOA) and now Alcoa Inc. Upon his death in 1914, Hall left one-third of his estate to Oberlin College.*

—Ohio Historical Marker at the Jewett House, dedicated on October 14, 2003

The Oberlin Community Center at the former U.S. Automatic frozen food plant on South Main Street in Oberlin, before its demolition in 1997.

ing the disadvantaged, education, and strengthening families. Eric noted the value of a broad mission statement that would allow for changes and expressed hope that the foundation would remain approachable, with a humble attitude toward its status and mission.

In his years as executive director, Mullaney, who serves also as program officer for grants in education and arts and culture, has kept The Nord Family Foundation focused on the effectiveness of its gifts. He writes that the maturing foundation's work "is far more than grantmaking; it requires thought and deliberation on how the assets can have the highest impact in the communities it serves." In addition to reevaluating a few of its commitments, the foundation has ventured beyond meeting immediate needs, to, in Mullaney's words, supporting "programs that bring stakeholders together to ask better questions about how public and private monies can best serve the needs of the community." One example in 2003 was sponsorship of a study by Dr. Harriet Alger on families coping with welfare reform, undertaken with the Oberlin Early Childhood Center; a

The Oberlin Community Services building at 285 South Professor Street, completed in 2001, was designed to blend with the Oberlin Depot, seen here at the far left and more fully on page 118.

Eric Nord (left), Kathleen (Mrs. John R.) Clark, Past President Ruth Haff, and Evan Nord at an August 2003 Amherst Historical Society event. Behind them is the 1840s Harris-Dute House, added to the society's Sandstone Museum Center complex in 2001. (Photograph courtesy of John R. Clark)

second, a conference on public policy change sponsored by Cleveland's Center for Families and Children. The foundation's leadership role within the philanthropic community in financial support and community involvement and in encouraging and motivating others to serve was acknowledged by the Association of Fundraising Professionals / Greater Cleveland Chapter in 2004. The organization selected the foundation to receive its Foundation Leadership Award, which was presented to President Gini Barbato at the National Philanthropy Day awards ceremony in Westlake on November 12, 2004.

"Another challenge before this foundation," according to Mullaney, "is to pass the legacy to future generations of Nord family members . . . to work with the individual families to compliment their own sense of philanthropy." As the foundation looks toward the future, it is preparing for a time when the family is even more geographically dispersed and further removed in years from the founding generation. In its new headquarters in Amherst, which was the vision of Evan, the foundation is designed to

The Octagonal Barn, part of the Amherst Historical Society's Sandstone Museum Center, photographed in 2003. Eight-sided barns, designed to conserve lumber and to withstand strong winds, are rare in the United States. This early-twentieth-century example was moved from its original site on Middle Ridge Road when it was threatened by demolition. (Reproduced courtesy of The Nord Family Foundation)

Constance Haqq, executive
director of The Nordson
Corporation Foundation
since 1991, pictured about
2000. (Reproduced
courtesy of The Nordson
Corporation Foundation)

*You get a sense here that
these people really do care,
that these people are really
involved and want to help.
. . . A lot of corporations
think that giving money is
enough—which is fine—
but that's all they do. The
Nord family has really
gotten involved. They
understand what it takes
to run a foundation and a
nonprofit organization.*

—Constance Haqq,
quoted in
Glenn Gamboa,
"Nord Family Legacy
Makes a Difference,"
*Lorain Morning Journal,*
December 20, 1992

serve as an anchor, a place where all the generations can come to absorb and appreciate the history of the family and its tradition of commitment to the community.[4]

## THE NORDSON CORPORATION FOUNDATION

In October 2002 Nordson Corporation published a booklet entitled *Seasons of Growth and Change,* commemorating the fiftieth anniversary of Walter's establishment of The U.S. Automatic Foundation and summarizing the history and mission of The Nordson Corporation Foundation. Since its beginning in 1988, the latter has been the centerpiece of the company's charitable program, designed to give 5 percent of domestic pretax profits back to its communities.

By 2003 The Nordson Corporation Foundation had awarded more than $20 million in grants. In addition, the corporation itself had given more than $3 million in direct gifts, more than $3 million in employee and matching funds to United Way, and more than $2 million in grants to match employees' charitable donations (up to $6,000 per employee). That totaled nearly $27 million in monetary donations in northeast Ohio and several other Nordson locations in the United States. Added to that were gifts in kind: 50,000 volunteer hours in more than 200 projects of the Nordson Time 'n Talent program.

For the first two years after its organization, Jim Doughman handled the staffing of the new foundation, which was—and still is—guided by a board of the corporation's executives, elected annually by the foundation's members (the corporation's Board of Directors). But soon the need was felt for full-time staff, and in 1991 Constance Haqq was hired as the foundation's first executive director. Haqq, a Cleveland native, earned her bachelor's degree from Tufts University and her master of science degree in social administration from Case Western Reserve University. Before joining Nordson she had nearly two decades of experience in nonprofit agencies, including eleven years with INROADS of Northeast Ohio, which provides corporate internships for African Americans, Hispanics, and Native Americans. As managing director of INROADS, she had made the acquaintance of Bill Madar, who served on its board—yet another example of fortunate circumstance in the Nord family's ventures.

Haqq and her four trustees, among them Madar, began with a planning effort. As she wrote in her first annual report, in 1991 "the foundation trustees and staff visited more than 50 community groups to learn firsthand the efforts currently being made and the tasks that lie ahead. The trustees met regularly to redefine strategies for guiding grantmaking decisions."

Haqq remains at the helm of the foundation. Important in assisting her have been former staff members Karen Sayre, program officer (1991–1999), and Carolyn Gibson of the Atlanta office (1993–1998), as well as her current staff: Symone McClain, manager of community relations in Atlanta; Cecilia Render, program officer in Ohio; Eddie Williams, manager of community relations in Ohio; and Kathy Ladiner, program assistant.

In general, The Nordson Corporation Foundation usually gives at least 70 percent of its funds to educational and health and welfare programs and the rest to civic, arts, and cultural organizations. Its grant priorities, as a central element in Nordson's coordinated philanthropy program, begin with each geographical area and its needs. "Although needs can change quickly," wrote Haqq in the fiftieth-anniversary booklet, "our vision is long term. We pursue and support results-oriented opportunities that prepare individuals for full and equal participation in the economic and social mainstream."

In Lorain County, a major example of that stated mission has been generous annual support since 1992 of the Center for Leadership in Education. Other major beneficiaries include the scholarship program of the Ohio Foundation of Independent Colleges, Lorain County 2020, Neighborhood House, the Child Care Resource Center, and Leadership Lorain County. Among the many grantees elsewhere in Ohio and in Georgia, Alabama, Rhode Island, and California are Habitat for Humanity in Atlanta, Baldwin-Wallace College in Berea, Ohio, for its programs for single mothers, and the Cleveland Clinic Foundation's Nordson Fellows program at the Morehouse School of Medicine, a multiyear program that

In 2002, Nordson Time 'n Talent volunteers Dawn LaRosa and Tom Jewell worked on "Make a Blanket Day" for Project Linus, a national organization with a Lorain County branch started by Barb Raymond, another Nordson employee. (Reproduced courtesy of The Nordson Corporation Foundation)

brings medical students from Morehouse to the Cleveland Clinic as researchers. Over the years, as with The Nord Family Foundation, the number of grants The Nordson Corporation Foundation has awarded in areas beyond Lorain County has grown. This has been accomplished through the establishment of employee decision-making committees (called "community affairs committees") in California, Atlanta, and Rhode Island.

As for employee giving, Haqq has clear goals. "The overriding theme that I came into the job with," she said in a recent interview, "was inclusion of as many Nordson employees and their families as possible in the overall corporate philanthropy." An important outgrowth of this philosophy has been the Time 'n Talent program. Not long after assuming her position, Haqq decided that Nordson needed an organized, company-wide employee volunteer program. She presented her proposal to Madar; he was enthusiastic, and in 1993 the Time 'n Talent program was born. "It's a strategy," Haqq said of Nordson's vital philanthropic and volunteer program, "that strengthens the relations between the company and the community, and strengthens the relationship between employees and their community."[5]

## NORDSON CORPORATION: RECENT HISTORY

In the last two decades of the twentieth century and the first years of the twenty-first, American corporations have gone through all sorts of convolutions in order to survive and achieve profitability in the ever-changing, intensely competitive global business environment. Many companies have disappeared. Others are nearly unrecognizable compared with what they were just a few years ago. Long-term planning has become more difficult. And in the United States untold numbers of persons have been adversely affected.

Nordson Corporation has been challenged by these changes, but it has survived—and thrived. Its strengths, maintained and increased by steadfast management, have been many: a culture of excellence and innovation; a culture of oneness with the customer and related manufacturers; a culture of trust and equality among all elements of the company, from

Eric Nord with Nordson President and Chief Executive Officer William Madar, as pictured in the 1995 *Nordson Corporation Annual Report*. (Reproduced courtesy of Nordson Corporation)

the board and top management to hourly employees; and a culture of community involvement and service. All are directly traceable to the influence of Walter, Eric, and Evan Nord. Conservative financial management, offices throughout the world, a diversified product offering that is of help to a variety of industries and can supply balance to the company when some sectors are in trouble, a relatively nonpolluting process of manufacturing— these values, too, began with Walter and his sons.

The corporation has one major vulnerability, however: As a manufacturer of machinery, it has suffered in times of economic downturn and recession, when customers reduce their capital purchases. Such has been the case in every decade since the 1970s, including the first three years of the new century, when conditions were especially severe. Financial unpredictability for a global enterprise can also flow from fluctuations in world currencies.

Edward Campbell, chief executive officer of the Nordson Corporation since 1997, was named chairman of its board in 2004. (Reproduced courtesy of Nordson Corporation)

## CONTINUED GROWTH AND EXPANSION

Despite one such domestic slowdown in the early 1990s and severe problems in Asia in the later 1990s, for Nordson it was mostly full speed ahead throughout the decade, under the leadership of Madar and his successor, Edward P. "Ed" Campbell. Sales almost tripled, from $245 million in 1988 to $700 million in 1999. The largest segment of the business has proved to be that devoted to applying adhesives and nonwoven fibers, which represented 63 percent of all sales by 1999.

Those technologies were gradually perfected, and many other landmarks were noted, such as the announcement in the 1993 annual report that Nordson had installed its first system for an automotive manufacturer that could powder-coat an entire car body. In the adhesives field, Nordson continued to work closely with adhesive manufacturers; a number, in fact, were located within a few miles of the company, facilitating close cooperation.

In those years Nordson Corporation made several important acquisitions, to further widen its capabilities and increase its capacity. In 1989 the corporation acquired a company in Lüneberg, Germany, known as Meltex, which, among other products, made equipment to apply adhesives to labels and tapes. In 1992 it purchased the Slautterback Corporation of Sand City, California, a maker of hot-melt-dispensing equipment. The next year saw the purchase of Mountaingate Engineering, Inc. of Campbell, California, through which Nordson gained the ability to manufacture dryers and ovens for the container coatings industry. And in 1994 Nordson acquired Electrostatic Technology, Inc., a Connecticut firm making electrostatic powder-coating systems.

*Top:* Nordson's European headquarters, Erkrath, Germany, pictured ca. 1990. (Reproduced courtesy of Nordson Corporation)

*Bottom:* Equipment made at Nordson's Asymtek unit in Carlsbad, California, applies fluids to circuit boards and other electronics surfaces. (Reproduced courtesy of Nordson Corporation)

In 1995 Walcom Benelux BV, a Dutch company that manufactures liquid-dispensing systems, was added; and in 1996 Asymptotic Technologies, Inc. (Asymtek) of Carlsbad, California, joined Nordson with its advanced capabilities in applying fluids to electronic components such as circuit-board assemblies. Also in 1996 came Spectral Technology Group Ltd., a British firm making drying and curing systems for the graphic arts and other industries.

The years 1997–1999 saw the acquisition of Applied Curing Technology plants in Norwalk, Ohio, and Malvern Link, England, another maker of ultraviolet curing equipment; J&M Laboratories, Inc. of Dawsonville, Georgia, a manufacturer of equipment for the nonwovens industry; Advanced Plasma Systems, Inc. of Saint Petersburg, Florida, and March Instruments, Inc. of Concord, California, both of which gave Nordson new capabilities in using gas plasma in the manufacture of printed circuit assemblies and other products for advanced technologies; and VeriTec™ Technologies, Inc. of Fairfield, New Jersey, maker of adhesive-dispensing systems. In 2000 Nordson made its largest acquisition, EFD, Inc. of East Providence, Rhode Island, a maker of low-pressure precision dispensing systems.

The 1990s saw another major expansion in Nordson's international reach. Sales outside North America more than doubled between 1989 and 1999, and various facilities were opened or enhanced in Italy, Portugal, Denmark, Austria, Poland, the Netherlands, the Czech Republic, Venezuela, Mexico, Colombia, India, South Korea, Malaysia, Thailand, Vietnam, and China, among others. Well established in Japan since the 1960s, the company was gratified to see its Chinese market develop with the blossoming of the Chinese free-market economy. By 1993 Nordson powder-coating and adhesive-applying equipment was being used in the manufacture of many Chinese consumer goods.

In 1994, nearly 60 percent of Nordson's sales were in foreign countries. In 1989, the company had received its second award for increasing trade abroad, the "President's 'E Star' Award for Exports," a follow-up to its similar recognition in 1969. More praise has come Nordson's way. An article in the 1995 *International Directory of Company Histories* noted Nordson's high rate of innovation and number of employee patents, its 1993 decision to obtain ISO 9000 certification of quality manufacturing standards from the International Organization for Standardization in Switzerland, and its highest possible recommendation from *Value Line*.

A number of new facilities were completed, including plants in Duluth, Georgia, and Monterey, California, as well as one in Amherst, Ohio, that focused on automotive coating equipment. Nordson continued to contribute substantially to the economies of its various locations and to offer a work environment that was hospitable to highly trained engineers and equally skilled workers, men and women, minorities, and people with disabilities. Each year, all who had received patents were honored at an inventors' gathering for both employees and retirees. Long-term employees and retired workers continued to enjoy the Old Timers banquets. As part of its community mission, along with monetary donations and thousands of employee volunteer hours, the company contin-

An aerial view of the Nordson Corporation complex in Amherst, ca. 1996. See pages 73 and 124 for aerial photographs taken in the 1950s and the 1970s, respectively. (Reproduced courtesy of Nordson Corporation)

ued to contract out some of its work, such as painting strips on nozzles, to the Elyria Contract Shop of Vocational Guidance Services, descendant of Walter's Center for the Sightless. No doubt Walter would have been much pleased.[6]

## An Orderly Transition

As of October 31, 1997, at the end of Nordson's fiscal year, Eric retired from the chairmanship of the board. Madar retired from his position as chief executive officer to take Eric's place as chairman. Forty-seven-year-old Campbell, who had joined Nordson as a vice president in 1988, became the new chief executive officer.

Eric was honored with a special presentation at the Old Timers Dinner on September 4, 1997, including both a videotape and a leather-bound "Memory Book" tracing the history of U.S. Automatic and Nordson. In comments to the *Amherst News-Times* that May, Eric had said that his forty-seven-year career had been "very rewarding . . . and a lot of fun" and explained that he would remain active on the board and continue to work for "sharing our good fortune with others."

New members of the Nordson Old Timers Club, honored for their fifteen years of service to the company, pose with Nordson President and Chief Executive Officer William Madar at the annual Old Timers Dinner in 1989. Left to right: Mary Ann Kastl, Robert Enlow, Nancy Scott, Robert Allsop, Marilyn Lewis, Jeffrey Noss, Paul Larrow, Richard Denger, Delores Horvath, Clifford Piar, Doris Bowyer, Leroy Coffin, George Norton, Maria Mrosek, Wesley Schmitt, Anna Bodach, Leonard Noster, Douglas Beattie, Mary Ann Shipula, Vincent Espitia, Allan Kuehn, Cheryl Musolf, Mary Keith, Rita Garza, Karl Veverka, Arlys Miller, Madar, and Ruth Wolfe. Thirty-one additional new members are not pictured. In all, 280 employees and 91 retirees were members of the club in 1989, some of whom had worked for the company for nearly half a century. When this book went to press in 2004, membership stood at 631. (Reproduced courtesy of Nordson Corporation)

Madar, just fifty-seven at his retirement, had led the company to a fourfold increase in sales since his arrival in 1986. But in a characteristic metaphor he told the *Lorain Morning Journal,* "You have to put yourself in a new pot every 10 years or so if you want to remain vital and growing. . . . I think it's generally unwise that anyone be responsible for an institution for more than 10 years. And this is going on 12." And he told the *Amherst News-Times,* "The election of Ed Campbell to chief executive officer represents the final phase of a succession strategy put into place several years ago to ensure the smooth transition of Nordson's leadership into the future." He praised Campbell's "vision, energy and experience."

Campbell, a graduate of the University of Notre Dame and the Harvard Business School, was, like Madar, a former vice president at Standard Oil before joining Nordson. The two had worked closely together since Campbell's elevation to president and chief operating officer in 1996, and they were beginning to institute some changes to streamline operations and further update technologies. After becoming chief executive officer on November 1, 1997, Campbell continued this process with an eye to further boosting productivity and reducing costs wherever possible. Under a program called "Action 2000," some operations were combined and centralized, and the company accelerated its use of advanced computer technology, including Internet communications and SAP enterprise management systems software.[7]

## Surviving Rough Waters

Nordson's sales rose to $740 million in 2000, but that year brought the first signs of the gradual slide in the economy that became a prolonged crisis. As a maker of capital goods, Nordson suffered severely. Sales for the year 2002 fell to $647 million, down nearly $93 million from 2000's high. By 2001, in fact, the company had embarked on a program to close nine plants worldwide and reduce employment by 15 percent. Business realities required that all jobs be reassessed for realignment or release. As Eric noted in a 2003 interview, "We're still very reluctant to reduce employment unless it's absolutely imperative. But we have had four years of hard times."

Eric also made the point, however, that there was much hope for the future, highlighting the fact that Nordson's "culture of innovation is very strong." In early 2003 the corporation introduced three totally redesigned adhesive melters called the Blue Series, representing a $10 million investment in research and development. And Nordson continued to work on internal processes designed to reduce costs and lay the foundation for future growth. In particular, the corporation successfully implemented the concept of "lean" manufacturing, dramatically restructured and reduced inventories, and made many other cost-effective improvements.

*I have always maintained that through the years almost all the employees felt they were working with you as a team rather than just working for you.*

—Former Nordson Corporation employee, in a letter to Eric Nord, August 12, 1993

As economic conditions began to improve, total sales in 2003 rose by $20 million over 2002, to $667 million. In the 2003 annual report, Campbell described the year as a "turning-point." He reported that Nordson Corporation, strengthened by its cost savings and by recovering sales, was ready to move forward more aggressively in search of new applications, markets, and possible acquisitions. Interviewed by Dow Jones for a March 12, 2004 Internet article, Campbell hailed quickly rising sales and earnings in certain segments of the business. In the first quarter of the new fiscal year, the company experienced an increase in orders of 11 percent over the previous year.

Following the 2004 meeting, the Board of Directors named the fifty-four-year-old Campbell chairman, to succeed Madar, and he continues as chief executive officer. Peter S. Hellman, also fifty-four, formerly executive vice president, was named president and continues as chief financial and administrative officer.

Among the points stressed in the Dow Jones article is that international sales continue to make up a large portion of Nordson's sales—now more than 60 percent. Exciting growth is taking place in China, where products made with Nordson machinery are rising in response to demand by a swelling middle class. Business, very definitely, was improving for Nordson as this book went to press.[8]

## RETIRED . . . BUT NOT RETIRING

### ERIC AND JANE

Eric, in his upper eighties, remained active and involved during his retirement, still serving on the board of Nordson Corporation and still participating in community projects. He and Jane continued to come up with new philanthropic ideas. In 2002, for example, they gave funds to Case Western Reserve University to provide the engineering school with a building of its own—the latest of several major gifts by the Nords to Case, including two endowed professorships and one scholarship.

Some years ago Eric was deeply involved in a community controversy and, not for the first time, took a stand that was initially unpopular. For many years Oberlin College's venerable Carnegie Library had housed not only the college library but also the Oberlin Public Library—on separate floors. Right after the college built the massive new Seeley G. Mudd Center, which houses its main library, in 1974, the public library was allowed to remain on Carnegie's first floor for a nominal rent. Later, however, the college determined that it needed to use the entire Carnegie building and that the public library would have to find another home. This provoked a considerable outcry from the public library's Board of Trustees and the community.

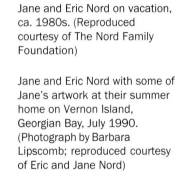

Jane and Eric Nord on vacation, ca. 1980s. (Reproduced courtesy of The Nord Family Foundation)

Jane and Eric Nord with some of Jane's artwork at their summer home on Vernon Island, Georgian Bay, July 1990. (Photograph by Barbara Lipscomb; reproduced courtesy of Eric and Jane Nord)

Eric jumped into the fray by offering to head a bond-issue campaign on behalf of the library board. The plan was to remodel a former supermarket on South Main Street, to adapt it for use as the Oberlin Public Library. Resistance was considerable at first. Eric remembered, "Some people just didn't want to move. They believed that re-doing an old food market would not be a good place for a library." One member of the library board was especially vocal in his opposition. However, Eric was able to generate considerable public support for the bond-issue campaign as plans for the new library were developed and made public. The bond issue passed easily, and in 1990 the library opened its bright and spacious quarters in its new, central location with ample parking space, to the acclaim of all. From April 1991 to December 1996 Patricia Holsworth served as the first director of the public library in its new quarters. "That was a big break," Eric told the historian Marlene Merrill. "Pat really did a fantastic job."

Another long-term project came to fruition at the turn of the millennium. For decades Eric had worked with concerned citizens and city officials to secure public swimming facilities for Oberlin residents. Several sites and options were considered, but each presented obstacles and none materialized. Community input was gathered in a series of meetings held throughout Oberlin. In 1994 Jep Carrell and community activist and O.H.I.O. Trustee Sigrid Boe sought and received Eric's strong support for an architectural study exploring options for a pool to be constructed on city-owned land. The city did not seem particularly interested, but Boe and other community members continued to explore new strategies.

In 1997 the city, together with the Public Services Institute of Lorain County Community College, surveyed residents' wishes and desires for a variety of types of recreational facilities. Eric approached Dan Martin, director of the Lorain County Metro Parks, to discuss the possibility of a regional facility that would be part of the Metro Parks system. This soon led to discussions with the Lorain County Board of Park Commissioners, who decided to conduct a countywide user/opinion survey about whether a regional pool might be a viable option. When the survey produced positive findings, Eric offered to raise $2 million if the balance of the needed funds could be raised from other sources and if the Metro Parks would construct and manage the facility.

Once again Eric was the catalyst for community improvement, successfully rallying family and friends to meet his pledge. In the meantime, a capital campaign committee of area residents and civic leaders solicited pledges from businesses, foundations, and other individuals, while another committee encouraged voters to pass a tax levy to raise $1.4 million over five years.

The Splash Zone, just south of downtown Oberlin, was completed in 2001. It is the area's first public facility for indoor/outdoor swimming and fitness. (Reproduced courtesy of Lorain County Metro Parks)

All of this community effort paid off when a $5.6 million year-round recreational facility opened in 2001. The Splash Zone is located on a 25-acre site leased from the city just south of town and includes a large outdoor pool, a water slide, an eight-lane indoor pool with bleachers that seat 200 people, a fitness room, a volleyball court, and a playground. Modest membership fees are charged for use of the facility, but financial aid is available to assist low-income families.

Eric was extremely satisfied with the results, saying, "Every kid ought to have the opportunity to swim well for safety and recreation." The Splash Zone now makes this possible for Oberlin and Lorain County children, in contrast to when Eric was a child. He had taught himself to swim—not very well, he pointed out—in what was the most easily available place: an Amherst quarry hole.

Eric still spent some time in his workshop. For a number of years he had designed devices to help his disabled friends, such as a swivel mechanism to make it simpler to move into an automobile from a wheelchair. His full schedule helped keep Eric and Jane in Oberlin most of the time; another draw was the frequent concerts and other cultural activities in the Oberlin community. For a few weeks every year the Nords, their children, and their grandchildren do, however, enjoy a respite together at their summer home on Georgian Bay, an extension of Lake Huron.

In recent interviews Eric did not dwell a great deal on history, but if he had looked back over the past dozen or so years he would have recalled several important recognitions of his achievements. On May 28, 1990 Oberlin College awarded him an honorary doctor of science de-

On April 30, 1997 the Governor's Arts Patron Award was bestowed on Jane Nord (left) at the Ohio Arts Council's Arts Day luncheon and ceremony in Columbus. Also in attendance was Betsy Manderen (right), executive director of the Firelands Association for the Visual Arts. (Photograph courtesy of Eric and Jane Nord)

gree. In 1991 his alma mater, Case Western Reserve University, gave him the Case Alumni Association Gold Medal based on his achievements in design, business management, and public service. In 1995 the Adhesive and Sealant Council, a trade organization of adhesive manufacturers, bestowed on him its "ASC" award for lifetime achievement. That same year, Leadership Lorain County honored him at its tenth-anniversary celebration by presenting him with an award named in his honor, the Eric Nord Award for Excellence in Community Leadership. In 1998 he received his second honorary degree, an honorary doctorate of science from Case. And in October 2001 he was inducted into the Northeast Ohio Business Hall of Fame of *Inside Business* magazine.

One especially satisfying memory was of something he decided to do in 1993. As he told the interviewer Barbara Griffith, he had been concerned for some time that people who had retired from Nordson in earlier years were receiving much less in retirement benefits than were recent retirees. "So," he said, "I decided . . . to take a one-time shot at trying to level up some of these people by giving them [some of] my personal stock." Shares of Eric and Jane's Nordson stock were distributed to retirees all over the nation and beyond, and in return Eric, though not asking for a reply, received many grateful and newsy letters. He kept and treasured them all.

Another letter Eric received that year gave him special delight. It was from a woman he had never met, whose father had been a close friend of

Walter's and who, many years ago, had purchased two shares of American Specialty stock. By 1993 the stock had become 15,120 shares of Nordson and was worth more than $800,000.

Jane, too, received special recognition in the 1990s. At its commencement on May 27, 1996 Oberlin College bestowed its Community Service Award on her, noting "her philanthropic work, her support for the arts and her advocacy of educational and economic opportunity for the citizens of Lorain County." The award cited her work as a trustee of The Nord Family Foundation, her role in the founding of FAVA and the renovation of the New Union Center for the Arts, her years as a Girl Scout leader, and her service for the Cleveland Center for Contemporary Art, the Allen Memorial Art Museum at Oberlin College, and the Frances Lehman Loch Art Center at Vassar College.

On April 30, 1997, in Columbus, Jane received the Governor's Arts Patron Award, praising her for "her philanthropic generosity, participation in the arts and unstinting encouragement of others." In addition to the activities noted in the Oberlin College award, it cited her work with the Lorain County Arts Council, her performance as a pianist with the Oberlin Friday Music Club, and her membership in the Christ Church choir.[9]

## EVAN AND CINDY

Evan and Cindy Nord enjoyed a life filled with family, animals, nature, and meaningful work. Their home in Blythewood near Columbia, South Carolina, is set in a rambling expanse of woods, pastures, meadows, streams, and lakes. Cindy's horse farm, which she began with just a few horses in 1979, had an equine population of more than thirty-five in 2004, along with a number of dogs she rescued from abuse. Evan and Cindy's many community contributions in South Carolina were recognized by the Palmetto Society of United Way of the Midlands, which named them Humanitarians of the Year in January 1995.

Four days a week Cindy spent most of her time at the nearby Nurturing Center, interacting with the children as a play therapist and working on a variety of projects in her office. A resource center was developed for use by parents and care providers. In addition, she remained closely connected to Common Ground, the secluded retreat center near Oberlin. In 2002 Cindy completed work for a doctorate from Union Institute and University, and she wrote and illustrated a book on child abuse, *The Nickel Run* (2002). In a recent interview she spoke of her great interest in ways of using animals to promote healing.

Evan had just as many interests and involvements. After a short hiatus he returned to the board of The Nord Family Foundation, and only in 2002 did he retire from the Nordson Corporation Board of Directors. At

*Above:* Among Cindy Nord's distinctions are five World Amateur Pleasure Driving Championships. Four of these, 1997–2000, were with Opies Boy, shown here at the 2000 Grand National & World Championship Morgan Horse Show in Oklahoma City, Oklahoma. No one else has ever won four consecutive world championships with the same horse. (Reproduced courtesy of the photographer, Howard Schatzberg)

*Right:* Cindy Nord greeting "Dirk," a Friesian horse from Holland, at Meadow Ridge Farm in Blythewood, South Carolina, on a misty day in September 2003. (Photograph by Richard Holsworth)

*Above:* Among The Nord Family Foundation trustees who attended a board meeting in 2002 were, left to right, Evan Nord, Randall Barbato, Emily Nord McClintock, Virginia Nord Barbato, and Jane Nord. Behind them is St. George's Chapel, part of the Amherst Historical Society's Sandstone Museum Center. (Reproduced courtesy of The Nord Family Foundation)

*Left:* Evan relaxing with "Mr. Pickens" at the Nords' Meadow Ridge Farm in Blythewood, South Carolina.

*Above:* The new head-quarters of The Nord Family Foundation on Milan Avenue, Amherst, Ohio, at the time of its June 19, 2003 dedica-tion. The landscaping for the headquarters received a Lorain County Beautiful Award in August 2003. (Repro-duced courtesy of The Nord Family Foundation)

*Right:* The foyer of the new Nord Family Foundation headquar-ters features a World War II–era photograph of Joseph A. and Mary Nord Ignat and their sons, David (left) and Joseph N. For a closer view of the photograph, see page 67. (Reproduced courtesy of The Nord Family Foundation)

his retirement ceremony the company's "Resolution of Appreciation" commended him for "over sixty years of exceptionally varied and dedicated service," mentioning specifically his work on the tungsten carbide flat-spray nozzle, his interest in the welfare of Nordson's employees and retirees, and his participation in charitable organizations.

In South Carolina, Evan served on the boards of the South Carolina State Museum Foundation, the New Morning Foundation, the Heathwood Hall Foundation, and, formerly, the South Carolina Children's Home. Daughter Katie, and now son Ethan, carry on his role on the board of the Central Carolina Community Foundation, which had assets of nearly $50 million and served an eleven-county area in 2003.

Many ties drew Evan back to Amherst and Oberlin for extended visits. One was friendship. He did not forget or abandon friends with whom he had worked for so many years in the shops at U.S. Automatic and Nordson. With each trip, for example, he made sure to spend some time with Cliff Berry, his close friend who retired in 1978 as a supervisor in the turret lathe department after forty-three years with the company. Berry's retirement was financially comfortable, thanks to Nordson's employee stock-ownership plan and other benefits, and the two enjoyed many activities together. Evan would also look in on other Nordson friends who were his contemporaries and might need help of some kind.

In Oberlin, Evan would often go to the Oberlin Early Childhood Center and visit with Director Nancy Sabath and her dedicated staff—as she said, "to see how things are going." An O.H.I.O. honorary trustee since 1994, he also made sure to stop in and see Executive Director Pat Murphy and all his friends at the Oberlin Heritage Center. He enjoyed the celebration and dedication of an Ohio Historical Marker at the Burrell-King House on May 24, 2003 as part of the Ohio Bicentennial. Murphy honored him in her remarks during the ceremony:

> Let us dedicate this historic marker in remembrance and appreciation of Lorain Countians past and present who have helped to make Oberlin and Lorain County a better place to live, learn, work and visit: people like Jabez Burrell and Henry Churchill King, who were great leaders in our community's first century, and, more recently, people like Evan Nord, who have worked so hard to build our community, to educate our children and young adults, and to help us to preserve and share our history with future generations.

Projects also drew Evan back. He and his longtime friends Jack Clark and Bill Ginn, as well as Eric, were still responding to the community's needs with new ideas. Evan's memories and his love of history took him to Amherst for visits to the Outdoor Life Association's grounds, the Nordson plant, the Nordson Depot, and the various buildings of the Sandstone Museum Center. He also played a leadership role in planning the renovation that is currently under way to transform the long-neglected sec-

*If Evan Nord were given a certificate of appreciation every time he did something that was significant for one of his two communities, Oberlin or Columbia, S.C., he could stay in great physical shape just by getting up to receive them! Here at O.H.I.O. each of us offers up a silent but fervent "Thanks" for one or more of the things he has done to assure that O.H.I.O. can continue to serve our community well. . . . What he has done is often not known by the general public or even some of our members because this consummately modest man doesn't let people know about his good deeds. . . . Perhaps most important of all, this thoughtful and exceptionally capable Oberlinian had a vision. He had a vision of how to make the community conscious of its heritage; that was to assemble a few historic buildings and a number of artifacts on adjoining sites in a location easily reached by all residents.*

—Jeptha Carrell, honoring Evan Nord during the O.H.I.O. Annual Meeting, March 6, 1996

*Right:* John Mullaney, executive director of The Nord Family Foundation since 1998, was one of several speakers who addressed family members and guests at the dedication of the foundation's headquarters at the Sandstone Museum Center on June 19, 2003. (Reproduced courtesy of The Nord Family Foundation)

*Below:* The staff of The Nord Family Foundation, gathered in front of their new headquarters in June 2003. Left to right: Ann Allison, office manager; Joy Anderson, program officer; Sharon White, controller; John Mullaney, executive director; Karen Cook, program officer; Juliet Mishak, administrative assistant. (Reproduced courtesy of The Nord Family Foundation)

ond floor of the sandstone Amherst City Hall (originally called the "Town Hall") for use as a community auditorium.

Near the Amherst Historical Society's Quigley Museum stands another of Amherst's early structures, the two-story Henry Walker house, also built of sandstone. In 2003 Evan completed a project that had long been foremost in his mind: renovating the house and constructing a large addition to serve as new headquarters for The Nord Family Foundation. At its formal dedication, on June 19, the restored and expanded building was dedicated to the memory of Joseph A. and Mary Nord Ignat. Incorporated into its design are rooms for welcoming both the family and the Lorain County community for meetings and special events, as well as a library where history of the family and community will be preserved. With his deep concern for the family's cohesiveness, Evan served as the family's historian and, together with Eric, its conscience.[10]

## A LOSS IN THE FAMILY

On June 21, 2004, as this book was about to go to press, Evan died in Columbia. His health had long been declining, so perhaps the news should not have come as a shock. But it did, in part because he had seemed so energetic when he visited Lorain County in mid-May. He had worked for long hours with Pat Murphy and Jack Clark at the Oberlin Heritage Center, fine-tuning portions of this narrative, and had visited other friends in the area. In South Carolina he had been looking forward to a meeting of The Nord Family Foundation members and, characteristically, had especially wanted to watch David Ignat play tennis. Touchingly, because most of the family were gathered in Columbia, they were able to bid him adieu.

The tributes that appeared in newspapers and on the Internet in the days following Evan's death reflected the widespread esteem and affection he elicited, not only for his professional prowess but also, especially, for his dedication to the communities in which he lived and worked. The *Elyria Chronicle-Telegram* editorialized, "As a patriot, an innovator and a charitable soul, Evan embodied the American spirit at its finest. . . . In an era when we've been deluged by headlines about corporate millionaires gone wrong, it is refreshing to be reminded of one who did so much good. Evan Nord will be missed." In the *Oberlin News-Tribune* Ann Fuller, executive director of Oberlin Community Services, commented, "He did a huge amount for the town, certainly for historic preservation, which is what he was interested in. He was enormously generous in so many ways." In the same article Nancy Sabath commented that Evan was "a philanthropist in the truest sense of the word. He didn't just give money. He stayed committed to the project. He just visited us three weeks ago. We may talk about benefactors in a distant way, but he was never distant."

*I want to add my voice to the list of people, especially those in Lorain County, who today mourn the loss of Evan Nord. He was a longtime benefactor of that community who gave unstintingly of himself and his resources. It was a privilege to know him, to work with him and to learn from him what it means to be a caring philanthropist. Would that more people of wealth might learn from his example.*

*Perhaps a fitting tribute to Evan is one of his own favorite quotations. In light of our nation's heavy emphasis on physical fitness, Evan always delighted in saying that to be truly fit, we should also learn how "to exercise our giving muscles." Amen.*

— Henry C. Doll,
"Evan Nord: True
Humanitarian,"
*Plain Dealer,*
June 28, 2004

Condolences and accolades came from South Carolina and other parts of the United States, too. A reporter for *The State,* a Columbia newspaper, quoted family friends as saying, "Evan Nord might not have been South Carolina bred, but his kind heart and generous nature made him one of the community's finer members." And Mac Bennett, executive director of the Central Carolina Community Foundation, told the Associated Press that Evan and Cindy "could have moved anywhere 20 to 25 years ago, but it was our community's good fortune that they came here. His passing away is going to be a devastating blow to the community."

The Nord family received friends on June 24 at The State Museum in Columbia, and on June 27 Evan's long and productive life was celebrated in Oberlin. Several hundred people from many of his varied communities gathered in the college's Finney Chapel. Ed Campbell, speaking on behalf of Nordson Corporation and its employees around the world, concluded his remarks thus:

> The impact of what Evan helped create goes far beyond what even he knew. After learning of Evan's passing, I notified Nordson's worldwide employees of our loss. I heard back from our employees with e-mails from around the world. These were messages, filled with love and respect, from people Evan never knew, but whose lives have been and continue to be profoundly affected in a very positive way.

> From an employee in Shanghai, China, "I am very sorry to hear the bad news. Thanks a lot to Evan for his dedication to our Nordson Corporation. Let's show our deepest respect for Evan and remember him forever. We will undertake his spirit, and build Nordson Corporation better and better."

> From another employee from our company in Mexico, "It may be the Nord family do not know who I am, but please send to them my personal condolences. Please tell them we are proud to represent the Nord family name in our country and we join to them in this deep and hard loss."

> I don't know how to say it any better than that.

> Evan, on behalf of your Nordson family worldwide, thank you.

In her tribute, Pat Murphy emphasized Evan's investment in community and involvement in heritage preservation:

> Evan personified duty, honor, humility, economy, and service to one's community. He loved life, he loved his family and he loved people. He loved his country and particularly his hometowns of Amherst, Oberlin, and Columbia. He believed in the importance of understanding history to appreciate the present and plan for the future.

> Without Evan's leadership, Lorain County would not be nearly as rich in cultural and historical resources, educational opportunities, and community services as; it is today. Evan did not want fanfare for his accomplishments. I think he would be pleased, however, if we each pay tribute to him in our own ways by doing what we can to improve our communities and to preserve and share our heritage.

Evan's nephew Joe Ignat shared personal memories—some humorous, many poignant—in remarks so insightful and eloquent that they are reproduced in full as Appendix 3.

After the memorial service a public reception was held on the college's large and leafy Tappan Square, just across the street from the chapel and only a stone's throw from the Oberlin Inn, where Evan and Eric had attended so many family, corporation, and foundation gatherings and community events. Later that Sunday, in the privacy of the family circle, Evan was interred in Oberlin's Westwood Cemetery, close to Walter and Virginia, Joe and Mary, and Chip.[11]

# 9

# A LEGACY OF LOVE AND RESPONSIBILITY

The sandstone industry that has dominated the Amherst area for more than 150 years has been difficult for laborers, due to the strenuous nature of the work and to the inherently unsafe conditions. But the prolonged efforts of its thousands of workers have made possible the building of countless beautiful structures and landscaping features. The quarries have brought families from far and wide to Lorain County—among them Walter Nord and his family.

The Nords, too, have been builders, in Lorain County and beyond, of business and employment, of nonprofit institutions and communities, of family. This has been the story particularly of Walter and his two sons: Walter, who was born to poor, Swedish-speaking parents, who grew up with five brothers and sisters in a small Ohio farmhouse, and who, through a lifetime of incessant work, thought, and caring involvement, became one of the most prominent and beloved citizens of northeast Ohio. Walter, whose combination of ingenuity, energy, honesty, conscience, humility, humor, love, common sense, and dogged perseverance brought so many accomplishments. Walter, whose spirit still lives in his descendants.

Walter seems to have had enough energy and ideas for two people, and both Eric and Evan inherited these characteristics. Eric, the older brother, to whom Walter gave management duties in addition to engineering ones from the beginning, provided the principal guiding hand since the 1950s in finding and fostering the products, people, markets, and methods to develop Nordson Corporation through innumerable changes and also, over his forty-seven-year business career, embraced many forms of community leadership, repeatedly facing risk and controversy. Evan, the younger brother, who supported Walter and Eric with design and engineering feats, ideas, and compassionate plant management for thirty-seven years, also combined his loves of history, buildings, family, friends, and youth in many significant and enduring community projects.

Others in the Nord family have, of course, played essential roles in its history and legacy, although at times they have been less visible: Herman, the oldest of Walter's generation, upon whom he relied greatly; Virginia, Walter's steadfast, serious, hardworking, frugal, and beautiful wife, whose "backbone" helped create character and whose love flowed out from the family to the homeless and others not so fortunate; Eric and Evan's two memorable grandmothers, Mary and Elizabeth; Mary Nord Ignat, who provided inestimable support to her brothers and the Oberlin community; the elder Joe Ignat, who brought so much life, vitality, creativity, and a fresh perspective to the Nords' world; Jane, whose life, character, and love of family, music, and the arts so enriched the life of Eric and the Oberlin community; Cindy, who brought family life to Evan and whose knowledge of child psychology and advocacy of women's and children's causes helped shape the family's philanthropy and move it forward in important new ways.

Many not related by blood to Walter, Eric, or Evan, far too numerous to try to list here, played major parts as well. Beginning with Otto and Mary's helpful neighbors in Ashtabula County and continuing with Walter's close friends and advisers in college, Walter and Virginia's friends, neighbors, associates, and employees in Amherst and Oberlin, they were close to the family and immeasurably valued by them.

In the early years of the twenty-first century the image of American business is, to say the least, not totally favorable. Almost every day comes a new story of the greed and dishonest practices of some large corporation or highly placed executive. The image of millionaires is not so favorable, either. The outsized mansions, the gated communities, the excesses in personal spending and waste of every kind continually mock the lives and efforts of the majority, of more average and poorer people, who often cannot afford many of the basic necessities of life.

The era is ripe for reform, in need of new heroes and new visions. The Nords and their businesses and philanthropies provide an instructive model, as well as being important in their own right. The model begins with an eagerness to work and learn and with the decision to run a business not only ethically but also on the basis of equality and sharing, not as a personal possession but as a joint undertaking and an adventure that benefits customers, employees, and communities just as much as shareholders. More benefits then flow to the economy, to suppliers, and to allied industries. A large share of the profits flow back into improvements, innovations, and contributions rather than into the owners' pockets.

When it comes to philanthropy, a few million dollars can go amazingly far, especially when they are thoughtfully placed and when the programs for which they are used are well nurtured. Philanthropy is actually another profitable exercise in innovation and frugality, and it brings great returns to the givers in personal satisfaction. In the case of the Nords, giving dollars has not been enough; personal involvement has been equally important.

With the help of seed money and planning provided by the Nords and their associates, four viable charitable foundations have grown: The Nord Family Foundation, The Nordson Corporation Foundation, the

*I am one of a lot of people who understand that they owe what they have received to a large component of luck or divine intervention. . . . I, for one, feel our family was very fortunate. . . . It's almost as if we had drilled for oil in our backyard and hit a gusher. It doesn't mean that we're any smarter. We did work hard and we took big chances that paid off, but we owe a lot to good fortune.*

*When you are lucky enough to have money, it is not enough to give it away. . . . You also have to be involved. You will never know what the problems are if all you do for a community is send out checks.*

—Eric Nord, quoted in Glenn Gamboa, "Nord Family Legacy Makes Difference," *Lorain Morning Journal,* December 20, 1992

*Between W.G. and Eric and Evan, there is a very strong ethic, almost like a religion, that life is tough. If you have a little bit of good luck, and you can share it and help somebody, that's what you should do.*

—David Ignat, interview with Jeanne Harrah, September 14, 1992

Community Foundation of Greater Lorain County, and the Central Carolina Community Foundation. Because of the Nords' personal involvement and their dollars, literally hundreds of charitable, educational, and cultural institutions have been strengthened. In some cases they owe their very existence to the creative dedication of Walter, Evan, Eric, and their key employees. Undergirding all their gifts of time, ingenuity, and money, the Nords have revealed over and over again an attitude of humility, of equality, of simply helping others solve problems.

An especially dynamic aspect of the Nord's philosophy of giving is its impact on employees and others who have volunteered their time and their talents. Volunteering asks something extra of people, and Walter began the tradition by gently but firmly insisting that his U.S. Automatic workers promote the purchase of war bonds, give blood, and do cleanup work in the community. Today volunteerism is solidly built into the structure of the company in all its locations.

Nordson Corporation's ethical excellence is now widely recognized. For the past four years the corporation has ranked among the "100 Best Corporate Citizens" in the United States, a listing compiled by *Business*

The June 19, 2003 dedication of The Nord Family Foundation headquarters in Amherst was also a family reunion. Pictured in the front row, left to right, are: Todd Ignat, Lydia Mayo, Eleanor Ignat, Evan Nord, Virginia Barbato, Emily McClintock, Jane Nord, Eric Thomas Nord, Pamela Ignat. Middle row: Elizabeth Bausch, Emily Porter. Back row: Nicholas McClintock, Matthew Barbato, David Barbato, Randall Barbato, David Ignat, Joseph Ignat, Brian Ignat, Erin Ignat, Courtney Nord, Eric Charles Nord. Foundation members (exclusive of the community trustees: Camille Hamlin Allen, Emma Mason, and Luis Villarreal) not pictured: Justin Bausch, Carlotte Berk, Samuel Berk, T. K. McClintock, Angel Nord, Bruce Nord, Cindy Nord, Eric Townsend Nord, Ethan Nord, Kathleen Nord, Richard Nord, Shannon Nord, Kathleen Peterson, Scott Peterson, Marc Porter, Michele Thornton, Allyson Wandtke, Todd Wandtke. (Reproduced courtesy of The Nord Family Foundation)

*Ethics* magazine (Nordson was rated 65th in 2004). The publisher noted, "The aim of the project is to identify firms that excel at serving a variety of stakeholders well: shareholders, community, minorities and women, employees, environment, non-U.S. stakeholders, and customers." Crediting the Nord family tradition, Chairman Campbell writes: "Quite simply, good corporate citizenship is good business and good for society." It would be most gratifying to Walter Nord to know of this honor.[1]

The story of the succeeding generation of the Nord family, now mostly in middle life, and of their children, has not been told here; that remains for a future undertaking. Experts who analyze family businesses and foundations warn that family institutions can split apart after the founder is gone, as the various branches become more distant in one way or another. The Nord family is no longer a nuclear family; it has become an extended one, with members in many parts of the United States. It is too early to tell the directions this extended family will take, but certain members are emerging as leaders with a strong desire for family cohesion. This, too, can be a model for others to follow in this time when so many families are fragmented and must rely on travel, the telephone, and e-mail to know one another.

And so, for almost a century, beginning with Walter and Virginia, the Nords, builders and innovators, have given generously of themselves and their financial resources—have invested in community—while helping to sustain others' faith in humankind.

*The philosophy has always been, going back to our parents . . . that if you have a foundation of this sort it doesn't relieve you as a person to do your own charitable works in the community. It isn't finding an alternative way of expressing your own obligations.*

—Eric Nord, in Jeanne Harrah, *The History of The Nord Family Foundation,* October 9, 1992

# THE NORD FAMILY

| | |
|---|---|
| 1848 | Otto Nord born in Sweden |
| 1856 | Mary Erickson born in Sweden |
| 1872 | Otto emigrates to the United States |
| 1874 | Mary emigrates to the United States |
| ca. 1876 | Otto Nord and Mary Erickson married |
| 1877 | Herman Joel Nord, Otto and Mary's first child, born |
| 1881 | Otto becomes a U.S. citizen |
| 1882 | Otto purchases land in Denmark Township, Ashtabula County, Ohio |
| 1884 | Walter Godfrey Nord, Otto and Mary's fourth child, born |
| 1888 | Virginia Grieve born |
| 1909 | Walter graduates from Western Reserve University / Case School of Applied Science, in Cleveland, Ohio |
| 1913 | Walter Nord and Virginia Grieve married |
| 1913 or 1914 | Walter begins working for the Cleveland Stone Company in Amherst, Ohio |
| 1914 | Mary Elizabeth Nord born |
| 1917 | Eric Thomas Nord born |
| 1919 | Evan Walter Nord born |
| ca. 1920 | Walter, Virginia, their children, and Elizabeth Grieve, Virginia's mother, move to Spring Street, Amherst |
| 1920 | Walter elected to the Amherst Board of Education |
| 1920 | American Specialty Company purchases land that becomes the Outdoor Life Park in Amherst |
| 1923 | Walter elected president of the Amherst Board of Education |
| 1924–1925 | Walter serves as mayor of Amherst |
| 1926 | Otto Nord dies |
| 1931 | Mary Erickson Nord dies |
| 1936 | Mary Elizabeth Nord graduates from Bluffton College |
| 1938 | Elizabeth Grieve dies |
| 1938 | Mary Elizabeth Nord and Joseph Allen Ignat married |
| 1938 | Walter founds the Rotary Club in Amherst |

# APPENDIX 1

## CHRONOLOGIES

## THE NORD FAMILY, *continued*

|  |  |
|---|---|
| 1938 | Walter becomes president of the board of the Center for the Sightless, in Elyria, Ohio |
| 1939 | Eric graduates from the Case School of Applied Science |
| 1939 | Herman Nord dies |
| ca. 1939–1940 | Walter ill |
| 1940–1941 | Eric, Evan, and Joseph and Mary Ignat return to Amherst to help Walter at the U.S. Automatic Corporation |
| 1941 | Evan graduates from the Case School of Applied Science |
| 1941 | David Walter Ignat born |
| 1943 | Joseph Nord Ignat born |
| 1943 | Walter purchases a dairy farm near Wellington, Ohio |
| 1944 | Walter and Virginia move to Oberlin, Ohio |
| 1944 | Evan and Joe Ignat enlist in the U.S. Navy |
| 1948 | Eric Nord and Jane Baker married |
| 1949 | Walter elected president of the American Swedish Historical Foundation |
| 1950 | Virginia Louise Nord born |
| 1951 | Eric Baker Nord born |
| 1951 | Walter named Knight of the Royal Order of Vasa by the Swedish government |
| 1953 | Walter elected president of the Lorain County (Ohio) Mental Health Association board |
| 1954 | Emily Jane Nord born |
| 1954 | Walter elected president of the Ohio Mental Health Association |
| 1956 | Carlotte Ann Nord born |
| 1956 | Eric Townsend Nord born |
| 1958 | Walter receives an honorary doctorate from Oberlin College |
| 1958 | Bruce Beard Tinker Nord born |
| 1958 | Richard Elbert Nord born |
| 1959 | Eric elected to the Oberlin City Council |
| 1959 | Walter receives a second Swedish award, Commander of the Royal Order of Vasa |
| 1961 | Walter and Virginia establish the Walter and Virginia Nord Scholarship Fund |
| 1961 | Kathleen Tinker Nord born |
| 1965 | Mary Nord Ignat dies |
| 1966 | Evan Nord and Cynthia Whitehead Tinker married |
| 1966 | Walter named "Ohio Small Businessman of the Year" |
| 1967 | Ethan Walter Nord born |

1967   Walter Nord dies
1968   Allyson Mary Nord born
1969   Joseph Allen Ignat dies
1973   Virginia Nord dies
1974   Eric and Evan receive Community Service Awards
           from Oberlin College
1978   Evan and Cindy move to South Carolina
2004   Evan Nord dies

## THE COMPANIES

1908   U.S. Automatic Company founded
1919   American Specialty Company founded
1919   U.S. Automatic completes a large, all-electric plant
1922   General Stone Company founded
1929   Walter named receiver for U.S. Automatic
1935   U.S. Automatic Corporation incorporated
1936   General Stone Company closes
1940   U.S. Automatic begins to manufacture wartime products
1941   A frozen-food plant designed by Evan opens in Amherst
1942–1943   U.S. Automatic receives government awards for war-
           bond purchases and for excellence in production
1944   A frozen-food plant designed by Evan opens in Oberlin
1944   U.S. Automatic formalizes a policy to contribute 5 per-
           cent of pretax domestic profits to charity
1944   A frozen-food plant designed by Evan opens in Oberlin
1950   Walter becomes president of SuperVision, Inc.
1952   Half of U.S. Automatic's equipment auctioned
1954   Manufacturing rights to airless painting equipment
           purchased from Bede Products, of Cleveland
1954   Bede Products Corporation (later Nordson Corpora-
           tion) established
1954   Nordson reaffirms the U.S. Automatic policy of contrib-
           uting 5 percent of pretax domestic profits to charity
1957   Bede Products Corporation changes its name to
           Nordson Corporation
1960   Kenneth Daly hired as the first non-family upper-level
           Nordson executive
1960   Nordson reorganizes its sales system
1960   Nordson takes its first steps toward expansion into
           European markets
1962   Nordson begins to manufacture adhesive-applying
           equipment
1963   Nordson's first five-year plan completed

## THE COMPANIES, *continued*

1965   American Specialty Company merged into U.S. Automatic

1966   After a series of mergers of Nordson and its subsidiaries into U.S. Automatic, U.S. Automatic changes its name to Nordson

1965   Nordson establishes its European headquarters in Brussels

1968   New Nordson offices in Amherst completed

1969   Nordson receives its first award for export business from the U.S. government

1971   Nordson perfects its electrostatic powder-coating equipment

1972   Almost all of Nordson's screw machine contract business phased out

1973   Nordson celebrates large plant additions at an open house

1974   Kenneth Daly becomes the first non-family Nordson president

1975   Nordson completes its renovation of the railroad freight depot in Amherst

1975   Nordson founds an Old Timers Club

1978   Evan retires

1978   Nordson's purchase of packaging and robot technology begins

1979   Nordson's Norcross, Georgia, divisional headquarters opens

1979   Nordson's first robot marketed

1979   FoamMelt applying equipment marketed

1979   First Nordson shares traded in the over-the-counter market

1979   Nordson celebrates the twenty-fifth anniversary of its founding

1982   Eric retires as Nordson's chief executive officer; President James Taylor replaces him

1983   Nordson's Westlake office facility opens

1983   Sell-off of Nordson's packaging and robotic business begins

1985   Eric returns as Nordson's chief executive officer for six months

1986   William Madar becomes Nordson's president and chief executive officer

1986   Nordson reorganizes into geographical divisions

| 1987 | Nordson enters the nonwovens market |
|---|---|
| 1988 | Nordson begins to manufacture machinery to apply adhesives and coatings on electronic equipment |
| 1989–2000 | Nordson completes acquisitions of related companies |
| 1993 | Time 'n Talent employee volunteer program launched at Nordson |
| 1997 | Eric retires as Nordson's chairman of the board; William Madar replaces him; Edward Campbell named president |
| 2002 | Evan retires from Nordson's board of directors |
| 2004 | Chief Executive Officer Edward Campbell replaces William Madar as chairman of the board; Peter S. Hellman named president |

# THE FOUNDATIONS

| 1943 | U.S. Automatic Corporation makes gifts during a profitable period |
|---|---|
| 1952 | Walter founds The U.S. Automatic Foundation as a trust |
| 1964 | Eric becomes a trustee of The U.S. Automatic Foundation |
| 1966 | William Ginn becomes a trustee of The U.S. Automatic Foundation |
| 1967 | U.S. Automatic Foundation changes its name to Nordson Foundation |
| 1967 | Evan becomes a trustee and president of Nordson Foundation |
| 1969 | Nordson Foundation launches its first initiative project with approval of purchase of the former railroad passenger depot in Oberlin |
| 1969 | Federal Tax Reform Act mandates partial divestiture in fifteen years of Nordson stock by Nordson Foundation |
| 1976 | Oberlin Early Childhood Center completed |
| 1979 | Jeptha Carrell hired as the first full-time executive director of Nordson Foundation |
| 1980 | Community Foundation of Greater Lorain County established |
| 1982 | County Cupboard established to provide relief in a recession period |
| 1983 | Nordson Foundation's Policy Advisory Committee, including members of the Nord family, created |

## THE FOUNDATIONS, *continued*

1988    Public Services Institute at Lorain County Community
        College opens

1988    Child Care Resource Center opens in Lorain

1988    Nordson Foundation splits into The Nord Family
        Foundation and The Nordson Corporation
        Foundation

1988    Nord Family Foundation has Nordson Corporation
        redeem $38 million of shares; continues to hold
        2 percent of the company's outstanding shares

1989    Nord Family Foundation holds its first membership
        meeting

1989    Linden School opens in Elyria

1989    Henry Doll appointed executive director of The Nord
        Family Foundation

1990    Nord Family Foundation spends the year in intensive
        planning

1990    Lorain County 2020, a major community planning
        effort, begins

1991    David Ignat elected the first president of The Nord
        Family Foundation from his generation

1991    Lorain County Access to Higher Education program
        launched

1991    Constance Haqq appointed the first executive director
        of The Nordson Corporation Foundation

1992    Center for Leadership in Education founded under
        the auspices of the Community Foundation of
        Greater Lorain County

1998    John Mullaney appointed executive director of The
        Nord Family Foundation

2003    New headquarters of The Nord Family Foundation
        dedicated in Amherst

2004    Oberlin Depot opened as a community meeting
        facility

The subject I would like to speak to you about today should not come as a surprise because I have, over the past two years, touched on it many times. Nevertheless, this is the first formal announcement.

At their regular meeting last week, the Board of Directors accepted my plan to step down as Chief Executive Officer at the end of this fiscal year, a date which closely coincides with my 65th birthday. I plan to continue as a Nordson employee and as Chairman of the Board, serving in that capacity at the pleasure of the Board.

My reasons for this change are simple.

1. I feel that together we have built an organization of very capable people and that we must provide them the opportunity to move up into top positions.

2. I can continue to make a strong input into the general conduct of the business without full-time or detailed involvement.

3. I feel that as one grows older, one often becomes less vigorous and less likely to take risks. As I will tell you later, that would not be in keeping with our corporate character of the past.

4. I have been in the management of the company or its predecessor company for 42 years, the last 28 years as head of Nordson since its inception. That is long enough.

The Board accepted my recommendation and unanimously elected Jim Taylor as President and Chief Executive Officer effective November 1, 1982. The post of Chief Operating Officer will cease to exist, at least for now. I'm sure you will agree that Jim is very well qualified and I am confident that he can count on your strong support as he can on mine.

While this opportunity is at hand, I would like to add a few remarks about how I have viewed my role in the past and about the corporate philosophy and objectives which have evolved over the last several decades.

Because the company was closely-held by my family in the years following 1935, the character of the company was largely synonymous with the character of the owner-operators. I can truthfully say that my parents brought up my sister, brother and me without any desire to become wealthy. We were "programmed" by example to try to develop a

# APPENDIX 2

## ADDRESS BY ERIC NORD TO THE NORDSON MANAGEMENT AND PROFESSIONAL CLUB, AUGUST 26, 1982

"good" company and so the understanding came about that as owner-operators we had two principal tasks:

> First, to make the business highly productive.
>
> Second, to see to it that the fruits of that productivity were shared, in some reasonable manner, by all of our constituents: Customers, employees, shareholders, suppliers and our community.

We came to hold certain operating philosophies. For example, we believed we should:

> Work and invest for the long term.
>
> Accept risk-taking as normal.
>
> Strive for an ambience in which people would like to work.
>
> Seek excellence in personnel and product.
>
> Encourage innovation.
>
> Encourage entrepreneurship through stock ownership.
>
> And last, but very important, treat customers as we would want to be treated.

Some might feel that as our family members become less directly involved, the company's character might change. Of course, it has already changed some. Nordson's very success has led to growth and growth has meant that many of us are not as close to one another as we once were. I am saddened by the thought that there are now many members of the company team whom I do not know personally. On the other hand, the company is in a very strong position and the Nord families are not leaving the scene. We are, to an increasing extent, leaving the future success and internal harmony of Nordson to you—our extended family.

Before I say anything about my hopes for Nordson in the next decade, let me tell you a little of the early history which helped to mold Nordson. Nordson was born in adversity. Its predecessor company, U. S. Automatic Corporation, rose out of the ashes of failure.

In 1929, my father was appointed by the court as receiver for a bankrupt company. Starting with a plant full of run-down machinery, no capital, and in the midst of the Great Depression characterized by the stock market crash in 1929 and the bank holiday of 1933, he and some very loyal employees brought the company out of bankruptcy and reorganized it in 1935. I refer to that period as "out of bankruptcy into poverty." I was working in the machine shop then and can remember often waiting for small, inexpensive tools to arrive—always C.O.D.

Business began to improve a little and then came the sharp recession of 1937. Hitler invaded Poland in 1939 and the United States started rearming and we became heavily involved. By 1941, the activity was frantic. During the period 1939 through 1945, more machine tool production capacity was created in the United States than existed in the country prior to that period. When the war was over, productive capacity in our segment of industry was hopelessly overbuilt; our business was again marginal. The company soon was short of working capital. In 1946, we borrowed $100,000 from a Cleveland bank. They charged us a premium of ½% because of our credit risk—that brought the interest rate from 2% up to 2½%. That same year, as a frame of reference, my father's salary, as President of the company, was $18,000.

Business continued to be cut-throat in the face of tremendous over-capacity. By 1949, the company was in a severe cash-flow bind because our friendly Cleveland bank would not renew our loan. The only money available to us was $75,000 at the unheard of interest rate of 6% and that was from an individual on the basis of our pledging all of our property and equipment as collateral.

It was under the pressure of this traumatic period that my father, brother and I decided to find some way to change the basic nature of the business. Since we had no free time nor any money to work with, we decided to shrink the business to about half its volume by keeping only our best customers and selling at auction the equipment not needed to support the lower volume. During the next two years, we let employment fall by attrition, started to cull customers and made preparations for the auction which took place in January, 1952. The proceeds of about $600,000 allowed us to pay all of our debts. We also gained time to plan our future and, curiously, we found that with lower capacity we could be more selective and the business we took was more profitable. We had turned a corner but now where should we go?

In 1954 we bought the rights to the Bede Airless Spray Process and Equipment. It was almost a disaster for the first couple of years but we used the meager profits from our screw machine products business to cover the start-up costs of getting into this proprietary equipment business. Any one of the several established spray equipment manufacturers could probably have wiped us out during that period if they had decided to enter the Airless Spray Equipment business. Happily that didn't happen and by 1960 we were well established in the special niches we chose to pursue in the paint spraying equipment field.

In 1963–64 we entered the hot melt equipment field through our internal product development activities. Again, we used the profits from our other businesses to pay the large start-up costs. Again, the then dominant equipment manufacturer could have murdered us during the 1965–70 period but by 1972 it was they who had lost the market. During the late 1960's we found ourselves in patent litigation on electrostatic equipment which we had developed several years earlier. The stakes were substantially over a million dollars. It was a stressful period because we had no way of getting that much money if we were to lose.

I cite these historical notes to make the point that things have not always been easy and risks have often been high. That probably will often be the case with anything that is really worth pursuing. My hope for Nordson is that we continue to be a venturesome company operating somewhere out on the leading edge and moving out of activities which have become commonplace and taken on the characteristics of a "commodity" business. This can only happen if we continue to encourage innovators and entrepreneurs. I see the country's industrial sectors as being in the midst of a technological revolution which will strongly challenge us for the next decades.

The question is often asked, "How secure is Nordson from a takeover by another company?" At the present time, the Nordson stock is held approximately in the following way: Nord families, 40%, Nordson Foundation (all of my mother's stock), 10%; Directors plus the 10 largest employee holdings and 10 largest retiree holdings, 15% When the holdings of the other employees are added, the total is about 70% in these groups; this is a very secure picture. The next question might be "How likely is it that the Nords would sell their stock?" I cannot speak for each of the family members. However, I feel quite confident that they share my belief that as long as Nordson follows the principles that formed it, each of us are best served by continuing our ownership. I am quite certain each of us values that ownership more than short-term financial gain.

One more hope is that while we must continue to emphasize the importance of brains and reason, we continue to pay attention to "heart." In 1644 a French mathematician/philosopher made what was probably the first mechanical calculator. Today many know his name because a computer language is named for him—Pascal. I would like to suggest that we remember him for his observation, "The heart has reasons that reason may never know."

I would like to thank all Nordson employees everywhere, present and past, for your efforts and support, and look forward to continuing to work with you and for you.

Evan Nord was my uncle, my mother's brother. All who knew him would agree that he was a remarkable man, a quiet presence, a diligent worker, and a man who not only cared about but cared for his fellow man. He had an extraordinary passion for helping those who were struggling with life, especially if their struggle was from no fault of their own. He had a passion for preserving history for future generations. Today, I want to tell you a few stories about Evan, which I hope in a personal way will describe the man I knew and loved.

During the time that my brother, David, and I were growing up, Evan lived just down the street from us here in Oberlin. He was a bachelor at the time, and was a frequent visitor to our home. He was our favorite guest. It seems that nearly every Saturday morning we would accompany him to "the shop" while he cleaned up a few things, and we familiarized ourselves with the sights and considerable smells of a machine shop. We waited anxiously for the candy bar that was always bought for us from that green vending machine in the central building. David had a Baby Ruth; I would get a Clark bar.

He loved that place. He loved the look of the steel parts. He would show them to us, admire the finishes. He carried this love with him into his restoration projects. While his arrival was always characterized by a storm of activity and plaster dust, his departure left a wake of restored exteriors and interiors decorated with surfaces and appliances of gleaming stainless steel. I think he was born to be a mechanical engineer.

He would join us for part of our annual vacation. He would come to the cottage on Lake Michigan and, as our guest, our pal, our entertainer, was a central part of some of our best times there. He and my mother were as close as siblings can be. He and my father were the best of friends. He was a part of the family in those days, and I am sure we were one of his few diversions in a period when the work of maintaining a struggling business and starting up a new one were particularly challenging.

He was young then, and he taught us how to wink at girls (mostly from afar) and mutter, "Hey, babe" (mostly when the car windows were shut) at the cute girls on the sidewalk as he drove by. In spite of this obvious interest, and also in spite of my parents' diligent efforts to get him (as we boys put it) hitched, nothing worked. We had many "dinners at the house" where poor Evan was introduced to various single women in what I'm sure were long and difficult evenings. I don't know how he put up with it.

Then, on the tennis court, he met Cindy—and that was the end of that.

Evan married Cindy and adopted her three children—Eric, Bruce, and Katie—as his own. They bought, from my father, the house in which I grew up, and there he and Cindy had Ethan and Allyson together. Evan, of course, immediately virtually dismantled the building and restored it with great care into the beautiful place it is today. I visited the house from time to time, and while I know that it was full of life, activity, and neighborhood kids when we were there, it seemed even more full of life with Evan and Cindy's family.

I remember being slack jawed visiting while I was on leave from the navy. Evan was great with us when we were kids, but there was "no roughhousing." We sat in the living room and carried on a conversation with kids coming in and out, Allyson hanging from one of Daddy's arms, dogs barking and running around. It was amazing. I, being a squared-away naval officer, asked, "Evan, how do you put up with this?" His answer: "Put up with what?" This was not the man I grew up with.

Even though he now had a young and growing family, he did what he always had done, both led and labored to improve the community and help those in need. He became the president of what was by then Nordson Foundation, and, with the help of that foundation, his own resources, his family, and countless others, he helped or started the Oberlin Early Childhood Center, the Oberlin Depot, the Center for the Sightless, the old Oberlin Community Center, O.H.I.O. and several of its properties, two community foundations, and on and on and on. As I say, he was indefatigable.

Evan was a younger brother, living in the penumbra of a brilliant "older" brother. While I can tell you from experience that this is not a bad thing, it has its own tensions and challenges. Evan handled it well, and together (along with countless others) he and Eric transformed a struggling machine shop into Nordson, an equipment manufacturing company that remains independent in a time of merger mania and successful beyond what I expect was either of the brothers' wildest expectations.

I worked there for a time, and in spite of being 25 years his junior, I could never keep up with him. But he was my mentor, my teacher—and he was also clairvoyant. It seemed that each and every time I turned off my machine to adjust something or change a tool, he was there, at my elbow, asking what was wrong. How he knew, I will never understand. It couldn't have been the sound—the din in that place was deafening. It must have been telepathy.

As time went on, daughter Katie wanted a horse. Just one. Maybe a little one. That little horse would start them on a path that would change their lives—completely. As time went on, he decided to retire from Nordson, while staying on the board until very recently, and move to South Carolina. As time went on, he and Cindy built the most beautiful horse farm I have ever seen, one that is now home to dozens of horses and countless show and competition awards. True to form, they take in foundling dogs at the farm—nearly two dozen of them have found shelter and sustenance at Meadow Ridge Farm. Someone who has been to the farm told me that when he passes on, he wants to come back as a Nord dog or a Nord horse. Whatever Evan or his family did, Evan wanted them to do and be the best.

Even though he moved away from Lorain County in body, he never moved away in spirit. The Nordson board meetings brought him back fairly often, as did foundation work, but often he just came to be with his friends. It would be breakfast at IHOP and golf with old friends, followed by fried perch at the Polish Community Center in Lorain.

He was the first president of The Nord Family Foundation at its conversion in 1987. As its first president, he did a lot to establish and instill the traditions with which that foundation operates today. I illustrate those principles as follows: Every three years the members of the foundation gather together for a retreat. The trustees report on the projects and progress of the foundation, and the members give their advice and counsel to the trustees as to what they would like to see the foundation do in the future. Several years ago we, the members, more or less formally did what we had been doing informally for some time: We asked Eric and Evan for comment about where they would like to see the foundation go. In the foundation world this is called "donor intent."

The brothers were pretty tight lipped. They said very little about the "what," noting that the trustees would be far better informed about community needs at the time of such decisions than they could be now. Evan spoke somewhat more forcefully about the "where." He wanted to be sure that the foundation continued to apply most of its future efforts in Lorain County.

But Evan was adamant about the "how." He described in no uncertain terms that he wanted the foundation as an organization and the trustees as individuals to conduct the business of the foundation and relations with grant seekers as he always did, with honesty, unselfishness, forthrightness, and sensitivity to preserve the dignity of the grant seeker. He wanted us always to view grants not as gifts but as investments, investments in the community.

I will tell you a story, one that I told at the opening of the headquarters of the foundation at the Sandstone Museum Center in Amherst.

Evan had donated that building to the foundation for its use and for the use of the community. He had dedicated it to the memory of his sister, Mary, and of my father and had given it as an anonymous gift. I was the president of the foundation when he made his wishes known during a meeting with lawyers and architects. I could only smile and say to him, "Sure, Evan, a gift this size, to the foundation, to be kept anonymous in Lorain County. Right."

But he insisted.

I know some of you were there at the dedication of that building, where I told the story, but I believe it is fitting to retell it today. It illustrates what kind of man Evan was:

Evan had promised his father, Walter Nord, that he, Evan, would see to it that a sandstone museum and historical society was built in Amherst. Walter came to this part of the country to take a job as an engineer in the quarries and wanted to see that sandstone quarry history preserved.

Evan was mulling over where the center could be built, and one night, in a dream, he saw the old sandstone Grange Hall on Milan Avenue. He thought that that hall and the surrounding largely vacant property would be ideal for the center. He mustered his real estate and legal buddies and wrangled an invitation to the next grange meeting.

At that meeting, they presented their proposal to the small number of graying heads that represented what was still extant of agriculture in Amherst, Ohio. The proposal was this: He, Evan, would buy the Grange Hall, restore it, endow it, and make it the centerpiece of the Sandstone Museum Center. They, the grange members, would have a lease to meet at the property for as long as they liked.

The gray heads huddled, took a vote, and accepted the proposal in minutes. They had no concerns as to whether Evan was a man of his word. No one ever had that worry.

After the meeting and on the way out, one of the gentlemen came to Evan personally, shook his hand, and thanked him with these words: "Mr. Nord, during our last meeting, we all struggled with the question of how we, the few remaining grange members, could afford to keep the place going and open. None of us had an answer. So we then had a short prayer meeting to ask God for help.

"Mr. Nord, *you* are the answer to our prayer."

Evan Nord was the answer to a lot of people's prayers.

Evan spent his last days of good health preparing for a gathering of most of his extended family at the farm: It was a trustees' and members' meeting of the foundation. He spent his days making sure the place was shipshape and his evenings looking over the family tree, to make sure he would keep the names of all the children straight. He fell ill as we gathered. He slept most of the time during his final illness, but he would awaken from time to time. Each of us had a chance to visit him, talk to him, and have our hand squeezed in response. He saw most of his family during that final time.

If you can keep a secret, I will tell you that his family smuggled his beloved dog, Mr. Pickens, in to see him in the hospital. The little dog sensed that there was trouble and gently snuggled next to him. Evan patted his head one last time. Not long after that, Evan slipped away.

Now he returns to his beloved Lorain County to join his mother, his father, his sister, Mary, her husband, Joe, and the first of my generation to pass on, Chip, in the family plot at Westwood.

So all of us can be confident that—though not today, it is after all Sunday, a day of rest, but tomorrow—the angels will be organized into work groups. They will be given their assignments and told where to go pick up their tools. Some, but probably not quite enough, instructions will be given about what to do and how to do it. Evan will probably miss a few details, because he will assume that the angels are as smart and knowledgeable about the tasks at hand as he is. Most of them will not be. But he will make it right, by making rounds, visiting each work group, and straightening things out as they go along.

They will forge ahead. The tasks may vary, but they will no doubt all fit under the rubric of: "Let's clean this place up." Yes, Evan will find chores in Paradise.

Most of the crews will be devoted to cleanup and fix up, but not all of them. He will organize some other, special crews to whom he will devote particular attention. These crews will be devoted to helping those . . . fallen angels. Those crews will be busy helping where they can, inspiring others, and always bringing and keeping humility in their thoughts and demeanor. They will work together and make investments in those who are not so well adjusted to their surroundings.

Early some morning, not long from now, you might find yourself outside, just before dawn. Should that happen, I urge you to look up to the heavens. There you might see the Morning Star, the brightest star in the sky. Actually, it is not a star but the planet Venus, sort of a younger brother. On that day you might notice that it somehow looks different. If it does, join me in believing that Evan noticed it too, and saw it as a beautiful historic property worthy of care, restoration, and preservation. His crews got busy, and, like so many properties around us here, it was restored, beautified, and burnished for our enjoyment and for the enjoy-ment of generations to come.

That Venus will be like Evan was when he was among us: shining brilliantly, full of energy, reflective, and up early in the morning.

All who have known either cannot help but be inspired and awed by their light.

# INITIALS, ACRONYMS, AND ABBREVIATIONS

NOTES

| | |
|---|---|
| AHS | Amherst Historical Society, Amherst, Ohio |
| ANT | *Amherst* [Ohio] *News-Times;* microfilm, Amherst Public Library; clippings, AHS |
| AS | Alvin Silverman, "He Must Be an Inventor," *Case Alumnus,* April 1945, 14–15 (reprint); NCVA |
| ASHFY | *American Swedish Historical Foundation Yearbook;* American Swedish Historical Museum |
| AWN | *Amherst* [Ohio] *Weekly News;* microfilm, Amherst Public Library |
| BC | Bob Cotleur, "Eric and Evan Nord: They Have a Philosophy," *Lorain Journal,* January 26, 1970; NFP |
| BG | Barbara Griffith, interviewer, Nordson Corporation Oral History Project, 1995–1996; transcripts, NCW, access restricted |
| BGC | Chronology created by Barbara Griffith for the Nordson Corporation Oral History Project (unpaginated, appended to BGS); NCW |
| BGS | "Nordson Corporation Oral History Project: Summary by Barbara S. Griffith, 1998"; NCW |
| CB | Cindy Binns, "Nordson Corporation: History of Acquisitions, Mergers and Divestitures," April 23, 1992; NFP |
| CN | Cynthia "Cindy" Nord |
| CWRUA | Case Western Reserve University Archives, Cleveland, Ohio |
| DWI | David Walter Ignat |
| EAB | "E" Award Booklet: *Presenting,* dinner souvenir booklet by Walter G. Nord, 1943; NFP |
| ECT | *Elyria* [Ohio] *Chronicle-Telegram;* microfilm, OHS |
| ETN | Eric Thomas Nord |
| EWN | Evan Walter Nord |
| FAVA | Firelands Association for the Visual Arts, Oberlin, Ohio |
| FRP | Fred R. Powers, author of histories, ca. 1974–1976; manuscripts, AHS |
| FVO | Fay Van Nuys Ott, *Amherst Pictorial History.* Amherst, Ohio: N.p., 2001 |
| INT | Interview with . . . |
| JAI | Joseph Allen "Joe" Ignat (father) |
| JBN | Jane Baker Nord |
| JC | Jeptha "Jep" Carrell |
| JD | James "Jim" Doughman |
| JH | Jeanne Harrah, interviewer, The Nord Family Foundation Oral History Project, 1992 |
| JNI | Joseph Nord "Joe" Ignat (son) |
| JRC | John R. "Jack" Clark |
| KHD | Kenneth H. "Ken" Daly |

| | |
|---|---|
| LJ | *Lorain* [Ohio] *Journal;* microfilm, Lorain Public Library |
| LMJ | *Lorain* [Ohio] *Morning Journal;* microfilm, Lorain Public Library; undated clippings, AHS |
| MAH | Mary Ann Hellrigel, "The Nordson Corporation: Global Leader in Industry and Still a Good Neighbor," 1992; manuscript, NFP |
| MDM | Marlene Deahl Merrill, interviewer, OHIO Oberlin Oral History Project, 2002–2003; audiotapes and transcripts, OHIO |
| MP | Martha Pickrell, interviewer, OHIO Nord history book, 2001–2004; audiotapes, transcripts, and notes, OHIO |
| NCAB | "Walter G. Nord," *National Cyclopedia of American Biography* (Clifton, N.J.: James T. White & Co., 1975), 56: 165–166 |
| NCAR | *Nordson Corporation Annual Report;* NCW |
| NCVA | Nordson Corporation vault (engineering building), Amherst, Ohio |
| NCW | Nordson Corporation, Westlake, Ohio |
| NFAR | *Nordson Foundation Annual Report;* NFF |
| NFF | The Nord Family Foundation, Amherst, Ohio |
| NFFAR | *The Nord Family Foundation Annual Report;* NFF |
| NFFV92 | Jeanne Harrah, *The History of The Nord Family Foundation, October 9, 1992;* videotape and transcript, NFF |
| NFFV99 | The Nord Family Foundation, *Nord Family Foundation Member Retreat, June 25–27, 1999;* videotape and transcript, NFF |
| NFP | Nord family papers |
| NN | *Nordson News;* NCVA, NFP |
| NNL | *Nordson Newsletter;* NFP |
| OECC | Oberlin Early Childhood Center, Oberlin, Ohio |
| OHIO | Oberlin Historical and Improvement Organization / Oberlin Heritage Center, Oberlin, Ohio; pre-1993 records housed at the Oberlin College Archives, newer records and research material compiled for this volume housed at the Monroe House |
| OHS | Ohio Historical Society, Columbus, Ohio |
| ONT | *Oberlin News-Tribune;* NFP |
| OSS | Ohio Secretary of State, Columbus, Ohio |
| PM | Patricia "Pat" Murphy |
| RFL | Roy F. Larson, "Walter G. Nord, 1884–1967," *American Swedish Historical Foundation Yearbook,* 1967, 51–55; NFP |
| TH | Thompson Hine LLP archives, Cleveland, Ohio |
| USA | U.S. Automatic Company/Corporation, Amherst, Ohio |
| WDG | William D. "Bill" Ginn |
| WGN | Walter G. "W.G." Nord |
| WRHS | Western Reserve Historical Society, Cleveland, Ohio, repository for Nordson Foundation / Nordson Family Foundation records and for The Nord Family Foundation Oral History Project, 1992 |

## CHAPTER 1

1. Account of ETN's trip: ETN and EWN, INT MP, August 23, 2002. Otto's origins and forebears: Research was conducted in Sweden and reported to WGN in letters dated November 29, 1953 and April 10, 1954 from Gustav Adolfsson, Stockholm, who had hired Osvald Stockefors as the researcher. A more complete genealogy, entitled "Walter G. Nord: His Father's Family Back-

ground," was prepared later and translated by Ann B. Weissmann (manuscript, n.d.). The facts in that genealogy, which is at NFF, are the same as those printed in the two letters mentioned in the text, so one may assume that Stockefors wrote it. Swedish historical information: Vilhelm Moberg, *A History of the Swedish People* (translated by Paul Britten Austin; New York: Pantheon Books, 1972), quotations on p. 39. An excellent source on the lives of nineteenth-century Swedes in the United States is Moberg's trilogy: *The Emigrants, a Novel* (translated by Gustaf Lannestock; New York: Simon and Schuster, 1951); *Unto a Good Land: A Novel* (translated by Gustaf Lannestock; New York: Simon and Schuster, 1954); and *The Last Letter Home, a Novel* (translated by Gustaf Lannestock; New York: Simon and Schuster, 1961).

2. Steamboat and Minnesota stories: ETN and EWN, INT MP, August 23, 2002. Otto's arrival, age, and naturalization information, Otto and Mary's marriage, Mary's family information: Ashtabula County (Ohio) Probate Court, Naturalization Record No. 2, 195 (Ashtabula County Genealogical Society microfilm reel 1, frame 138); "Walter G. Nord: His Father's Family Background" (translated by Ann B. Weissmann; manuscript, n.d.), NFF. Ashtabula information: Ashtabula County Genealogical Society, *Ashtabula County History Then and Now: A History of the People of the County by the People of the County* (Dallas, Tex.: Taylor Publishing Co., 1985), 39. Otto's occupation: Ashtabula County Probate Court, Birth Registrations and Corrections #3339, Emily A. Nord Birth Application, 1953. Children's birth dates: two-page genealogical summary, NFP; Ashtabula County Genealogical Society, Birth Records, 1867–1909 (Olive, Emily, Frank, Walter). Federal Census 1880, Ohio, ABAB, 273B (Ashtabula County, Ashtabula Township).

3. Movement of Scandinavians to Denmark Township: *Ellsworth's Historical Sketches of Ashtabula Co., Ohio* (Ashtabula, Ohio: Ashtabula Star-Beacon, 1986–1988), quotations on p. 171. Land purchase: Ashtabula County, Recorder's Deed Index, Denmark Township, 103. WGN's recollections: "W.G. Nord Designed New Products, New Jobs," *Everybody's Business,* November 1945, 20. Help in construction of house and memories of Denmark village: ETN and EWN, INT MP, August 23, 2002. Federal Census, Ohio, Ashtabula County, 1900, Denmark Township, Census Microfilm Records, Roll 1238, Book 2, 35a.

4. Description of crops: WGN, "Axel Hallstrom in Memoriam," ASHFY, 1966, 74. WGN's values and early education: ETN and EWN, INT MP, August 23, 2002; NFFV92; ETN, INT MP, October 17, 2001.

5. Federal Census, 1900, Ohio, Ashtabula County, 1900, Denmark Township, Census Microfilm Records, Roll 1238, Book 2, 35a. Herman's graduation information: Nord family data prepared by James P. Conway, Case Western Reserve University, NFP. Additional information on Herman: "Dedication of the Herman J. Nord Memorial Library," ASHFY, 1957, 72–78. Frank's teaching: ETN and EWN, INT MP, August 23, 2002. WGN's early interests and ambitions: ETN, INT BG; ETN, INT MP, October 17, 2001. Otto's ambition to become self-sufficient: RFL, 51. WGN's high school, including the quotation: *Jefferson Educational Institute* (pamphlet), 1908, 7–8, Henderson Memorial Public Library, Jefferson, Ohio; WGN's diploma (copy), NFP.

6. WGN's life at college: obituary, LJ, May 17, 1967; FRP, "An Industry Grows in Amherst," 9; AS, 14–15; ETN, INT JH. WGN's grades: Registrar's Office, Adelbert College, 1909 transcript, CWRUA. WGN's friends: WGN, EAB, 6–7, 38–39, NFP; and the following CWRUA items: *The Reserve* [Western Reserve University year-

NOTES
TO
PAGES
5–12

book], 1903; *The Differential* [Case School of Applied Science yearbook], 1907, 50; *The Differential,* 1910, 39, 42. WGN's degrees and thesis: commencement programs of Adelbert College and Case, 1909, NFP; WGN's thesis (copy), CWRUA.

7. Chronology of WGN's positions: his genealogical notes, NFP; NCAB, 165. Meeting Virginia Grieve: EWN, INT MP, August 23, 2002. Information on Virginia and her family: Virginia's obituary, ONT, November 8, 1973; RFL, 51; ETN and EWN, INT MP, August 23, 2002; Federal Census 1880, Ohio, Cleveland, vol. 13, Dist. 27, Sheet 59; Cleveland city directories, 1880, 1885, 1891; ETN, INT MP, October 16, 2002. Death of Thomas Grieve: August 17, 1901, Woodland Cemetery records, Cleveland; Cleveland Public Library necrology index. Virginia's grade school: report cards, NFP. Virginia's high school and premarriage work: ETN, INT JH. Virginia and WGN's wedding: Grace Church, marriage certificate, NFP. Elizabeth Grieve's arrival in Amherst: her obituary, ANT, June 17, 1938.

## CHAPTER 2

1. Quarrying in Amherst and South Amherst: Robert G. Armstrong, *Amherst's Story* (Amherst, Ohio: Amherst Old Home Week Committee, 1914), 81–84; Stephen H. Paschen, *Quarry Town: The History of Amherst, Ohio, 1811–1900* (Amherst, Ohio: Amherst Historical Society, 2003), 47–68; numerous items in AHS files, including "The Largest Sand Stone Quarry in the World," *North Amherst Argus,* November 28, 1901, and Peggy Engel, "The Quarries: One Hundred Years of Hazards, Low Pay and Crude Conditions," LJ, January 12, 1975, and articles from the *Lorain Daily News,* April 3, 1913; ECT, February, 1960; ETN, INT JH. Early history of Amherst: FVO, 4, 178, 180–185; E. Valerie Jenkins and Elizabeth Anderson, *Amherst, Our Community* (Amherst, Ohio: Amherst Exempted Village Schools, 1992), 15–16; Valerie Jenkins, "The Past Is Not Forgotten," ANT, July 19, 1979. Passenger station date: *All Aboard!* ca. 1990, Nordson Corporation brochure, NFP, [4]. Central School construction: FVO, 172. The school was largely rebuilt after a fire in 1907. Stonecutters' quotation from the monument.

2. WGN's work and the Cleveland Stone Company: FRP, "An Industry Grows in Amherst," 10; Robert G. Armstrong, *Amherst's Story* (Amherst, Ohio: Amherst Old Home Week Committee, 1914), 88. Egeland's chronology of WGN and Virginia's coming to Amherst and various quotations: FRP, "But Whom Say Ye That I Am?" Early locations of the Nord family in Amherst: ETN, INT MP, October 16, 2002. Mary's birth date: handwritten genealogy by WGN, NFP. WGN's difficulties: ETN, INT BG; ETN, INT MP, August 23, 2002, including the quotation.

3. Purchase of the lot and construction of the house on Spring Street: Lorain County Deed Records, vol. 165, 248. Loan: mortgage deed (copy), NFP. Description of the house and neighborhood: ETN and EWN, INT MP, August 23, 2002; ETN, INT JH. History of the church: *Dedication, St. George's Chapel at Amherst Sandstone Center, May 17, 1998,* AHS; George Franklin Smythe, *A History of the Diocese of Ohio to 1918* (Cleveland: Diocese of Ohio, 1931), 510. Size of the congregation: ETN, INT JH. Services: ANT, April 18, 1919. Amherst's population: FVO, 4. Community life: various issues, ANT, 1919–1924, at the Amherst Public Library. USA: Robert G. Armstrong, *Amherst's Story* (Amherst, Ohio: Amherst Old Home Week Committee, 1914), 187; AWN, February 27, 1919; ANT, January 1, 1920, January 15, 1920. Location of USA: JD, INT JH. Nabakowski: FVO, 20. Editor's feelings: ANT, February 19, 1920. Examples of town spirit: ANT, May 6, 1920,

July 1, 1920, October 28, 1920, ANT, August 18, 1921; Valerie Jenkins, "The Past Is Not Forgotten," ANT, July 19, 1979; E. Valerie Jenkins and Elizabeth Anderson, *Amherst, Our Community* (Amherst, Ohio: Amherst Exempted Village Schools, 1992), 17; FVO, 162–163. Smythe and Powers examples: ANT, July 29, 1920, January 15, 1920. Smythe as youngest mayor: EAB, [23]. Biographical sketch of Powers: FVO, 176.

4. Articles of incorporation at OSS: American Specialty, vol. 226, 652; General Stone Co., vol. 257, 171. American Specialty products: ETN, INT MP, August 23, 2002, November 7, 2002; ETN, INT BG. Repair business: ANT, May 8, 1924. ETN's young ambitions: ETN, INT JH. Locations: FRP, "An Industry Grows in Amherst," 10. First-year sales: Nordson Corp. records, NCVA, Box 19. Elizabeth Nord's mortgage: deed (copy), NFP. Machinists coming with WGN from quarries: ETN and EWN, INT MP, August 23, 2002, October 16, 2002; ETN, INT JH. Virginia's office help: ETN, INT JH.

5. Articles of incorporation at OSS: General Stone, vol. 257, 171. Description of business and travels to Opekiska: ETN, INT BG; ETN, INT JH; FRP, "An Industry Grows in Amherst," 13–15, quotation on p. 13; ETN and EWN interviews, NFFV92; ETN and EWN, INT MP, August 23, 2002.

6. Accounts of childhood visits to Denmark Township: ETN, INT JH; ETN and EWN, INT MP, August 23, 2002. Deaths of Otto and Mary, Otto's estate: ETN and EWN, INT MP, August 23, 2002; obituaries, *Ashtabula Star-Beacon,* October 11, 1926, February 20, 1931; Edgewood Cemetery, Ashtabula, interment files, Ashtabula County Genealogical Society microfilm, Ashtabula Township, 16; State of Ohio, Death Certificate of Otto Nord, October 11, 1926; Ashtabula County Probate Court records (microfilm), 1926, 1927, 1931. Otto's second land purchase, 1897: Ashtabula County Deed Records, book 144, 555. Family life: EWN and ETN, INT JH; NFFV99. Mary: ETN, INT MP, June 16, 2003.

7. WGN and school events and problems: ANT, March 16, 1920, April 15, 1920, January 18, 1923, March 1, 1923, March 8, 1923, June 7, 1923, August 2, 1923, September 6, 1923, December 6, 1923, May 1, 1924; ECT, February 20, 1924. Marion Steele: FVO, 176.

8. Clark and Post: JRC, INT PM, May 11, 2004, May 12, 2004. Silsbee noted in ANT, March 1, 1923. According to JRC and Ronald Cocco ("A Brief History of Clark and Post Architects, Inc."; manuscript, May 2004; OHIO), the history of the firm "started in the early 1900s, when Ralph S. Silsbee, a 1903 graduate of Princeton University, came to Lorain County from Chicago to attend to the building of structures at Oberlin College. Projects included the Men's Building (Wilder Hall) and the Memorial Arch on Tappan Square, dedicated to Oberlin missionaries and their children who perished in the Boxer Rebellion in China. These structures were designed by Joseph Lyman Silsbee, father of Ralph Silsbee, in his office in downtown Chicago. Silsbee also proposed a plan for Tappan Square; a record of this plan is in the Oberlin College Archives. Ralph Silsbee and his wife, Esther, lived in Oberlin briefly and moved to Elyria in 1911. The firm then known as J. L. and R. S. Silsbee, Architects, moved its offices from the Elyria Block Building to the Masonic Temple Building in 1912. J. L. Silsbee died in Chicago in February 1913. Frank Lloyd Wright received his first job from J. L. Silsbee. Wright wrote of this first job in several of his books, and much of his early work is reported to have been 'in the Silsbee manner.' Wright and Ralph Silsbee were friends and would meet when Wright was in the Cleveland area.

After J. L. Silsbee died, his son Ralph continued to practice architecture in his own name in Elyria. The practice was extensive and included many of the public schools in Elyria and elsewhere in Lorain County. He was also involved in planning most of the evolving manufacturing facilities in Elyria and designed many of the city's grandest homes. When World War I ended, Alva C. Smith joined Silsbee as an apprentice, and later the partnership of Silsbee and Smith, Architects was formed. The partnership endured through the Great Depression and World War II and terminated with Silsbee's death in 1950. During the depression the firm resorted to designing toys and creating 'stock' plans for homes because of the utter lack of construction projects. Silsbee developed the concept of Gulf Farms in Elyria, which is still considered one of the finest residential developments in the area. In 1950 the firm took the name of Alva C. Smith and Associates. Alva L. Smith and John R. Clark associated with the firm in 1952. The partnership of Smith, Smith and Clark, Architects was formed in 1953 and existed until the death of Alva C. Smith in 1966. Shortly after his death, Smith and Clark, Architects was formed as a partnership and then as a professional corporation. It existed until the death of Alva L. Smith in 1975. In 1976 John Clark and Robert Post continued the practice as Clark and Post Architects, Inc. Clark retired in 1996; Post, in 2003. The firm is now owned by three of its longtime members: Ronald Cocco, Daniel Weaver, and John Mazze. Measured by continuity, Clark and Post is probably one of the oldest architectural firms in Ohio. Some of the relationships between the architectural firm and local manufacturing are of long standing. Ralph S. Silsbee, Architect, performed services for Walter Nord for many years, and the relationship has continued through the various iterations of the architectural firm and the Nords' companies. Architectural services have included the design of Nordson Corporation's world headquarters building in Westlake, Ohio and its manufacturing and engineering facilities in Amherst, in South Carolina, and in Georgia. Clark and Post and its predecessors have also participated in planning facilities sponsored by Nordson Foundation and The Nord Family Foundation, such as the Oberlin Early Childhood Center, the Firelands Association for the Visual Arts, the New Union Center for the Arts, Oberlin Community Services, the Nord Family Foundation headquarters, and the renovation of Oberlin's former passenger depot. Other facilities designed by the firm in its recent history include: the world headquarters of Moen, Inc. in North Olmsted, Ohio; the National Association of College Stores and the Lorain County Children's Home (Green Acres) in Oberlin; the Bell System Center for Technical Education in Lisle, Illinois; the Lorain County Metro Parks' French Creek Interpretive Center in Sheffield, Ohio; the Center for Leadership in Education in Elyria; the main offices of the Lorain National Bank and many of its branch facilities; and many banking facilities for the Elyria Savings and Trust Company and the Central Bank Company."

9. Mayoral election: ANT, August 16, 1923, November 8, 1923, November 15, 1923, December 13, 1923. Ohio's problems in controlling Prohibition law violators: ECT, December 9, 1924. Amherst formerly a whiskey-making center: ECT, December 5, 1924. Amherst ordinances: ANT, January 17, 1924; Amherst, Village Board, January 22, 1924–January 6, 1925, AHS. Court: Mayor's Criminal Docket, 1923–1924, Mayor's Record of Fines, 1910–1928, AHS. WGN and Virginia's stance on liquor: ETN and EWN, INT MP, August 23, 2002; ETN, INT JH. Virginia's membership in the WCTU: ANT, May 18, 1922. Various problems addressed by

the Village Board: ANT, April 3, 1924, April 17, 1924, May 8, 1924; LJ, August 6, 1924. Sewer backup quotation: ANT, April 3, 1924. Tornado response: LJ, July 10, 1924, July 12, 1924. Amherst mayoral records for the year 1925 cannot be located. School events: ECT, February 8, 1924, including the quotation, February 26, 1924; LJ, October 1, 1924, October 30, 1924.

10. Outdoor Life Park purchase: Lorain County Deed Records, vol. 163, 401–403; ETN, INT MP, June 16, 2003. News items: ANT, April 10, 1924, April 24, 1924; LJ, September 17, 1924, September 25, 1924, November 14, 1924, November 25, 1924; ANT, April 19, 1928. EWN's and ETN's memories of the park: EWN, INT JH; ETN, INT MP, August 22, 2002; ETN, INT MP, June 26, 2003. EWN's recent visits: JRC, INT PM, May 11, 2004.

## CHAPTER 3

1. Events concerning the Amherst Savings and Banking Co., William H. Schibley, USA receivership: ANT, December 20, 1928, January 3, 1929, including the quotation, January 31, 1929, February 7, 1929, February 14, 1929, February 21, 1929, February 28, 1929, March 7, 1929, March 14, 1929, March 21, 1929. FRP quotation: FRP, "An Industry Grows in Amherst," 16. ETN quotation: ETN, INT BG. Schibley died in Ashland on January 3, 1944 (ANT, January 6, 1944). Number of employees in 1935: ANT, August 9, 1935.

2. Savings bank history: ANT, January 15, 1931, July 9, 1931, July 30, 1931, August 6, 1931, August 27, 1931, September 3, 1931. Problems in the school system: ANT, January 9, 1930, October 16, 1930, October 23, 1930, October 30, 1930, April 30, 1931, May 4, 1933. Problems in the local government: ANT, February 18, 1932, March 3, 1932, March 16, 1933, May 16, 1933, July 3, 1933, January 4, 1934. Aid drives: ANT, December 24, 1930, November 10, 1932; clipping describing the Community Fund, 1930, AHS. Quotations on Amherst and Virginia: ETN, INT JH. Homeless men in jail: ANT, April 9, 1931. Virginia's food for homeless men: ETN and EWN, INT MP, August 23, 2002. Noon Day Club: ANT, December 3, 1942. Businessmen's Association, Taxpayers League: ANT, February 11, 1932, February 25, 1932, March 10, 1932.

3. Cigarette rollers: ETN, INT BG. Chuck device and fitting: ETN, INT BG; AS. Rotoscope: ETN, INT BG; clipping about Oberlin branch of company, June 30, 1949, and other Wottring documents, NCVA, Box 17; ETN, NFFV92; JRC, INT PM, May 11, 2004. ETN and EWN at American Specialty: ETN and EWN, INT MP, August 23, 2002; ETN, INT MP, October 16, 2002. Mary at Bluffton: ANT, November 29, 1935. Graduation information: Bluffton College registrar, March 22, 2004. JAI's background: JNI, INT MP, June 13, 2003. ETN in high school: ANT, September 27, 1934. Tennis quotation: EWN, INT JH. Mary Erickson Nord's death: *Ashtabula Star-Beacon,* February 20, 1931. ETN's experience at Christ Church, Oberlin: ETN, INT JH. Confirmation dates: Richard P. Lothrop, Christ Church historiographer, September 18, 2003. Virginia's activities: ETN, INT JH; ANT, April 25, 1929, May 9, 1929, November 1, 1940. Fan collection: EWN, INT JH; EWN and ETN, INT MP, August 23, 2002. The collection of about 800 fans was later given to the WRHS. School board dinner: ANT, January 4, 1934.

4. General Stone Co.: ETN, INT BG; records, NCVA, Box 17. USA incorporation: OSS, vol. 434, 210; ANT, August 9, 1935; "Record of Proceedings of U.S. Automatic Corporation," October 16, 1935, OSS; MAH, 5–15. Incorporators: ETN,

INT JH. Corporate culture: Clifford Berry, INT MP, August 22, 2002. Union benefits: ANT, January 14, 1943; MAH, 17.

5. Slowdown and WGN's response: MAH, 17–21. Zerk fitting problem: ETN, INT BG. American Specialty financial statistics: handwritten sheets, NCVA, Box 17. Vegetable washers, comment on convenience: JD, INT JH. Quotation: EWN, INT JH. Harold Ricket: FRP, "An Industry Grows in Amherst," 12. Size of washers: two-page handwritten letter, unsigned, NFP.

6. Reminiscence: Marilyn Jenne, INT MP, February 21, 2002. School board matters: ANT, August 13, 1937, March 18, 1938, April 29, 1938, June 17, 1938, July 8, 1938, July 15, 1938, August 12, 1938. Power plant controversy: ANT, February 17, 1939, February 24, 1939. Center for the Sightless: ETN, INT MP, January 28, 2003; NCAB, 165. A workshop, Skills Division, was established in 1959 and became Diversified Skills, Inc. in 1981. The workshop component split off in 1983 and is now administered by Vocational Guidance Services, which provided this information. Rotary Club activities: ANT, May 12, 1939, June 9, 1939. Elizabeth's death: ANT, June 17, 1938. Mary Nord and JAI's wedding: *Oberlin Times,* October 20, 1938; ANT, October 21, 1938. Characterization of JAI: WDG, INT JH. ETN's graduation: commencement program, NFP; notice in ANT, June 2, 1939; Case School of Applied Science, 1939 yearbook, *The Differential,* CWRUA. The name of the school was changed to Case Institute of Technology in 1947, and it merged with Western Reserve University in 1967. Herman Nord's death and burial: Cleveland Public Library necrology files. WGN's ill health: ETN, INT JH. Anniversary celebration: ANT, September 16, 1938, December 16, 1938, August 18, 1939, September 1, 1939, September 22, 1939.

## CHAPTER 4

1. Summary of World War II military service and home-front activities of Amherst residents: "Amherst Community War Record," a special issue of *Chips,* November 1946, AHS. Newspaper items: ANT, July 19, 1940, August 30, 1940. Rhodes: <http://mikeblog.blogspot.com/>.

2. Start of war manufacturing and coming of ETN and EWN to USA: MAH, 23–25; ETN, INT BG; NFFV92; ETN and EWN, INT MP, August 23, 2002, including the quotation; *Chips,* February 1945, [4]. The start of war production is dated by some sources to 1940; however, the first mention of defense work in the USA minutes is May 8, 1941, TH. WGN's secretary: Marilyn Jenne, INT JH; *Chips,* December 1941, 7. ETN's first jobs at USA: MAH, 72; ETN, INT BG; ETN, INT MP, December 16, 2002. ETN on the board: USA minutes, September 25, 1941, TH. Government contracts: ETN, INT MP, December 16, 2002. Norden bombsight quotation: ETN's address, Atlanta, October 18, 1979 (press release), NFP. Bombsight manufacture: MAH, 49, 70; *Chips,* October 1941, 1, 8. Complying with government regulations: *Chips,* September 1941, 6, November 1941, 1; ANT, July 11, 1941. Amherst Cold Storage building: USA minutes, July 3, 1941, TH; FVO, 165. EWN's responsibilities and undertakings: EWN, INT BG; ETN, INT MP, December 16, 2002; MAH, 73; *Chips,* September 1941, 8, October 1941, 8, November 1941, 8, January 1946, [4]; ANT, November 7, 1941, December 5, 1941; Clifford Berry, INT MP, June 24, 2003. EWN on the board: USA minutes, December 26, 1942, TH. Number of employees: MAH, 52 (from JAI's *Oberlin Times* interview, December 24, 1942).

3.  Launching of *Chips:* first issue, September 1941. First Christmas party: *Chips,* December 1941. Press Club: *Chips,* September 1941, 5; ANT, September 5, 1941.

4.  New construction: MAH, 49–50. Women hired: MAH, 53–56; *Chips,* April 1942, 7. Workers from surrounding areas: MAH, 83. Uniforms: *Chips,* May 1942, 8. Vacation pay: *Chips,* April 1942, 8. Number of employees: MAH, 52, n. 2. Modernization: Clifford Berry, INT MP, August 22, 2002. Product list: MAH, 48, based on *Chips,* March 1943, 1. War bonds: MAH, 53. American Specialty plating: *Chips,* February 1942, 1, 5; ETN, INT MP, December 16, 2002.

5.  Recognition of USA: ANT, September 3, 1942, December 24, 1942; MAH, 46–47. Press coverage of the "E" Award: ANT, January 14, 1943, including Karch quotation; *Chips,* "E" Award program issue, January 1943, including Patterson letter on p. 5, WGN quotation on p. 7, Lach quotation on p. 7; scrapbook made by company employees, including congratulatory telegrams, clippings, etc., NFP; *Screw Machine Engineering,* February 1943, 44.

6.  WGN's salary: MAH, 75, 77. Purchase of the house in Oberlin: Lorain County Deed Records, vol. 335, 261–262 and vol. 350, 224. JAI and his family in Oberlin: *Chips,* October 1941, 5; JNI, INT MP, June 13, 2003. The Nords' friends in Oberlin: ETN and EWN, INT MP, August 23, 2002. Living in Oberlin: ETN, INT MDM, May 21, 2002. Purchase of the Wellington farm: Lorain County Deed Records, vol. 327, 441–442, vol. 328, 517–519; AS, quotation on p. 15; ETN and EWN, INT MP, August 23, 2002. Oberlin frozen food locker: USA minutes, October 20, 1943, TH; ANT, May 11, 1944; *Chips,* June 1944, 3, January 1946, [4]; MAH, 114–115. Acquisition of SuperVision: MAH, 76. American Specialty products: *Chips,* May 1943, quotation on p. 6, August 1943, 7; AS.

7.  USA charitable contributions: MAH, 84–85; ANT, November 4, 1943; *Chips,* November 1943, 8, August 18, 1944; letter: USA minutes, 1944, TH. U.S. statistics from F. Emerson Andrews, *Corporation Giving* (New Brunswick, N.J.: Transaction Publishers, 1993 [1952]), 42 (on pp. 44–45 Andrews notes that the smallest companies gave the largest percentages). The subject was also addressed by Michael Useem, "Corporate Philanthropy," in Walter W. Powell, ed., *The Nonprofit Sector: A Research Handbook* (New Haven, Conn.: Yale University Press, 1987), 341. WGN's volunteer activities: ANT, May 13, 1943, June 3, 1943, July 15, 1943, November 11, 1943. Blood-donation facility: *Chips,* November 1946, [17]. WGN's connections with Swedish Americans: ANT, November 11, 1943; EAB, 7; RFL, 51; NCAB, 165. History of the foundation: *Welcome to the American Swedish Historical Museum . . . the 75th Anniversary,* June 2, 2001 (Philadelphia: American Swedish Historical Foundation, 2001), 10; Esther Chilstrom Meixner, "Amandus Johnson," ASHFY, 1963, 59–63. ETN's activities: ANT, October 31, 1941, November 7, 1941, March 13, 1942, April 13, 1944, September 14, 1944, September 27, 1945. ETN's draft status: ETN, INT MP, December 16, 2002. EWN's and JAI's navy service: ANT, July 13, 1944; EWN, INT JH; EWN, INT BG; *Chips,* May 1946, [2]; EWN, INT PM, May 11, 2004. Mary Ignat's editorship: *Chips,* July 1944, August 1944–August 1946.

8.  Characteristics of an effective corporate culture: Terrence E. Deal and Allan A. Kennedy, *Corporate Cultures: The Rites and Rituals of Corporate Life* (Cambridge, Mass.: Perseus Publishing, 2000), 23–103.

9.  Christmas parties: *Chips,* December 1941, 1, 4; ANT, December 26, 1941. Picnics: ANT, July 23, 1942, August 6, 1942, July 29, 1943, August 5, 1943. Baseball field: *Chips,* April 1942, 2. Health club: ANT, June 25, 1942, including the quotation.

10.  ETN's reliance on consultants, including the quotations: ETN, INT BG. Quotation: Clifford Berry, INT MP, August 22, 2002. Steps toward organization: *Chips,* May 1942, 2–4. Notifying foremen of absences: *Chips,* December 1941, 6. Hands: *Chips,* October 1941, 3. Slogan: *Chips,* April 1942, 3. Work stoppage, union vote: ANT, June 24, 1943, July 15, 1943, July 22, 1943; *Chips,* January 1944, 4, 6; EWN and Clifford Berry, INT MP, August 22, 2002; EWN, INT BG.

11.  Bond drives: ANT, June 29, 1944, July 13, 1944. Blood drives: *Chips,* July 1944, [9], September 1944, [3]. Drive to employ women: ANT, September 23, 1943, April 13, 1944. Mrs. Taft: ANT, October 26, 1944, including the quotation. Foremen's Club: *Chips,* April 1944, 3, May 1944, 4; Job evaluation system: *Chips,* May 1944, quotation on p. 2, September 1944, 8; ETN, INT MP, December 16, 2002; BGS, 23–24. EWN quotation: EWN, INT BG. WGN quotation: *Chips,* January 1945, 4. Pitching in: *Chips,* February 1945, [3], October 1944, [5]. Conversion advertisements: NCVA, Box 19. ETN's first patent: family records, noted in ETN, INT MP, April 14, 2003.

12.  Veterans committee: ANT, March 15, 1945. USA war statistics: *Chips,* September 1945, [8]. Parade: ANT, September 13, 1945, including the quotation. Picnic: ANT, August 2, 1945, August 9, 1945. Athletic field gifts: ANT, November 1, 1945, May 2, 1946, June 27, 1946. Virginia Nord's committee: ANT, October 11, 1945.

# CHAPTER 5

1.  EWN's return: *Chips,* May 1946, [2]. New products: MAH, 104. WGN's design and packing machine: ETN, INT MP, January 28, 2003. Expanding the vegetable washer business: *Chips,* April 1947, 3, January 1948, 6. Move: *Chips,* Spring 1948, 3. Open house: *Chips,* June 1946, [8]. Giving: *Chips,* October 1946, [4, 8]; ANT, May 2, 1946. Purchase of machinery: MAH, 86–88. American Cast Products: USA minutes, December 27, 1945, TH; MAH, 93–94; *Chips,* December 1946, [2]; *Orrville Courier-Crescent,* January 21, 1946. ETN's speech: *Chips,* March 1947, quotation on p. [3]. His position in the trade organization: *Chips,* January 1946, [3]. Declining sales: MAH, 92; ETN, INT BG. Sales strategies: *Chips,* Spring 1948, [2].

2.  Henry Petrosky, *Invention by Design: How Engineers Get from Thought to Thing* (Cambridge, Mass.: Harvard University Press, 1996), quotation on p. 54. More on the $75,000 loan and subsequent events: MAH, 95–96, 125; NFFV92, including the quotations; BGS, 30–33. Approval of the $75,000 loan at 6 percent interest: USA minutes, April 2, 1949, TH. Auction total: FRP, "Nordson Foundation," 11. Sale of interest in American Cast Products: USA minutes, September 26, 1952, TH; MAH, 129–130. ETN's "gamble" quotations: NFFV92; ETN, INT JH. EWN's work in the factory: WGN and Virginia Nord, letter to EWN, August 4, 1952, NFP; EWN, INT BG; Clifford Berry, INT MP, June 24, 2003. ETN's "prospecting" quotation: ETN, INT MP, January 28, 2003. New product experiments: BGS, 33.

3.  SuperVision: ETN, INT MP, June 16, 2003. JAI's role: JNI, INT JH; EWN, INT BG. Benefits of airless process: JD, INT JH. Chronology: USA minutes, July 1–6, 1954, TH; MAH, 94, 105–113; BGS, 33–42; ETN, INT MP, June 16, 2003. Bede articles of incorporation: OSS, vol. 682, 547. According to *The Cleveland Directory* (Cleveland, Ohio: Cleveland Directory Co., 1954), 334, James H. Frier Jr. was president and general manager of Bede Products. Naming the new company: BGS, 42–44, WDG quotation on pp. 43–44. Early difficulties: ETN, INT BG; WDG, INT BG.

4. Refinement of the airless equipment and information on Rosen and Libicki: BGS, 45–48; ETN, including the quotations, and EWN, INT BG. Secrecy in nozzle work: WDG, INT BG; MAH, 118. Role of the Banor Corp.: BGC. Dates of subsidiaries: CB. Attribution of the *Nordson Newsletter:* ETN, INT MP, January 28, 2003. Coors projects: ETN, INT BG; ETN, INT MP, January 28, 2003. Other businesses: MAH, 115–116.

5. Open houses: Richard P. Lothrop, INT MP, September 19, 2003. Trips: *Chips,* Spring 1948, [4]; WGN and Virginia, letter to EWN, August 4, 1952, NFP. Ignat house: Geoffrey Blodgett, *Oberlin Architecture, College and Town: A Guide to Its Social History* (Oberlin, Ohio: Oberlin College, 1985), 177–178. Discussions and JAI's projects: JNI, INT MP, June 13, 2003. Mary's activities and qualities: JNI, INT MP, June 13, 2003; DWI, letter to MP, June 16, 2003; Mary's obituary, ONT, May 13, 1965. EWN and JAI's family: DWI and JNI, INT JH. EWN's influence on and employment of DWI and JNI: EWN, INT MP, March 17, 2003; DWI, letter to MP, May 15, 2003; JAI, INT MP, June 13, 2003. ETN's marriage: *Chips,* Spring 1948, [7]. ETN's meeting with JBN: ETN, INT MP, January 28, 2003. JBN's interests: ETN, INT MDM, May 21, 2002. Elbert Hall Baker Jr.: ETN, INT MP, April 21, 2004. JBN's memories: JBN, INT MDM, May 21, 2003; ETN, INT MP, June 16, 2003.

6. WGN's activities: NCAB, 165–166. Bank: *Oberlin, Ohio 1956 City Directory* (Oberlin, Ohio: Oberlin Printing Co.), 62. Case award: *Case Alumnus,* August 1951, 13. Lorain County Tuberculosis and Health Association: "Walter Nord Is Honored by TB Group," ONT, May 13, 1965; EWN and JRC, INT PM, May 12, 2004. The association also provided services to the county tuberculosis sanatorium, which was housed in the building at the intersection of State Route 58 (Leavitt Road) and North Ridge Road that is now the Golden Acres Lorain County Home; EWN, INT PM, May 12, 2004. American Swedish Historical Foundation activities: RFL, 54–55. Associate chapters: ASHFY, 1958, 78. Herman Nord Library: ASHFY, 1957, 72–78. Examples of writings: "Emil Tyden," ASHFY, 1964, 1–11; WGN, "Axel Hallstrom in Memoriam," ASHFY, 1966, 74–77. Vasa awards: ANT, May 11, 1951; ASHFY, 1960, photograph page; correspondence, medal description received by MP from the Swedish consul in New York, May 9, 2002; "Royal Order of Vasa Honor Conferred on W. G. Nord," clipping, NCVA, Box 11; "Orders and Medals," <http://www.royalcourt.se/net/Royal+Court/The+Monarchy +in+Sweden/Orders+and+Medals>. Prince Bertil's visit: ASHFY, 1959, 3–6. Princesses' visit: ASHFY, 1960, 111–112 and photograph pages. Opinions of the Eisenhowers: ETN, INT MP, January 28, 2003.

7. Origin of WGN's interest in mental health: ETN, including the quotation, EWN, and Marilyn Jenne, INT JH. Chronology of the mental health movement in Lorain County: *Leading and Caring for 40 Years — W. G. Nord Community Mental Health Center,* October 17, 1987 (copy), NFP (including the memories of Marilyn Jenne, EWN, WDG, and others), and accompanying typed historical data. EWN's recollection of use of the center: EWN, INT JH. JAI's role in mental health levy campaigns: WDG, INT JH; EWN, INT MP, March 17, 2003. Ohio Mental Health Association: 1965 Annual Meeting program, NFP. Presidency: NCAB, 165. Brussels meeting: WGN and Virginia, letter to EWN, August 4, 1952, NFP.

8. Reasons for establishing the USA Foundation: ETN, INT JH, including the quotations; NFFV92. Beginnings of the trust: NFFV92; WDG, INT JH, including the quotations; WDG, INT BG; Marilyn Jenne, INT JH. Note that Ginn's law

firm changed its name to Thompson Hine in 2001. Warner's position: *Oberlin, Ohio 1956 City Directory* (Oberlin, Ohio: Oberlin Printing Co.), 81. Process of giving: NFFV92. Early financial and donation information: USA and Nordson Foundation minutes, 1952–1976, TH. Policy of Nordson Corp.: WDG, INT JH; WDG, e-mail messages to MP, January 15, 2003, January 23, 2003. F. Emerson Andrews (*Corporation Giving* [New Brunswick, N.J.: Transaction Publishers, 1993]), in his 1951 survey of more than 300 companies, found that only 30 percent had a contributions budget and that only a few large companies had established corporate foundations. Some smaller companies were making contributions of 5 percent or more. The 1951 Revenue Act stimulated more giving (Andrews, *Corporation Giving,* 64–65, 90, 101, 247). Dayton Hudson data: "The Dayton Family," *Foundation News & Commentary,* January-February 2003, 25–26. WGN's honors: NCAB, 165; Upsala College catalog, 1954, 133, from the Swenson Center, Augustana College; Lynn Ayers, Wilberforce University Library, email message to MP, June 3, 2004; *Oberlin Alumni Magazine,* December 1958, 11–16, quotation on p. 14.

## CHAPTER 6

1. WGN's approach: JD, INT JH. WGN's bank position: *Oberlin, Ohio 1956 City Directory* (Oberlin, Ohio: Oberlin Printing Co.), 62. WGN's position at Christ Church: Richard P. Lothrop, INT MP, September 19, 2003. JAI's purchase of the Oberlin depot: ETN, INT MP, January 28, 2003. Oberlin Community Center and other OHIO projects: Bob Thomas, "Walter Nord Family Feted in Oberlin," LJ, December 9, 1965; ETN, INT MP, January 28, 2003; OHIO minutes, July 8, 1964, December 16, 1964, February 2, 1967, OHIO; president's correspondence, July 6, 1964, August 12, 1965, November 11, 1965, November 17, 1965, OHIO; WDG, e-mail message to PM, May 27, 2004. Farm management: ETN, INT MP, June 16, 2003. Frank's blindness: ETN and EWN, INT MP, August 23, 2002. Skills Division chronology: "Elyria Center Timeline," Vocational Guidance Services. Scholarship fund: scholarship fund leaflet, AHS. Lorain County Community College: Max J. Lerner, *Thirty Years of Service: The First Three Decades of Ohio's Independently Governed Two-Year Colleges, with Special Emphasis on Lorain County Community College* (N.p.: M. J. Lerner, 1995), xi, 139, 144, 148–151; "Unit to Push Levy for County College," ECT, September 20, 1963; ETN, INT MP, May 22, 2003. Student training program: ASHFY 1960, 104, 1961, 109, 1962, 93, 1963, 15, 1964, 104, 1965, 98, 1966, 91, 1967, 73. Mental health progress: LJ, May 15, 1964. Ohio Mental Health Association meeting chair: 1965 Annual Meeting program, NFP. Oberlin banquet: program, "Honoring the Nords of Oberlin," December 8, 1965, NFP; Bob Thomas, "Walter Nord Family Feted in Oberlin," LJ, December 9, 1965. Businessman honor: program, "Recognition Luncheon Honoring Walter G. Nord, Oberlin, May 26, 1966," NFP; "Nord Hailed as Inspiration to All Small Businessmen," undated article, including the quotation, NCVA, Box 11.

2. Mary's death and its impact: her obituary, ONT, May 13, 1965; WDG, EWN and JNI, INT JH; WGN obituary, ONT, May 18, 1967 (mentions gift in Mary's memory); CN, INT MP, July 15, 2002. EWN's hobbies: BC. EWN and CN: BC, including the quotation; EWN, INT JH; CN, INT MP, July 15, 2002; marriage notice, ONT, June 2, 1966. WGN's death: obituaries, LJ, May 17, 1967; ONT, May 18, 1967. OHIO meeting: OHIO records, Close/Tear file, May 22, 1967. WGN funeral: program, including the quotation, NCVA, Box 15; ETN, INT MP, January

28, 2003. Resolution: Ohio Senate Concurrent Resolution No. 25 (copy), NFP. Farm sale: ETN, INT MP, January 28, 2003. Naming of the mental health center: *Leading and Caring for 40 Years — W. G. Nord Community Mental Health Center,* October 17, 1987, [12] (copy), NFP. Naming of the junior high school: FVO, 179. JAI's death: JNI, INT JH. JAI's obituary: ONT, May 29, 1969. Virginia's obituary: ONT, November 1, 1973. Virginia's funeral program: NCVA, Box 15.

3. ETN's City Council leadership: ETN, INT MDM, May 21, 2002. Aaron Wildavsky, *Leadership in a Small Town* (Totowa, N.J.: Bedminster Press, 1964), as follows: ETN's coming to the council, 56–60, 81; housing code and first steps after February 1, 1960, 82–84, 101–108; open housing question, 110–140. Eric's role: ETN, INT MP, April 21, 2004. Also open-housing ordinance drafts, Oberlin Housing Corporation and Oberlin Community Welfare Council documents saved and annotated by ETN, NFP; Resulting public housing: Wildavsky, *Leadership in a Small Town,* 116–117; Geoffrey Blodgett, *Oberlin Architecture, College and Town: A Guide to Its Social History* (Oberlin, Ohio: Oberlin College, 1985), 215–216. Donald R. Reich, "The Oberlin Fair-Housing Ordinance," in Lynn W. Eley and Thomas W. Casstevens, eds., *The Politics of Fair-Housing Legislation: State and Local Case Studies* (San Francisco, Calif.: Chandler Publishing Company, 1968), 105–147. Industrial park: Wildavsky, *Leadership in a Small Town,* 158. Income tax: ETN, INT MDM, May 21, 2002; ETN, INT MP, January 28, 2003. School board service: ONT, June 17, 1965; ETN, INT MDM, May 21, 2002; ETN, including the quotation, INT MP, March 11, 2003. Joint Vocational School: ETN, INT MP, March 11, 2003; <www.lcjvs.com/about.shtml>; Tina L. Salyer, e-mail message to MP, April 26, 2004. Hospital board: ETN, INT MDM, May 21, 2002; ETN, INT MP, March 11, 2003.

4. ETN's concern: ETN, INT BG. ETN's speech quotations: manuscript, NFP. KHD's first position and background: NCAR, 1980; NNL, March 1960, [4]. Story of KHD's coming to the company: ETN, INT BG.

5. Items in NNL, September 1959–January 1963, NFP. Change needed in sales methods: ETN, INT BG; NNL, July 1960, 1. Taylor story: ETN, INT BG. Subsidiaries: NNL, July 1960, [1]; CB. Sales techniques: KHD, INT BG; *Nordson . . . The First Twenty-Five Years,* 1979, [10–11], NCVA, Box 11. Sales office example: *Western Manufacturing,* January 1966, 82–83, including the quotations. Each sales office was created as a separate company; reasons in WDG, INT BG.

6. International Nordson development detailed in ETN, INT BG, including the quotation; BGS, 49–50, 68–74; KHD, INT BG; CB; Ron House, "Far Reaching Subsidiary," *Case Alumnus,* April 1963, 29–33. On one trip ETN and JBN traveled to Brussels together: JBN, INT MDM, May 21, 2003. Subsidiary dates: BGC. Award: photograph in *Case Alumnus,* December 1969, 2.

7. Goal setting, etc.: BGS, 75–80; ETN, INT BG; KHD, INT BG. Corporate purpose: 1972 version, NFP. Quotation from John W. Gardner, *Self-Renewal: The Individual and the Innovative Society* (New York: Harper & Row, 1964), 5. ETN's acquaintance with Gardner: ETN, INT MP, January 28, 2003. Convertible-debentures plan: ETN, INT MP, October 6, 2003; WDG, e-mail message to MP, October 15, 2003. KHD's promotion: NCAR, 1980, inside front cover.

8. Product improvements: Ron House, "Far Reaching Subsidiary," *Case Alumnus,* April 1963, 29–33. Examples: NNL, November 1960, [1], September 1961, [4], February 1962, [1], November 1962, [1]. Legal problems with the electrostatic process: BGS, 58–60. Idea for hot-melt equipment: ETN, INT BG; Robert Crowell:

Larry Anderson, "An Interview with Eric Nord, Winner of the ASC Award," *Adhesives Age,* 1996 (reprint), NFP. Early hot-melt equipment: NNL, February 1962, [1]. Improvement necessary: ETN, INT BG; BGS, 62–65. Help from adhesive salesmen: ETN, INT BG. Start of hot melt in Europe: BGS, 73–74. Total focus on hot melt in Japan: KHD, INT BG. Financial statistics: ETN, NFP. Legal problems and hiring of Thomas Moorhead: BGS, 56–60; WDG, including the quotation, INT MP, October 13, 2003.

9.  Contract business: Ron House, "Far Reaching Subsidiary," *Case Alumnus,* April 1963, 29–33; *Imagineering* brochure, ca. 1960–1965, NCVA, Box 16. Vegetable washer sale: WDG, documents in permanent attorney files, TH. Legal changes: CB; BGC; OSS records, January 12, 1965, roll B390, frames 2229–2238, March 31, 1965, roll B400, frames 2148–2157, October 31, 1966, roll B479, frames 1–14, November 14, 1966, roll 480, frames 1446–1449. Office for WGN, headquarters: ETN, INT MP, January 28, 2003. Article: "Nordson Corp. . . . Successor to U.S. Automatic Co.," *Automatic Machining,* February 1968, 40–42, quotations on p. 40 (reprint), NFP. Phasing out contract work: BGS, 76; EWN, INT BG; Henry Libicki, INT JH; article in NN, Issue 4, 1972, [2], NCVA, Box 16. Corporate brochure: *The Role of Nordson Corporation in the Continuing Search for Better Ways to Apply Coatings and Adhesives,* July 1970 printing, quotations on p. [6], NCVA, Box 11. Minorities at Nordson: EWN, INT MP, June 26, 2003; JNI, INT JH.

10.  ETN's editorial: NN, Spring 1971, [3]. Process: NN, Fall 1971, [1]. First production: NN, Fall 1972, [1]. OSHA: BGS, 81–82. Quality assurance: NN, Fall 1972, [2]. New buildings: NN, Spring 1971, [1], Fall 1971, [2–3]. Open house 1973: *The Times* [Lorain, Ohio?], October 11, 1973. Meeting minutes: March 2, 1973, NFP. Stock-option plan: WDG, including the quotations, INT MP, September 22, 2003, October 13, 2003. Policy quotation: Meeting minutes, March 2, 1973, NFP.

11.  Skills Division nickname: "Elyria Center Timeline," Vocational Guidance Services. Reprint: "Nordson Corp . . . Successor to U.S. Automatic Co.," *Automatic Machining,* February 1968, 40–42, NFP. JD's responsibilities: ETN, INT JH; JD, INT JH; BC. JD's causes: JD, INT JH; NN, Winter 1971, [2], Spring 1971, [5], Fall 1972, [3]; ETN, INT MP, January 28, 2003. Strategy to not lay off workers: "Layoff with a Silver Lining," *Industry Week,* July 12, 1971, 23–25 (reprint), NFP.

12.  Growth of the foundation and changes in its leadership: USA Foundation and Nordson Foundation minutes, 1952–1976, NFF. EWN's activities: Ron House, "Far Reaching Subsidiary," *Case Alumnus,* April 1963, 29–33; OHIO minutes, November 1, 1967, May 28, 1969, OHIO. EWN's church position: Richard P. Lothrop, INT MP, September 19, 2003. CN and their home: CN, INT MP, July 15, 2002. EWN's mental health work: *Leading and Caring for 40 Years — W. G. Nord Community Mental Health Center,* October 17, 1987 (copy), NFP. Group home: Tom Oney, "Old Oberlin House 'Home' to Retarded," LJ, April 8, 1973; Ellen Payner, INT MP, October 10, 2003; OHIO minutes, September 28, 1972, December 12, 1972, OHIO.

13.  CN, EWN, and ETN and the Head Start project: CN, INT MP, July 15, 2002; ETN, including the quotation, INT MP, January 28, 2003; EWN, INT MP, March 17, 2003; Foundation minutes, April 1, 1969, December 1, 1969; Nordson Foundation records, Coll. 4641, Box 18, WRHS; WDG, letter to MP, February 19, 2003. Description of the new center: NN, Winter 1971, [4]. Caboose: EWN and JRC, INT PM, May 11, 2004. OECC: Foundation minutes, December 12, 1973,

Nordson Foundation records, WRHS; CN, INT MP, July 15, 2002; ETN, INT MP, January 28, 2003; JRC, INT PM, May 11, 2004. Burrell-King House: Geoffrey Blodgett, *Oberlin Architecture, College and Town: A Guide to Its Social History* (Oberlin, Ohio: Oberlin College, 1985), 65; JRC, INT PM, May 11, 2004. Note that the number of the Burrell-King House was changed from 317 to 315; 317 is now the OECC. Buildings in Amherst: Foundation minutes, June 30, 1972, February 1, 1973, NFF; FRP, "Nordson Foundation," 3; *Final Bulletin to the Board of Trustees of the Lorain County Tuberculosis and Health Association,* April 14, 1973, in JRC's files; EWN, letter to Harrison Comstock, February 20, 1973, in JRC's files. Tax Reform Act and its implications: Paul N. Ylvisaker, "Foundations and Nonprofit Organizations," in Walter W. Powell, ed., *The Nonprofit Sector* (New Haven, Conn.: Yale University Press, 1987), 360–379; WDG, e-mail message to PM, June 3, 2004.

# CHAPTER 7

1. Involvement in family businesses: Benjamin M. Becker and Fred A. Tillman, *The Family Owned Business* (2d ed.; Chicago: Commerce Clearing House, 1978), 17–18. KHD's appointment: Nordson Corporation minutes, December 12, 1973, TH; WDG, memorandum to MP, May 2, 2003. Response to oil crisis: NCAR, 1974, [1]. Engineering growth and good sales: NN, December 1974, [1]. FRP quotations: FRP, "An Industry Grows in Amherst," 4–5. ETN quotation: Mark Ellis, "The Nordson Corporation: Amherst Employer and Citizen," LJ, January 6, 1974. KHD's description of principles: KHD, INT BG; NCAR, 1977, 3. Citicorp Venture Capital: Peter G. Gerry, report to George A. Campbell at Nordson, October 23, 1974, NCW, quotation on p. 3. Work stoppage: clipping, October 26, 1974, AHS; NN, December 1974, [2]. Earlier stoppage: see chapter 4. The next three years: NCAR, 1975, 1–2, NCAR, 1976, 1, 4, quotation on the inside front cover; NCAR, 1977, 3. Branches: CB. Approach to management: NCAR, 1977, 10, including the quotation.

2. Karen Bair, "Meet Jim Doughman from Nordson: His Job Is to Help Communities," LJ, June 20, 1976. Amherst depot: *All Aboard!* ca. 1990, Nordson Corporation brochure, NFP; EWN, INT MP, March 17, 2003; JRC, INT PM, May 11, 2004; National Register Web site, <http://www.nr.nps.gov/iwisapi/explorer.dll?IWS_SCHEMA=NRIS1&IWS_1&IWS_REPORT=100000039>; Ohio State Historic Preservation office; special Nordson edition, ANT, September 27, 1979; Cecilia Render, INT PM, April 30, 2004. Featured workers: NN, [4–6, quotation on p. 4]. Old Timers Dinner: information from Barbara Shehan, Nordson; Nancy Scott, former employee.

3. Growth of the foundation: Nordson Foundation minutes, 1974–1979; NFAR, 1979, [3]. 1976 change: WDG, NFFV92; "The Nord Family Foundation, Summary of History and Organization," NFP. OECC: Nordson Foundation minutes, July 31, 1975; one-page typed history received from OECC; FRP, "Nordson Foundation," 3–4. Tuberculosis Association's building, Amherst: NFAR, 1979, [4]. The Sandstone Office on Aging now stands at this address; FVO, 158. Nord Center: NFAR, 1979, [3]; *Leading and Caring for 40 Years — W. G. Nord Community Mental Health Center,* October 17, 1987, [12] (copy), NFP. Committee of employees: FRP, "Nordson Foundation," 2. Cityview project: JD, INT JH; ETN, INT MP, March 11, 2003; JRC, INT PM, May 11, 2004. Employees as volunteers: "Nordson Corp. Salutes Seven Employees for Community Service," ANT, June 23, 1977;

*Leading and Caring,* [16]; Rosen, letter to United Way supporters, September 29, 1978, NCVA, Box 12.

4. ETN/EWN honors, May 26, 1974: commencement program, Oberlin College Archives. Stocker Center: Max J. Lerner, *Thirty Years of Service: The First Three Decades of Ohio's Independently Governed Two-Year Colleges, with Special Emphasis on Lorain County Community College* (N.p.: M. J. Lerner, 1995), 185–187; *Lorain County Community College Alumni Newsletter,* March, 1978, Lorain County Community College Library; ETN, INT MP, April 14, 2003. JBN's degree: *CWRU Magazine,* Fall 2002, 43. JBN's teaching and FAVA work: JBN, INT MDM, May 21, 2003; JBN, "A Brief History of FAVA" (manuscript; July 23, 1998), FAVA. Eric Baker Nord's death: obituary, ONT, May 1, 1980; JBN, INT MDM, May 21, 2003; ETN, INT MP, June 16, 2003. CN's activities: CN, INT MP, July 15, 2002. EWN head of scholarship fund: FRP, "Nordson Foundation," 5. EWN's OHIO work: OHIO minutes, January 15, 1973, OHIO; OHIO chronology file, 1972, 1976, 1977; EWN, INT MP, April 21, 2003. Move to South Carolina and foundation work: EWN, INT MP, March 17, 2003; ETN, INT MP, March 11, 2003; "A Brief History of the Foundation," Central Carolina Community Foundation. CN's injuries: CN, INT MP, July 15, 2002.

5. Purchases: CB; NCAR, 1979, 3, NCAR, 1980, 9; ETN, INT BG; ETN, INT MP, April 14, 2003. Robots, including the quotation: ETN, INT BG. Statistics and products: NCAR, 1979, 2–3, NCAR, 1980, 9; ETN, INT BG. Stock trading: NCAR, 1979, 3, including the quotation. Anniversary: ANT, July 12, 1979, September 27, 1979 (special Nordson edition), October 4, 1979; *Nordson . . . The First Twenty-Five Years,* 1979, NCVA, Box 11. ETN's address: Nordson news release, September 18, 1979, NFP. EWN's role in buildings: JRC, INT MP, September 22, 2003.

6. Tribute to KHD: NCAR, 1980, inside front cover, including the quotation. First report by Taylor and ETN: NCAR, 1980, 3. Problems in 1981: NCAR, 1981, 14, including the quotation. Measures taken in 1982: NCAR, 1982, 2. ETN's 1982 speech: NFP [complete text in Appendix 3, this volume]. Libicki's comment: DWI, letter to MP, May 15, 2003. ETN's retirement: ONT, November 3, 1983. New building, including the quotation: "Welcome to Nordson's Westlake Facility!" corporate brochure, 1983, NCVA, Box 10; JD, INT JH; JRC, INT MP, September 22, 2003. Branches: CB. Sale and new strategy announcements: NCAR, 1983, 2, NCAR, 1984, 2–3, 5; "No Room for Robots in Nordson's Future," LJ, March 4, 1984. ETN's view of robotics: ETN, INT BG. Donation of robots: Max J. Lerner, *Thirty Years of Service: The First Three Decades of Ohio's Independently Governed Two-Year Colleges, with Special Emphasis on Lorain County Community College* (N.p.: M. J. Lerner, 1995), 187–188; "Nordson Donates Robots," *Lorain County Times,* August 16, 1984. Taylor's resignation and ETN's reentry: LJ, July 4, 1985, July 5, 1985, July 8, 1985. Statement on not selling: ECT, July 8, 1985. ETN's address, including the quotation: NFP.

7. Madar's hiring, including the quotation: ETN, INT MP, April 14, 2003. Madar's credentials: ANT, August 14, 1996. Madar's approach: JD and Henry Libicki, INT JH; *International Directory of Company Histories* (Detroit: St. James Press, 1995), 11: 357; Nordson Corporation, *They Mean Business* (videotape), 1994, NFP; WDG, INT PM, May 28, 2004. Changes: NCAR, 1987, 2; Libicki, INT JH. Move to Westlake: NCAR, 1986, inside front cover; JRC, INT MP, September 22, 2003. New branches: CB. New products: NCAR, 1987, 15, NCAR, 1988, 17–18. Progress in sales: NCARs contain eleven-year summaries. Top 200 listings: "The 200 Best Small Compa-

nies in America," *Forbes Magazine,* November 16, 1987, 216, November 14, 1988, 297. New building: NCAR, 1988, 2.

8. JC's story and role: JC, INT JH; JC, notes to MP, May 13, 2003. Community Foundation: Nordson Foundation minutes, 1980–1983, including November 1 organizational meeting [quotation], WRHS, Coll. 4641, Box 1; JC and WDG, INT JH; ETN, INT MP, March 11, 2003; NFFV99; EWN, INT MP, March 17, 2003; NFAR, 1980–1981, [5], NFAR, 1986 [4]. Community Foundation name change: November 1, 1985, filed December 9, 1985 (from the OSS Web site, <http://www.state.oh.us/sos/>). County Cupboard: NFAR, 1982–1983, [3], NFAR, 1986, 19.

9. Other JC projects: JC and Anne Marie Cronin, INT JH; NFAR, 1982–1983, [3]. Leadership Lorain County: NFAR, 1983–1984, [3]. JC's policies: JC, INT JH; NFAR, 1980–1981, [3]; Nordson Foundation minutes, January 21–22, 1980, August 12–18, 1982, June 27, 1983, WRHS, Coll. 4641, Box 1; DWI, letter to MP, May 15, 2003. Expansion to Cuyahoga County: NFAR, 1982–1983, [2]. Policy Advisory Committee: NFAR, 1982–1983, [2], NFAR, 1983–1984 [3]. Number of grants: NFAR, 1982–1983, [3]. Anne Marie Cronin: Cronin, INT JH. Interns: NFAR, 1984–1985, [3]. Philanthropic trend: Paul N. Ylvisaker, "Foundations and Nonprofit Organizations," in Walter W. Powell, ed., *The Nonprofit Sector* (New Haven, Conn.: Yale University Press, 1987), 370. Lucy Idol Center: Carol Peck, INT MP, August 27, 2003. Philanthropic growth and round table: JC, INT JH; JC, notes to MP, May 13, 2003.

10. Donation and transition: JC, INT JH; NFAR, 1986, 2, 18. Ranking: Dorothy Williams, "Eric Nord '39, 1991 Gold Medal Winner, Carries on Family Traditions," *Case Alumnus,* Summer 1991, 9. New initiatives: NFAR, 1987, 3; JC, INT JH. Public Services Institute: NFAR, 1987, 16, NFAR, 1988, 6. Child Care Resource Center and Linden School: Cronin, INT JH; WDG, INT JH; NFAR, 1987, 17, NFAR, 1988, 7–8, 1989, 6. OECC and Kendal: JC, notes to MP, May 13, 2003; *New Choices,* December 1996/January 1997, 64–65, 68. Family meeting: NFAR, 1986, 20; DWI, INT JH.

## CHAPTER 8

1. Quotation: NFFAR, 1989, 2. Breakfast: "Foundation Split by Nords," ANT, November 30, 1988. Beginning of NFF: NFFV92; NFAR, 1988, 4, 18; NFF founding documents, 1988–1989, NFF records, NFF.

2. Chronology: NFF minutes, NFF founding documents, 1988–1989, NFF; NFFAR, 1989, 2. More on the Amherst historical project: ANT, February 1, 1989; information from the AHS office. St. George's reconstruction: "Foundation Split by Nords," ANT, November 30, 1988; *Dedication, St. George's Chapel at Amherst Sandstone Center, May 17, 1998,* AHS; quotation from WDG, e-mail message to MP, April 28, 2004. Family story told by EWN at NFF headquarters dedication, June 19, 2003. April 1989 meeting: NFFAR, 1989, 2, 8; NFF minutes, January 19, 1989, NFF; memorandum from WDG, 10, 1989, in NFF minutes, NFF. Quigley House: originally purchased by Nordson Foundation; transferred to the NFF on October 28, 1988 (Quit Claim Deed, Lorain County Auditor, Book 123, 576–583; copy at TH) and from the foundation to the AHS on August 18, 1999 (Quit Claim Deed, August 18, 1999; copy at TH). Ylvisaker documents from Harvard University Archives, HUGFP 142, Box 26 (discovered by DWI); biography from the Bethany Lutheran College Web site, <http://www.blc.edu /students/organizations/pyc/biography/>. Davis: DWI, letter to MP, June 4, 2003; NFF minutes,

January 19, 1989, NFF; Anne Marie Cronin, e-mail message to MP, April 21, 2004. Concept of public domain: Anne Marie Cronin, INT JH; e-mail message to MP, April 21, 2004. JC's retirement: LJ, June 28, 1989; NFF, press release, June 28, 1989, AHS. Doll appointment: LMJ, September 18, 1992; NFFAR, 1989, 2.

3. Doll's approach: Cronin and Doll, INT JH. Quotation: NFFAR, 1989, 3. Year of study: NFFAR, 1990, 3, 6; NFF minutes, 1990, NFF. May 1990 retreat: NFFAR, 1990, 6, including the quotation, NFFAR, 1991, 3; Cronin and Doll, INT JH; CN, INT MP, July 15, 2002; NFF minutes, April 23, 1990, May 22, 1990 (detailed report), NFF. Glebocki: NFFAR, 1990, 17. Nurturing Center: CN, INT MP, July 15, 2002; Emily Carswell Clay, "The Nurturing Center Offers Hope to Parents and Children," *Columbia Metropolitan,* Spring 1991, 67–69, NFF; NFFAR, 1990, 11. Lorain County 2020: NFFAR, 1990, quotation on p. 8, NFFAR, 1991, 3. Doll's two initiatives: Doll and Cronin, INT JH. DWI's election as president: NFF minutes, June 22, 1991. Second-year programs: NFFAR, 1991, 3, 4–7. 1992 programs: NFFAR, 1992, 3–8, quotation on p. 6. Doll's resignation: LMJ, September 18, 1992. Doll's view: Doll, INT JH. 1993 retreat: NFF minutes, June 23 and 24, 1993, NFF. History project, NFF: minutes, June 13, 1992, NFF. EWN's idea to hire Harrah: ETN, INT MP, April 14, 2003.

4. History since 1992: NFFARs, 1993–2002; CN, INT MP, July 15, 2002. Pyer: LMJ, February 13, 1993, June 1, 1994; NFFAR 1994, 8. Cronin: Anne Marie Cronin, e-mail message to MP, May 25, 2004. Ashenhurst: LMJ, February 5, 1995; NFFAR, 1995, 23, NFFAR, 1996, 29. Weiss: NFFAR, 1997, 33. Members in 2003: headquarters dedication program, June 19, 2003, 11. Public funding decline: NFFAR, 1995, 4–5. Grants in 2003: NFFAR, 2003. Mission statement: NFFAR, 1993, inside front cover. Barbato quotation: NFFAR, 1996, 7. Mullaney quotation: NFFAR, 1998, 7; names of supported organizations from various NFFARs; JRC, INT MP, May 11, 2004; Nancy Sabath, e-mail message to PM, May 14, 2004. Nord Center: current information from the center. Common Ground: <http://www.commonground-center.org/about/>; brochures. New Union Center: NFFAR, 1995; *New Union Center for the Arts Dedication, June 21, 1996,* NFF; OHIO Resource Center File on Union School, OHIO. JBN and ETN's role: JBN, INT MDM, May 21, 2003. OHIO: OHIO board minutes, July 28, 1993; John Mullaney, "NFF Grantmaking History and Review"; Oberlin Community Services Web site, <http://www.oberlincommunityservices.org/homepage.htm>. AHS sites: *Dedication, St. George's Chapel at Amherst Sandstone Center, May 17, 1998,* AHS; EWN, INT PM, May 11, 2004, May 14, 2004; JRC, INT MP, May 11, 2004, May 12, 2004, May 14, 2004. Train wreck and caboose: Valerie Jenkins, "The Past Is Not Forgotten," ANT, July 19, 1979; E. Valerie Jenkins and Elizabeth Anderson, *Amherst, Our Community* (Amherst, Ohio: Amherst Exempted Village Schools, 1992), 17; FVO, 162–163; "Caboose Pulls out of Town," ONT, June 22, 2004. Mullaney quotations: remarks prepared for OHIO's "Philanthropy Day," 2004. Examples: NFFAR, 2003, 6. Foundation Leadership Award: Anne Marie Cronin, chair, National Philanthropy Awards Committee, Association of Fundraising Professionals, letter to John Mullaney, June 21, 2004.

5. Anniversary booklet: *Seasons of Growth and Change: Nordson Corporation Foundation Celebrates 50 Years of Giving,* Nordson Corporation, 2002, statistics on p. 2. 2003 statistics: The Nordson Corporation Foundation; Cecilia Render, email message to PM, August 24, 2004. Haqq's background: Haqq, INT MP, April 1, 2003. Haqq's 1991 quotation: Nordson Corporation, *1991 Contributions Report to the Community,* 1. Haqq's 2002 quotation: *Seasons of Growth and Change,* 2. Ben-

eficiaries: annual Nordson Corporation Foundation brochures. Employee giving: Haqq, INT MP, April 1, 2003.

6. Statistics: NCARs, 1988–1999. Nearby adhesive manufacturers: Nordson Corporation, *They Mean Business* (videotape), 1994, NFP. Automobile powder coating: NCAR, 1993, 5. Acquisitions: BGC. Meltex: NCAR, 1989, 2, 10–11. Slautterback: NCAR, 1992, 3. Mountaingate, Electrostatic: NCAR, 1993, 5, NCAR, 1994, 3, 5. Walcom Benelux: NCAR, 1995, 6. Asymtek, Spectral: NCAR, 1996, 4. Applied Curing: NCAR, 1997, 3. J&M: NCAR, 1998, 11. Advanced Plasma, March Instruments: NCAR, 1999, 11. VeriTek: NCAR, 1999, 8. EFD: NCAR, 2000, 5. International statistics: NCAR, 1989, NCAR, 1999. Expansion: BGC; NCAR, 1989–1999. Chinese market: NCAR, 1993, 12–13. "E" Award: Larry Anderson, "An Interview with Eric Nord, Winner of the ASC Award," *Adhesives Age,* 1996, [1] (reprint), NFP. Praise: "Nordson Corporation," *International Directory of Company Histories* (Detroit: St. James Press, 1995), 11: 356–358. Minorities: ETN, INT MDM, May 21, 2002. Inventors' gatherings: ANT, June 7, 1995. Contract shop business: items from Vocational Guidance Services via board member Tom Petredis, December 16, 2002.

7. Personnel changes and quotations: LMJ, May 21, 1997; ANT, May 28, 1997. Campbell's background: ANT, August 14, 1996. New programs: NCAR, 1999, 2–5, NCAR, 2000, 4, NCAR, 2001, 4.

8. Sales figures: NCAR, 2000, 1, NCAR, 2002, 1. Cost cutting: NCAR, 2001, 4–5. ETN quotations, INT MP, April 14, 2003. Blue Series: NCAR, 2003, 3. "Lean" manufacturing: NCAR, 2003, 2–4, 7, 9–10. "Lean" principles are offered in a series of manuals by J. Ross Publishing, Inc. 2003 sales: NCAR, 2003, 1. Campbell quotation: NCAR, 2003, 2. Dow Jones article: Ralph E. Winter, "Nordson CEO Says Stronger Demand to Boost Results," March 12, 2004, Dow Jones Newswire.

9. ETN and JBN's gift to Case Western Reserve University: *CWRU Magazine,* Fall 2002, 42–43. Library campaign: ETN, INT MDM, May 21, 2002, including the second quotation; ETN, INT MP, March 11, 2003. Splash Zone: Molly Kavanaugh, "Community Rallying for Oberlin Pool," *Plain Dealer* [Cleveland, Ohio], April 6, 2001, §B, 3, including the quotation; ETN, INT MDM, May 21, 2002; ETN, INT MP, April 14, 2003; ETN, INT MP, April 21, 2004, including the first ETN quotation; Sigrid Boe and Keith Koenning, INT PM, June 5, 2004, June 9, 2004. Workshop projects: Larry Anderson, "An Interview with Eric Nord, Winner of the ASC Award," *Adhesives Age,* 1996, [3] (reprint), NFP; Michael Zawacki, "Bond for Success," *Inside Business,* October 2001, B42–B44, NFP. Honors list: "Business Hall of Fame Taps Nord as Member," ANT, November 7, 2001. Oberlin honorary degree: commencement program, May 28, 1990, 9; *Oberlin Alumni Magazine,* Summer 1990, 19, Oberlin College Archives. Case award: Dorothy Williams, "Eric Nord '39, 1991 Gold Medal Winner, Carries on Family Traditions," *Case Alumnus,* Summer 1991, 7. ASC award: "An Interview with Eric Nord . . . ." Leadership Lorain County: ECT, March 26, 1995. Case honorary degree: ONT, June 2, 1998. Hall of Fame award: Zawacki, "Bond for Success." Stock-gift thank-you letters and American Specialty stockholder letter: NFP. JBN's awards: programs of Oberlin commencement, 1996 and Arts Day '97 luncheon, Columbus (copies), furnished by FAVA.

10. Blythewood: EWN, INT MP, March 17, 2003. Recognition: clipping from a Columbia, South Carolina newspaper, January 1995, Nord file, OHIO. CN's activities: CN, INT MP, July 15, 2002. EWN's activities: Nordson Corporation,

"Resolution of Appreciation for Evan W. Nord March 7, 2002" (copy), NFP; *Worth,* March 2002, 83; LMJ, January 29, 2002; "A Brief History of the Foundation," Central Carolina Community Foundation; EWN and CN, interviews with MP, 2002–2003. EWN's visits to Amherst, EWN, INT MP, July 16, 2002; EWN and Clifford Berry, INT MP, August 22, 2002. New NFF headquarters: dedication program, June 19, 2003, NFP. JRC, INT MP, September 22, 2003, noted that this site was suggested as early as 1988.

11. Quotations about EWN: "Evan Nord's Unforgettable Contributions," ECT, July 1, 2004, §B, 4; "Philanthropist Left Mark on City," ONT, June 29, 2004, 1, 8; Devon Marrow, "Entrepreneur and Philanthropist Evan Nord Dies," *The State* [Columbia, S.C.], June 22, 2004, §B, 1; Associated Press release, June 22, 2004, carried as "One of Founders of Nordson Corp. Dies at Age 84," *Contra Costa* [California] *Times,* <http://www.contracostatimes.com/mld/cctimes/business/8984063.htm?1c> and as "S.C. Philanthropist Dies," *Island Packet* [Hilton Head Island, S.C.], <http://www.islandpacket.com/news/state/regional/story/3655511p_3257801c.html> and *The Herald* [Rock Hill, S.C.], <http://www.herald-online.com/scnews/state_regional_interest/v-print/story/3655509p_3257800c.html>, posted June 22, 2004; Henry C. Doll, "Evan Nord: True Humanitarian" [letter to the editor], *Plain Dealer* [Cleveland, Ohio], June 28, 2004, §B, 6; Michael C. Fitzpatrick, "Area Native Made 'Investments in People,'" LMJ, June 23, 2004, §C, 1, 7; Marilyn Jenne, "In Memory of a Dear Friend," *The Grindstone,* July-August 2004, <http://www.amhersthistorical.org>. Other press reports of EWN's death (located as of July 10, 2004): Alana Baranick and Richard M. Peery, "Evan Nord, Nordson Co-Founder, Dead at 84," *Plain Dealer* [Cleveland, Ohio], June 23, 2004, §B, 2, 5; Adrian Burns, "Philanthropy Defined Leader," ECT, June 23, 2004, §A, 1, 2; "Evan Nord," *Beaufort* [South Carolina] *Gazette,* <http://www.beaufortgazette.com/local_news/obituaries/v-print/story/3656810p_3258986c.html>, posted June 23, 2004; "Evan Nord," *The State* [Columbia, S.C.], <http://www.thestate.com/mld/thestate/8988994.htm?template=contentModules/printstory.jsp>, posted June 23, 2004; "Evan W. Nord, 84, Was Philanthropist," LMJ, June 23, 2004, §A, 6; "Evan Nord Deserves Praise for His Example of Generosity, Modesty" [editorial], LMJ, June 26, 2004, §A, 6; "Evan W. Nord," ONT, June 29, 2004, 7; "Institute Mourns the Passing of Evan Nord," University of South Carolina Institute for Families in Society, <http://ifs.sc.edu/default.asp>, downloaded July 1, 2004; "Obituary: Evan Nord," *Chronicle of Philanthropy,* <http://philanthropy.com/free/update/update.htm>, downloaded July 1, 2004. EWN's memorial service, including the quotations: "A Celebration of the Life of Evan W. Nord" (program); opening prayer by Rev. David W. Clark; Edward Campbell, "Remarks"; PM, "Remembering Evan"; JNI, "Evan W. Nord: Recollections." Copies of all materials cited in this note are on file at OHIO.

## CHAPTER 9

1. *Business Ethics* honor: <http://www.business-ethics.com/100best.htm>; NCAR, 2003, 11. Recent ranking and Campbell quotation: Nordson Corporation, news release, May 3, 2004.

The following is a partial list of sources used in the research for this book. Many more references can be found in the notes.

American Specialty Company.  Advertising scrapbooks, 1942–1950. Nordson Corporation vault (engineering building), Amherst, Ohio.
———.  Financial statistics, handwritten, 1930s. Nordson Corporation vault (engineering building), Amherst, Ohio.
———.  Incorporation documents, 1919–1921. Ohio Secretary of State, Columbus, Ohio.
———.  Root-washer letter, n.d. Nord family papers.
Amherst, Village of.  Mayor's Criminal Docket, 1923–1924. Amherst Historical Society, Amherst, Ohio.
———.  Mayor's Record of Fines, 1910–1928. Amherst Historical Society, Amherst, Ohio.
———.  Village Board Minutes, January 22, 1924–January 6, 1925. Amherst Historical Society, Amherst, Ohio.
Bede Products Corporation.  Various incorporation documents, 1946–1964. Ohio Secretary of State, Columbus, Ohio.
Case School of Applied Science.  Various publications, 1903–1909, 1939–1941. Case Western Reserve University Archives, Cleveland, Ohio.
General Stone Company.  Incorporation documents, 1922–1926. Ohio Secretary of State, Columbus, Ohio.
———.  Statistics, handwritten, 1930s. Nordson Corporation vault (engineering building), Amherst, Ohio.
Grieve, Virginia.  Report cards, 1890s. Nord family papers.
Griffith, Barbara S.  Interviews for the Nordson Corporation Oral History Project, 1995–1998. Transcripts. Nordson Corporation, Westlake, Ohio. Access restricted.
———.  Summary and Chronology for the Nordson Corporation Oral History Project, 1998. Nordson Corporation, Westlake, Ohio.
Harrah, Jeanne.  Interviews for The Nord Family Foundation Oral History Project, 1992–1993. Transcripts. Western Reserve Historical Society, Cleveland, Ohio. Access restricted.
Hellrigel, Mary Ann.  "The Nordson Corporation: Global Leader in Industry and Still a Good Neighbor," 1992. Manuscript. Nord family papers.
"History of the Sandstone Industry of Northern Ohio," n.d. Manuscript. Amherst Historical Society, Amherst, Ohio.
"Honoring the Nords of Oberlin," December 8, 1965. Testimonial program. Nord family papers.

# REFERENCES

## ARCHIVAL DOCUMENTS

ARCHIVAL
DOCUMENTS,
*continued*

Lorain County [Ohio]. Deed Records, 1920–1944. Copies. Nord family papers.

Merrill, Marlene Deahl. Interviews for the O.H.I.O. Oberlin Oral History Project, 2002–2003. Audiotapes and transcripts. Oberlin Heritage Center / Oberlin Historical and Improvement Organization, Oberlin, Ohio.

Mullaney, John. "Nord Family Foundation: Grant Making History and Review, 1987–2001," n.d. Manuscript. The Nord Family Foundation office, Amherst, Ohio.

Nord, Eric. Corporate mission statement, July 17, 1972. Nord family papers.

———. Financial statistics, handwritten notes, n.d. Nord family papers.

———. Minutes, March 2, 1973, officially adopting 5 percent donation policy. Nord family papers.

———. Service on the Oberlin City Council, various documents, 1960–1966. Nord family papers.

———. Speeches delivered, 1960, n.d., October 18, 1979, August 26, 1982, June 3, 1985. Nord family papers.

Nord, Otto and Mary. Records, 1874–1931. Copies. Nord family papers.

Nord, Walter. Order of Vasa awards, 1951, 1959. Documents. Nord family papers.

———, and Virginia Grieve. Marriage service, 1913. Booklet. Nord family papers.

———, and Virginia Nord. Letter to Evan Nord, August 4, 1952. Nord family papers.

Nord Family. Financial documents, 1920–1942. Copies. Nord family papers.

———. Genealogy notes. Nord family papers.

The Nord Family Foundation. Founding documents, October 26, 1988–February 15, 1991. The Nord Family Foundation office, Amherst, Ohio.

———. Minutes and retreat records, 1989–1993. The Nord Family Foundation office, Amherst, Ohio.

———. Oral History Project, 1992–1993. Western Reserve Historical Society, Cleveland, Ohio.

Nordson Corporation. Incorporation documents, 1957–1966. Ohio Secretary of State, Columbus, Ohio.

———. "Memory Book," 1997. Historical photograph album presented to Eric Nord on his retirement as chairman of the board. Nord family papers.

———. Old Timers Club, membership lists, 1976–1993. Nord family papers.

Nordson Foundation. Minutes and other official documents, October 16, 1952–October 31, 1976. The Nord Family Foundation office, Amherst, Ohio.

———. Minutes, 1980–1983. Western Reserve Historical Society, Cleveland, Ohio.

———. Oberlin Head Start, Oberlin Early Childhood Center, 1969–1976. Files. Western Reserve Historical Society, Cleveland, Ohio.

Oberlin Historical and Improvement Organization and predecessors. Minutes and other records, 1958–1993. Copies. Oberlin Heritage Center / Oberlin Historical and Improvement Organization, Oberlin, Ohio.

Pickrell, Martha M. Interviews for this volume, 2001–2004. Audiotapes, transcripts, and notes. Oberlin Heritage Center / Oberlin Historical and Improvement Organization, Oberlin, Ohio.

Powers, Fred R. "But Whom Say Ye That I Am?" ca. 1974–1976. Manuscript. Amherst Historical Society, Amherst, Ohio.

———. "An Industry Grows in Amherst," ca. 1974–1976. Manuscript. Amherst Historical Society, Amherst, Ohio.

———. "Nordson Foundation," ca. 1974–1976. Manuscript. Amherst Historical Society, Amherst, Ohio.

————. "Should Old Acquaintance Be Forgot," ca. 1974–1976. Manuscript. Amherst Historical Society, Amherst, Ohio.

"Recognition Luncheon Honoring Walter G. Nord, Oberlin, May 26, 1966." Testimonial program. Nord family papers.

Ryan, June. "Her Fancy Fans Fantastic Collection," ca. 1963. Clipping. Nord family papers.

[Stockefors, Osvald]. "Walter G. Nord: His Father's Family Background." Translated by Ann B. Weissmann. N.d. Manuscript. The Nord Family Foundation office, Amherst, Ohio.

"25-Day Strike at Nordson Ends," October 26, 1974. Clipping. Amherst Historical Society, Amherst, Ohio.

U.S. Automatic Corporation. Advertising scrapbooks, 1942–1950. Nordson Corporation vault (engineering building), Amherst, Ohio.

————. "E" Award scrapbook, 1943. Nord family papers.

————. Incorporation documents, 1935–1941. Ohio Secretary of State, Columbus, Ohio.

————. Minutes, scattered dates, 1935–1966. Copies. Nord family papers.

U.S. Automatic Foundation / Nordson Foundation. Minutes and other official documents, October 16, 1952–October 31, 1976. The Nord Family Foundation office, Amherst, Ohio.

U.S. Federal Census schedules, Ashtabula County, Ohio, 1880, 1900.

## PUBLISHED MATERIALS

*All Aboard!* Nordson Corporation brochure, ca. 1990. Nord family papers.

*American Swedish Historical Foundation Yearbooks,* 1952, 1957–1967. American Swedish Historical Museum, Philadelphia, Pennsylvania.

"Amherst Girl Honored at College," *Amherst News-Times,* November 29, 1935. Amherst Historical Society, Amherst, Ohio.

*Amherst* [Ohio] *News-Times,* May 8, 1919–May 8, 1924, August 14, 1924, April 18, 1928–December 19, 1946. Microfilm. Amherst Public Library, Amherst, Ohio.

————, September 27, 1979 (special Nordson edition). Nordson Corporation vault (engineering building), Amherst, Ohio.

————, Clippings from various issues. Amherst Historical Society, Amherst, Ohio.

*Amherst* [Ohio] *Weekly News,* 1918–May 1, 1919. Microfilm. Amherst Public Library, Amherst, Ohio.

Anderson, Larry. "An Interview with Eric Nord, Winner of the ASC Award," *Adhesives Age,* 1996. Reprint. Nord family papers.

Andrews, F. Emerson. *Corporation Giving.* New Brunswick, N.J.: Transaction Publishers, 1993 [1952].

Armstrong, Robert G. *Amherst's Story.* Amherst, Ohio: Amherst Old Home Week Committee, 1914.

Ashtabula County Genealogical Society. *Ashtabula County History Then and Now: A History of the People of the County by the People of the County.* Dallas, Tex.: Taylor Publishing Co., 1985.

Bair, Karen. "Meet Jim Doughman from Nordson: His Job Is to Help Communities," *Lorain Journal,* June 20, 1976. Nordson Corporation vault (engineering building), Amherst, Ohio.

Becker, Benjamin M., and Fred A. Tillman. *The Family Owned Business.* 2d ed. Chicago: Commerce Clearing House, 1978.

PUBLISHED
MATERIALS,
*continued*

Blodgett, Geoffrey. *Oberlin Architecture, College and Town: A Guide to Its Social History.* Oberlin, Ohio: Oberlin College, 1985.

*Chips* [U.S. Automatic Corporation magazine], September 1941–May 1942, January 1943, May–June 1943, August 1943–July 1945, September 1945–January 1946, March 1946, May 1946–May 1947, January, Spring 1948. Nordson Corporation vault (engineering building), Amherst, Ohio.

————, November 1946. Amherst Historical Society, Amherst, Ohio.

Clay, Emily Carswell. "The Nurturing Center Offers Hope to Parents and Children," *Columbia Metropolitan,* Spring 1991, 67–69. The Nord Family Foundation office, Amherst, Ohio.

*Cleveland Quarries Company.* Pamphlet, ca. 1950s. Copy. Amherst Historical Society, Amherst, Ohio.

Cotleur, Bob. "Eric and Evan Nord: They Have a Philosophy," *Lorain Journal,* January 26, 1970. Nord family papers.

"Cynthia Tinker Becomes Bride of Evan Nord. . . ," *Oberlin News-Tribune,* June 2, 1966. Nord family papers.

Deal, Terrence E., and Allan A. Kennedy. *Corporate Cultures: The Rites and Rituals of Corporate Life.* Cambridge, Mass.: Perseus Publishing, 2000.

*Dedication, St. George's Chapel at Amherst Sandstone Center, May 17, 1998.* Amherst Historical Society, Amherst, Ohio.

"Dedication of the Herman J. Nord Memorial Library," *American Swedish Historical Foundation Yearbook,* 1957, 72–78. American Swedish Historical Museum, Philadelphia, Pennsylvania.

Ellis, Mark. "The Nordson Corporation: Amherst Employer and Citizen," *Lorain Journal,* January 6, 1974. Nordson Corporation vault (engineering building), Amherst, Ohio.

*Elyria* [Ohio] *Chronicle-Telegram,* February 5, 1924–January 5, 1925. Microfilm. Ohio Historical Society, Columbus, Ohio.

Engel, Peggy. "The Quarries, One Hundred Years of Hazards, Low Pay and Crude Conditions," *Lorain Journal,* January 12, 1975. Amherst Historical Society, Amherst, Ohio.

"Eric Nord to Relinquish Nordson Chairmanship," *Amherst News-Times,* May 28, 1997. Amherst Historical Society, Amherst, Ohio.

Gardner, John W. *Excellence: Can We Be Equal and Excellent Too?* New York: Harper & Row, 1961.

————. *Self-Renewal: The Individual and the Innovative Society.* New York: Harper & Row, 1964.

Gersick, Kelin E. *Generation to Generation: Life Cycles of the Family Business.* Boston: Harvard Business School Press, 1997.

"Haqq to Lead Nordson [Corporation] Foundation," *Amherst News-Times,* June 26, 1991. Amherst Historical Society, Amherst, Ohio.

Harrah, Jeanne. *The History of The Nord Family Foundation, October 9, 1992.* Videotape and transcript. The Nord Family Foundation office, Amherst, Ohio.

House, Ron. "Far Reaching Subsidiary," *Case Alumnus,* April 1963, 29–33. Nord family papers.

*Imagineering.* Brochure, ca. 1960–1965. Nordson Corporation vault (engineering building), Amherst, Ohio.

Jenkins, E. Valerie, and Elizabeth Anderson. *Amherst, Our Community.* Amherst, Ohio: Amherst Exempted Village Schools, 1992.

Jenkins, Valerie. "The Past Is Not Forgotten," *Amherst News-Times,* July 19, 1979. Amherst Historical Society, Amherst, Ohio.

Johansson, Carl-Erik. *Cradled in Sweden.* Logan, Utah: Everton Publishers, 1972.

"The Largest Sand Stone Quarry in the World," *North Amherst Argus,* November 28, 1901. Amherst Historical Society, Amherst, Ohio.

Larson, Roy F. "Walter G. Nord, 1884–1967," *American Swedish Historical Foundation Yearbook,* 1967, 51–55. Nord family papers.

"Layoff with a Silver Lining," *Industry Week,* July 12, 1971, 23–25. Reprint. Nord family papers.

*Leading and Caring for 40 Years— W. G. Nord Community Mental Health Center,* October 17, 1987. Anniversary brochure. Copy. Nord family papers.

Lerner, Max J. *Thirty Years of Service: The First Three Decades of Ohio's Independently Governed Two-Year Colleges, with Special Emphasis on Lorain County Community College.* N.p.: M. J. Lerner, 1995.

*Lorain* [Ohio] *Journal,* August 1, 1924–February 6, 1925. Microfilm. Lorain Public Library, Lorain, Ohio.

*Lorain* [Ohio] *Morning Journal,* September 18, 1992–January 29, 2002 and undated clippings. Amherst Historical Society, Amherst, Ohio.

Moberg, Vilhelm. *A History of the Swedish People.* Translated by Paul Britten Austin. New York: Pantheon Books, 1972.

*New Union Center for the Arts Dedication, June 21, 1996.* Dedication brochure. The Nord Family Foundation office, Amherst, Ohio.

Nord, Walter G. *Presenting.* Booklet published by the U.S. Automatic Corporation and sent as a souvenir to those who had attended the "E" Award dinner held in Oberlin on January 13, 1943. Nord family papers.

The Nord Family Foundation. *Nord Family Foundation Member Retreat, June 25–27, 1999.* Videotape and transcript. The Nord Family Foundation office, Amherst, Ohio.

*The Nord Family Foundation Annual Reports,* 1989–2002. The Nord Family Foundation office, Amherst, Ohio.

*The Nord Family and Nordson Corporation: A Historical Overview,* 1997. Videotape. Nord family papers.

*Nordson . . . The First Twenty-Five Years,* 1979. Nordson Corporation vault (engineering building), Amherst, Ohio.

"Nordson Corp. . . . Successor to U.S. Automatic Co.," *Automatic Machining,* February 1968, 40–42. Reprint. Nord family papers.

Nordson Corporation. *Eric Nord's Presentation to the Nordson Corporation's Old Timers' Club on October 3, 1996.* Videotape. Nord family papers.

———. *They Mean Business,* 1994. Videotape. Nord family papers.

"Nordson Corporation," *International Directory of Company Histories,* 11: 356–358. Detroit: St. James Press, 1995.

*Nordson Corporation Annual Reports,* 1974–1984, 1986–2002. Nordson Corporation, Westlake, Ohio.

*Nordson Corporation Foundation, Annual Reports /* brochures for grant seekers, 1991–1999. Nordson Corporation, Westlake, Ohio.

*Nordson Foundation Annual Reports,* 1979–1988. The Nord Family Foundation office, Amherst, Ohio.

"Nordson Honors a Dozen Inventors with Patents," *Amherst News-Times,* June 7, 1995. Amherst Historical Society, Amherst, Ohio.

**PUBLISHED MATERIALS,** *continued*

*Nordson News,* Spring 1971, Fall 1971, Issue 4, 1972, December 1974, June 1975. Nordson Corporation vault (engineering building), Amherst, Ohio.

———, September 1974. Nord family papers.

*Nordson Newsletter,* September 1959–January 1963 (14 issues). Nord family papers.

"Nordson Recognized for Depot Restoration Effort," *Amherst News-Times,* July 12, 1979. Amherst Historical Society, Amherst, Ohio.

*Oberlin Alumni Magazine,* December 1958, 11–16. Article on honorary degrees awarded at 125th Anniversary Convocation. Nordson Corporation vault (engineering building), Amherst, Ohio.

*Oberlin* [Ohio] *News-Tribune,* various issues, May 13, 1965–June 2, 1998. Nord family papers.

*Oberlin* [Ohio] *Times,* October 20, 1938, December 24, 1942. Nord family papers.

Ott, Fay Van Nuys. *Amherst Pictorial History.* Amherst, Ohio: N.p., 2001.

Paschen, Stephen H. *Quarry Town: The History of Amherst, Ohio, 1811–1900.* Amherst, Ohio: Amherst Historical Society, 2003.

Petrosky, Henry. *Invention by Design: How Engineers Get from Thought to Thing.* Cambridge, Mass.: Harvard University Press, 1996.

Powell, Walter W., ed. *The Nonprofit Sector: A Research Handbook.* New Haven, Conn.: Yale University Press, 1987.

Reich, Donald R. "The Oberlin Fair-Housing Ordinance." In *The Politics of Fair-Housing Legislation: State and Local Case Studies,* edited by Lynn W. Eley and Thomas W. Casstevens, 105–147. San Francisco, Calif.: Chandler Publishing Company, 1968.

*The Role of Nordson Corporation in the Continuing Search for Better Ways to Apply Coatings and Adhesives,* July 1970. Brochure. Nordson Corporation vault (engineering building), Amherst, Ohio.

*Seasons of Growth and Change: Nordson Corporation Foundation Celebrates 50 Years of Giving,* 2002. Nordson Corporation, Westlake, Ohio.

Silverman, Alvin. "He Must Be an Inventor," *Case Alumnus,* April 1945, 14–15. Nordson Corporation vault (engineering building), Amherst, Ohio.

Thomas, Bob. "Walter Nord Family Feted in Oberlin," *Lorain Journal,* December 9, 1965. Nord family papers.

Trager, Jane. "Father's Lessons Basis of Nord Success," *Elyria Chronicle-Telegram,* May 25, 1997. Nord family papers.

"The 200 Best Small Companies in America," *Forbes Magazine,* November 16, 1987, 216; November 14, 1988, 297.

"U.S. Honors Nordson Corp.," *Case Alumnus,* December 1969, 2. Nordson Corporation vault (engineering building), Amherst, Ohio.

Van Cleef, Frank Chapman. *Gathering Horse Feathers: Over a Quarter of a Century in Active Retirement.* Oberlin, Ohio: Oberlin Historical and Improvement Organization, 1976.

"W.G. Nord Honored by King of Sweden," *Amherst News-Times,* May 11, 1951. Amherst Historical Society, Amherst, Ohio.

"Walter G. Nord," *National Cyclopaedia of American Biography,* 56: 165–166. Clifton, N.J.: James T. White & Co., 1975.

"Walter Godfrey Nord," *Who Was Who,* 5: 536. Chicago: Marquis Who's Who, Inc. 1973.

"Walter Nord, 83, Industrialist, Civic Leader, Dies," *Lorain Journal,* May 17, 1967. Nord family papers.

*Welcome to the American Swedish Historical Museum . . . the 75th Anniversary,* June 2, 2001. Historical brochure. American Swedish Historical Museum, Philadelphia, Pennsylvania.

*Welcome to Nordson's Westlake Facility,* 1983. Brochure. Nordson Corporation vault (engineering building), Amherst, Ohio.

Wildavsky, Aaron. *Leadership in a Small Town.* Totowa, N.J.: Bedminster Press, 1964.

Williams, Dorothy. "Eric Nord '39, 1991 Gold Medal Winner, Carries on Family Traditions," *Case Alumnus,* Summer 1991, 7–9. Reprint. Nord family papers.

Zawacki, Michael. "Bond for Success," *Inside Business,* October 2001, B42–B46. Nord family papers.

BAKER–
CASE

## G

Garcia, Roberta, 158
Gardner, John W., 106, 123
Garza, Rita, 170
General Electric Company (Fairfield, Connecticut), 110
General Stone Company (Amherst, Ohio), 25–26, 41
George Gund Foundation (Cleveland, Ohio), 144, 149
German language, and the Grieve family, 27, 30
Germans in Amherst, 18, 30, 32
Gerstenberger, Valerie Jenkins, 134–135
Gestalt Institute (Cleveland, Ohio), 131
Gibson, Carolyn, 165
Gillman, J. H., 26
Ginn, William D. "Bill," 77, 86–88, 102, 106, 108–109, 112–115, 120, 131, 140–141, 143, 146–148, 152, 181
Girl Scouts, in Oberlin, Ohio, 59, 177
Glebocki, Jeffrey M., 150
Glime, Zach, 159
Goodson, George, 110
Grace Episcopal Church (Cleveland, Ohio), 15
Grange. See Hickory Tree Grange
Great Lakes Naval Training Station (North Chicago, Illinois), 49
Great Lakes Science Center (Cleveland, Ohio), 153
Grennell, Howard, 85
Grieve, Elizabeth Stabe (Mrs. Thomas), 12, 14–15, 21–22, 27–28, 30, 33, 47–48, 187
Grieve, Thomas (father of Thomas and Virginia), 12, 14
Grieve, Thomas (son of Thomas and Elizabeth), 13–14
Grieve, Virginia. See Nord, Virginia Grieve
Griffith, Barbara S., 25, 66, 69, 73, 77–78, 104–108, 123, 133, 137, 176

Gustav VI Adolf, King, of Sweden, 84

## H

Habitat for Humanity (Atlanta, Georgia), 165
Haff, Ruth, 163
Hagan Corporation (Pittsburgh, Pennsylvania), 72, 74. See also American Cast Products, Inc.
Hall, Carl, 72
Hall, Charles Martin, 93–94, 158, 160–161
Hall, Julia, 160
Hallstrom, Axel, 8
Hansdotter, Helena, 4
Haqq, Constance, 164–166
Harrah, Jeanne, 30, 34, 41, 73, 85, 115, 140–143, 149–152
Harris, Josiah, 16, 48
Harris-Dute house (Amherst, Ohio), 161, 163
Hartville, Ohio, 44
The Hawk, 96
Head Start program (Oberlin, Ohio), 91, 116–119, 129
Heart Fund, 88
Heathwood Hall Foundation (Columbia, South Carolina), 181
Hedqvist, Jonas Olofsson. See Olofsson, Jonas Hedqvist
Hellman, Peter S., 172
Hellrigel, Mary Ann, 41–43, 52, 80
Heritage Ohio / Downtown Ohio, 158
Hickory Tree Grange (Amherst, Ohio), 147–148, 161, 204
High/Scope Educational Research Foundation (Ypsilanti, Michigan), 144
Hobbs, Glenn, 159
Hogstrom, Ed, 77
Hollstein, Walter, 11, 42
Holsworth, Patricia, 158, 174
Hoover, Herbert, 38
Horvath, Delores, 170
Howe, Charles, 33

HUBBARD–
KELCH

LORAIN–
NATIONAL

NORD–
NORD

OBERLIN–
OHIO

RAYMOND–
STEWART